Compiled by Chinese Academy of Cyberspace Studies (CACS)
China Internet Development Report 2023

Compiled by Chinese Academy of Cyberspace Studies (CACS)

China Internet Development Report 2023

sciendo

ISBN: 978-83-67405-93-5 PRINT
e-ISBN (PDF): 978-83-67405-86-7 ONLINE
e-ISBN (EPUB): 978-83-67405-99-7

10.2478/9788367405867-fm

Preface

2023 is the first year to fully implement the guiding principles of the 20th CPC National Congress, and a milestone in the development of Internet and information technology in China. The National Conference on Cybersecurity and Information Technology Work was successfully staged. General Secretary Xi Jinping gave important instructions on the work of the Internet and information technology. The new journey in a new era of high-quality development of the Internet and information technology in China has unfolded. Under the guidance of Xi Jinping's *Thought on Socialism with Chinese Characteristics for a New Era*, especially his important thoughts on building China into a country with strong cyber strength, positive progress and significant breakthroughs have been made in building China's strength in cyberspace and digital China. The *China Internet Development Report 2023* (hereinafter referred to as *The Report*) aims to showcase the great achievements and practices of China Internet development over the past year, forecast trends in Internet development, and provide abundant information and detailed data for readers and industrial researchers. *The Report* strives to:

First, adhere to General Secretary Xi Jinping's important thoughts on building China into a country with strong cyber strength and take these important thoughts as a scientific guide and fundamental guidelines for the compilation of *The Report*. Since the 18th CPC National Congress, General Secretary Xi Jinping has accurately understood the information era, clearly proposed the strategic goal of building China into a country with strong cyber strength, coordinated and promoted cybersecurity and information technology work, and theorized about the important thought on building China into a country with strong cyber strength with rich meaning and scientific systems. Under the scientific guidance of General Secretary Xi Jinping's important thoughts on building China into a country with strong cyberstrength, Internet and information technology in China has developed vigorously. China is making significant strides from a big country in cyberspace into a powerful country in cyberspace. General Secretary Xi Jinping's important thoughts on building China into a country with strong cyber strength plays an important part in his *Thought on Socialism with Chinese Characteristics for a New Era* and becomes a theoretical summary of the Party's practical experience in cyberspace governance and a guide to action in the development of Internet and information technology. In the compilation of *The Report*, we always adhere to General Secretary Xi Jinping's important thinking on building China into a country with strong cyberstrength, and focus on disseminating and interpreting significant achievements and vivid practices of China's Internet development from a theoretical perspective.

Second, thoroughly study, publicize, and implement the spirit of the 20th CPC National Congress, and fully demonstrate the latest achievements and vivid practices in China's Internet development. The report of the 20th CPC National

Congress clearly proposes to "accelerate the building of the country's cyber strength and a digital China, and "accelerate the development of digital economy, further integrate it with real economy, and build internationally competitive digital industry clusters," making clear arrangements for the future development of Internet and information technology. On this new journey, the development of Internet and information technology in China faces new situations, new goals, and new tasks. As the representative of advanced productivity, information technology will play an important role in Chinese modernization. Following the spirit of the 20th CPC National Congress, *The Report* highlights building the country's cyber strength and digital China and comprehensively represents the latest achievements and practices in Internet and information technology in China over the past year. In 2023, China continuously strengthened the top-level design in major fields of Internet and information technology and drew a blueprint for the future development of Internet and information technology. Relevant departments solidly and effectively promoted the implementation of various plans, emphasized the role of digital infrastructure as a major artery, continuously improved the strategic layout of digital economy, ensured that positive energy and mainstream values prevailed, continually consolidated the capability for safeguarding cybersecurity, continuously optimized the legal system in cyberspace, raised the efficiency of collaborative governance of digital government, and extensively carried out international cooperation and exchanges in the digital field. Noticeably, as digital culture thrives in China, *The Report* adds a new chapter of "The Construction of Digital Culture" to completely review and introduce the achievements in the construction of digital culture in China over the past year.

Third, evaluate Internet development comprehensively, objectively, and accurately in various provinces, autonomous regions, and municipalities directly under the central government (excluding Hong Kong, Macao, and Taiwan) across the country. Focusing on China's Internet development since 2022, *The Report* comprehensively evaluates Internet development in 31 provinces, autonomous regions, and municipalities directly under the central government (excluding Hong Kong, Macao, and Taiwan) from six dimensions (i.e., infrastructure construction, innovation capability, the development of digital economy, the development of digital society, cybersecurity and cyberspace governance). It reflects the level of Internet development in various regions and accurately displays their advantages, further clarifies the strategic goals and priorities for Internet development, and provides examples for promoting the development of Internet and information technology and building China into a country with strong cyber strength.

It is hoped that *The Report* truthfully records the progress of China's Internet development, comprehensively presents new achievements, practices, and experiences of China Internet development, and provides ideas for readers to understand China's Internet development.

Chinese Academy of Cyberspace Studies (CACS)
September 2023

10.2478/9788367405867-toc

Contents

10.2478/9788367405867-001

Overview

The 20th CPC National Congress focuses on the development of information revolution and current trends, aims to advance building a great country and national rejuvenation, makes a series of new judgments, arrangements, and requirements for building China into a country with strong cyber strength, raises clear requirements for accelerating the construction of a strong cyber nation and a digital China, promoting the development of digital economy, achieving self-reliance in high-level science and technology, improving comprehensive Internet governance system, forging a healthy Internet ecosystem, strengthening the construction of security systems for Internet, data, and other fields, enhancing personal information protection, and points out the direction for the development of Internet and information technology in this new era. In particular, in July 2023, the National Conference on Cybersecurity and Information Technology Work was successfully held. General Secretary Xi Jinping gave important instructions on the work of Internet and information technology, fully affirmed the major achievements made in Internet and information technology since the 18th CPC National Congress, deeply expounded the important role of Internet and information technology, and clearly proposed the mission and task of Internet and information technology to "rally public support, ward off risks and ensure security, strengthen governance and benefit people's lives, nurture growth momentum and boost development, and seek mutually-beneficial cooperation." The conference clarified important principles, further enriched and developed General Secretary Xi Jinping's thoughts on building China into a country with strong cyber strength, and provided scientific guidance for promoting the high-quality development of cybersecurity and information technology.

Over the past year, under the guidance of Xi Jinping's *Thought on Socialism with Chinese Characteristics for a New Era*, especially his important thoughts on building China into a country with strong cyber strength, China always adhered to the leadership of the Party on Internet and information technology in an all-round way, strengthened the top-level design for building China into a country with cyber strength, launched *Overall Layout and Planning for the Construction of Digital China*, proposed an overall framework for "2522," and outlined a blueprint for the construction of a digital China. The construction of digital infrastructure steadily advanced, and its role as an "artery" in socioeconomic development became increasingly prominent. The digital economy showed strong momentum and became an important engine for stabilizing growth and promoting transformation. The framework of a basic data system was determined, and the construction of data resources systems quickened. New Internet technologies were intensively applied in education, employment, social security, healthcare, transportation, and other fields, empowering people to meet their growing material and cultural needs. The creation and governance of online content continued to be strengthened, the mainstream public opinion in cyberspace was consolidated and developed, the layout of digital culture accelerated, the development of an Internet culture was deepened, a comprehensive Internet governance system was basically established, and the Internet ecology was continuously improved. Cybersecurity was comprehensively optimized, and the protection of data security and personal information was greatly strengthened. Law-based governance of cyberspace deepened, and multiple pillars of law in cyberspace took initial shape. More efforts were invested in Internet law enforcement, with law enforcement procedures being continuously standardized. International exchanges and cooperation in cyberspace kept deepening and expanding, and the idea of a community with a shared future in cyberspace won support among the international community.

Now, the overall strategy for the great rejuvenation of the Chinese nation, profound changes in the world unseen in a century, and the tide of the information revolution are historically intertwined, providing new opportunities and challenges for us to comprehensively build a modern socialist country. Internet and information technology have developed rapidly and been increasingly integrated into social life, which has profoundly reshaped the global economic and security landscape. Major countries around the world prioritize Internet development in economic growth and technological innovation and regard the Internet as a strategic tool for forging new competitive advantage. However, a few countries use the Internet as a tool to maintain hegemony, abuse information technology, and implement cyber hegemony, which increase the risks of confrontation in cyberspace. Some countries organize "small blocs" and pursue "decoupling and supply chain disruption," instigate fragmentation and confrontation in cyberspace, and complicate the situation in cyberspace.

To thoroughly implement major strategic arrangements of the 20th CPC National Congress, and tackle complex international situations and various challenges, China faces an important period of strategic opportunity, plays a leading role in Internet development, maintains the initiative to promote development, and solidly fosters the construction of a country with strong cyber strength. China continuously achieves new results in stimulating the vitality of the digital economy, promoting the construction of a digital ecosystem, creating a healthy cyberspace, and preventing cybersecurity risks. This encourages high-quality development and increases development efficiency, laying a solid foundation for building a community with a shared future in cyberspace and contributing Chinese wisdom to promoting world Internet development.

1. China's Internet Development

1.1 Digital infrastructure as a major artery becomes prominent, and China ranks at the top in the world in multiple indexes

China closely follows the trends of technological innovation and development. To meet major needs of socioeconomic development, China appropriately deploys the construction of digital infrastructure in advance, accelerates the improvement and digitization of traditional infrastructure, and leads the world in attaining achievements. China steps up efforts to build a high-speed, ubiquitous, intelligent, and comprehensive digital information infrastructure that integrates space and ground, the cloud and the Internet, which is green, low-carbon, secure, and controllable. Over the past year, China has steadily promoted the construction of communication network infrastructure, computing power infrastructure, new technological infrastructure, and application infrastructures, ranking at the top in the world in the deployment of 5G, gigabit optical network and IPv6, as well as the total scale of computing power.

5G comes to a critical period of large-scale applications. By the end of June 2023, China had constructed and opened more than 2.937 million 5G base stations. 5G network covered all urban areas of prefecture-level cities and counties nationwide. The number of 5G mobile phone users reached 676 million. The application scenarios of 5G continued to deepen, covering 52 major categories of the national economy. The number of "dual gigabit" (5G and gigabit optical network) use cases exceeded 50,000 households. The service capability of gigabit network continued to improve, and a total length of fiber-optic cables reached 61.06 million kilometers nationwide. With 110 "gigabit cities" built, gigabit optical network can cover more than 500 million households. The Internet of Things (IoT) sees rapid development. By June 2023, the scale of cellular IoT users had expanded quickly, and three basic telecom corporations owned 2.123 billion cellular IoT terminal users. The large-scale deployment and application of IPv6 deepened, and the number of active users of IPv6 reached 767 million, accounting for 71 percent of the total number of Internet users. 4G, 5G, and fixed broadband networks fully supported IPv6, and IPv6 accounted for more than 50 percent of mobile network traffic. Significant achievements have been made in empowering and improving space-based network infrastructure. China's Beidou Navigation Satellite System (BDS) is widely used in transportation, digital construction, express delivery, and other fields. Deeply integrated with emerging technologies like artificial intelligence (AI), BDS breeds new business models such as "Beidou + " and "+ Beidou." The application of satellite Internet accelerates. In May 2023, China achieved the first test and application of low-orbit satellite Internet for communication in remote areas. The layout and construction of "East Data, West Computing" and other national projects significantly increased the demand for computing power, and remarkably improved the comprehensive capabilities of computing infrastructure. According to statistics from the Ministry of Industry and Information Technology, by the end of 2022, the total scale of computing power had reached 180 EFLOPS ($18{,}000 \times 10^{16}$ floating-point operations per second), ranking second in the world, with an annual growth rate of about 30 percent. AI computing centers are continuously being built as important infrastructure for building national pilot zones for new-generation AI innovation and development. Blockchain and quantum infrastructure have developed quickly. The industrial Internet effectively empowers various industries, and key industrial Internet platforms connect more than 85 million sets of industrial devices. IoV (Internet of Vehicles) pilot zones accelerate the construction of infrastructure and the deployment of tests and demonstrations. More than 9,000 kilometers of test roads have been opened nationwide, and more than 1,900 test licenses have been issued, driving the coordinated development of multiple fields such as intelligent transportation and smart cities.

1.2 The strategic layout of the digital economy continues to improve, and basic data system and framework take shape

The digital economy provides important support for building a modern economic system. Over the past year, China continuously optimized its polices on the digital economy and explored how to innovate the data element market. The cycle of data resources was gradually cleared, and the value of data elements was quickly unleashed. This tremendously enhanced the innovation capability of digital industry and accelerated the digital transformation and upgrading of industries.

The top-level strategic planning system for the digital economy continues to improve. *Overall Layout and Planning for the Construction of Digital China* clearly proposes to strengthen, optimize, and expand the digital economy, cultivate and develop core industries in the digital economy, and build internationally competitive digital industry clusters. By April 2023, 31 provinces, autonomous regions, and municipalities directly under the central government of China had formulated plans for the development of the digital economy. The construction of basic data system quickens. *Opinions of the CPC Central Committee and the State Council on Building Basic Data System to Better Play the Role of Data Elements* (hereinafter referred to as *Twenty Articles on Data*) has been issued and implemented, providing systematic designs and a framework for a basic data system. Various regions promptly formulate the rules and regulations on data development and utilization, and explore innovations on data management mechanisms. The scale of data production and storage continues to increase. In 2022, China's data production reached 8.1 ZB, with a year-on-year increase of 22.7 percent, accounting for 10.5 percent of global total data production, ranking second in the world. China's data storage capacity reached 724.5 EB, accounting for 14.4 percent of total global data storage. China constantly explores innovations in the data element market, and the scale of data element industry keeps expanding. The scale of the big data industry in China reached 1.57 trillion *yuan*, with a year-on-year increase of 18 percent. According to relevant data, the scale of the digital economy in China reached 50.2 trillion *yuan* in 2022, ranking second in the world, and accounting for 41.5 percent of GDP.[1] The innovation

1 Cyberspace Administration of China. *Digital China Development Report 2022*, May 2023.

capability in digital industrialization significantly improves. In the first quarter of 2023, the decline in production of electronic information manufacturing industry narrowed, and software and the IT service industry steadily developed, realizing a business revenue of ten trillion *yuan*. The Internet and related service industries achieved positive growth in revenue, with a significant increase in total profit and a slight narrowing in the decrease of research and development (R & D) expenses. The digital transformation and upgrading of industries accelerate, and industrial digitalization penetrates all fields within the economy and society. Agricultural digitization develops comprehensively. Modern information technology is widely applied to aquaculture, agricultural planting, breeding, and other sectors. The IT rate of agricultural production exceeds 25 percent[2]. The pace of digital transformation of the manufacturing industry has quickened. The CNC (Computer Numerical Control) rate of key processes and the popularization rate of digital R & D and design tools in industrial enterprises nationwide reach 58.6 percent and 77.0 percent, respectively, which helps to reduce costs and increase efficiency in the manufacturing industry. The industrial Internet continues to expand. According to data from the Ministry of Industry and Information Technology, in the first quarter of 2023, the scale of core industries of the industrial Internet in China exceeded 1.2 trillion *yuan*, up by 15.5 percent over 2022. The digital economy and the modern service industry continue to integrate. Online retail maintains a trend of growth and plays an important role in promoting consumption. In the first half of 2023, national online retail sales reached 7.16 trillion *yuan*, with a year-on-year increase of 13.1 percent. Specifically, online retail sales of physical goods realized 6.06 trillion *yuan*, up by 10.8 percent.[3] According to customs bureaus, in the first half of 2023, the import and export volume of cross-border e-commerce in China reached 1.1 trillion *yuan*, with a year-on-year increase of 16 percent.[4]

1.3 Digital public services become inclusive and convenient, which raises the efficiency of collaborative governance

General Secretary Xi Jinping stresses that "we should meet the expectations and needs of the people and accelerate the popularization of information-based services"

2 Information Technology Development Bureau of Office of the Central Cyberspace Affairs Commission and Information Technology Center of Ministry of Agriculture and Rural Affairs. *China Digital Countryside Development Report 2022*, March 2023.

3 "The Total Retail Sales of Consumer Goods in the First Half of 2023 Increased by 8.2 percent". http://www.stats.gov.cn/sj/zxfb/202307/t20230715_1941269.html. Accessed August 2023.

4 "Picture-Text Record of the Press Conference on the Import and Export in the First Half of 2023 Held by the State Council Information Office." http://www.scio.gov.cn/xwfb/gwyxwbgsxwfbh/wqfbh_22841/49421/50133/wz50135/202307A20230724_729250.html. Accessed August 2023.

and that "the achievements of Internet development benefit hundreds of millions of citizens and enhance their sense of gain." Over the past year, new Internet technologies were intensively applied in various portions of society. The construction of the digital society improved people's livelihood and optimized public services. The construction of digital countryside and digital community advanced solidly. Digital services in various fields such as education, healthcare, employment, and elder care were continuously upgraded. The construction of digital government service platforms accelerated, the effectiveness of the sharing of government data deepened, and the performance of digital governance services significantly improved.

By June 2023, the number of Chinese Internet users reached 1.079 billion, and the penetration rate of Internet reached 76.4 percent.[5] Digital technologies were deeply integrated into the daily life of ordinary people, allowing them to spend more time on the Internet and to meet their diverse needs. The National Digital Education Strategy has been fully implemented, and National Smart Education Public Service Platform has been officially promulgated. China has established the largest education and teaching resources database in the world, and the pattern of the opening and sharing of high-quality educational resources has gradually taken shape. The coverage rate of Internet healthcare has been further enlarged, and its scale continuously expands. Remote medical services at the city and county levels achieved full coverage. By June 2023, the number of Internet healthcare users in China reached 364 million, with an increase of 1.62 million over December 2022, accounting for 33.8 percent of the total number of Internet users[6]. The standardization of Internet healthcare continues to improve. China released documents such as *Measures and Rules on the Regulation of Online Diagnosis and Treatment (Trial)* and *Measures on the Regulation and Management of Online Drug Sales*, which specify the procedures for online diagnosis and the treatment and management of online drug sales. The digitization of elder care, social security, sports, and other areas important to people's livelihood continues to improve, with significant achievements in the construction of a digital countryside. By June 2023, the penetration rate of the Internet in rural areas reached 60.5 percent, and a rural network infrastructure hade been basically achieved. The popularization and application of the Internet in rural areas accelerated. The number of online healthcare users in rural areas reached 68.75 million, with a penetration rate of 22.8 percent.[7] The digital literacy and skills of Internet users have been steadily enhanced. The digital adaptability of special groups such as people with disabilities, the elderly, and minors has been significantly raised. Every year, about 68,000 people with disabilities are employed via the Internet. China quickens the development of

5 CNNIC (China Internet Network Information Center). *The 52nd Statistical Report on China Internet Development*, August 2023.

6 CNNIC. *The 52nd Statistical Report on China Internet Development*, August 2023.

7 CNNIC. *The 52nd Statistical Report on China Internet Development*, August 2023.

standards for digital technology engineers and other digital professions. Professional training institutions are selected to cultivate digital technology personnel and raise the digital level of the entire society through multiple channels. The Chinese government accelerates the pace of digital transformation and strengthens the construction of digital government. According to the United Nations *E-Government Survey 2022*, China ranks 43rd globally (45th in 2020). In particular, China takes the lead in the "Online Services" index. Integrated government services are continuously improved, and the construction of "one-stop government services" and "cross-provincial government services" is continuously deepened. The efficiency and convenience of handling government affairs are tremendously raised. By March 2023, the real-name registered users of the National Integrated Government Service Platform exceeded one billion, including 820 million registered users of the national government service platform. The platform was visited, in total, 86 billion times. Significant achievements were made in the sharing and opening of government data. By April 2023, the national data sharing and exchange platform was connected to 82 departments at the central level, providing a total of 11.283 billion queries/verifications to relevant departments and local governments through service interfaces. The transparency of government affairs substantially enhanced digital governance. All sectors of society actively make suggestions and proposals to the important work of the CPC Central Committee and the State Council via online media platforms. The "Internet + supervision" platform, online investigation platform, and the performance platform of the National People's Congress constantly raise the digital and modern level of government affairs and improve the effectiveness of digital governance.

1.4 Positive energy and mainstream values prevail, and the development momentum of digital culture industry remains robust

The Internet provides new platforms and spaces for people's work and life, as well as new channels and opportunities for promoting cultural prosperity and development. General Secretary Xi Jinping stated that "As a major component of social etiquette and civility under new circumstances, Internet civilization is a key area of enhancing China's strength in cyberspace" and that "we must develop better online content, strengthen positive publicity, and work to foster a positive, healthy and upright online culture." Over the past year, online propaganda on the Party's innovation theory continued to be strengthened. Xi Jinping's *Thought on Socialism with Chinese Characteristics for a New Era* has been widely accepted. Remarkable results were made in online publicity about major themes. The supply of online content matched the needs of the public. The efficiency of online international communication was comprehensively promoted. Positive energy prevailed in cyberspace. Digital culture industry thrived, with a new prospect in the creation of an "Internet civilization."

Various activities were organized. "Managing Internet, Using Internet, Accessing Internet and Developing Internet in a Civilized Way" became an extensive consensus all of society, forming a mighty force for hundreds of millions of Internet users to build a beautiful home on the Internet.

China makes innovation based on tradition, promotes online propaganda of the Party's innovation theory, and accelerates the construction of *Li Xiang Zhong Guo*, an online propaganda brand of the Party's theories. The spirit of the 20th CPC National Congress has been deeply disseminated on the Internet. Major mainstream media, websites and local media focus on major themes, enrich communication forms, and create high-quality integrated media products, such as *Steering a Steady Course*, *Decoding the Past Decade*, *New Landscape of China*, *The Great Era*, etc. China has accelerated the construction of an all-media communication system, held the 2023 Forum on Internet Media of China, and launched the selection and broadcasting of excellent positive works on Internet. A group of excellent works have stood out. Remarkable results have been achieved in international online communication. Major websites build new contexts and narrative systems that integrate China and foreign countries and play an active role in telling the story of China and spreading the voice of China to the world. China has comprehensively begun the construction of an Internet civilization and built a strong momentum. The National Conference on the Promotion of Internet Civilization was convened, and the China Internet Civilization Conference was successfully staged in 2022 and 2023. China continuously cultivates new trends in online culture and diversifies the practices of Internet civilization, in which Internet celebrities with positive energy play an exemplary and leading role. The activities of "Learning National Conditions among Internet Celebrities," including "Finding the Footprints for the Centenary of the Communist Party of China," have been organized, vividly telling the stories of the new era. Online mass line has been implemented, and the activity of selecting 100 outstanding accounts in implementing online mass line hs been carried out. China has explored the construction of Internet literacy education bases for Internet users, built the China Internet Joint Platform for Refuting Rumors, strengthened the handling of online reports, and effectively formed a concentric circle online and offline. A comprehensive Internet governance system became more scientific and raised its levels of public participation and rule of law, which tremendously enhances cyberspace governance. The "Nationwide Campaign to Purify the Online Environment" has been carried out, focusing on combating Internet addiction, cyberbullying, and undesirable fan culture. The digital culture industry shows strong momentum. New business models and new application scenarios of cultural consumption continue to emerge. China has explored new mechanisms in various fields such as rural revitalization, cultural heritage protection, and tourism and museology; industrial development has entered the fast lane. AI kindles new models of cultural products, shapes new features, models and formats of digital culture industry, and promotes the deep integration and intelligent transformation of media.

1.5 The capability for safeguarding cybersecurity is gradually consolidated, and the foundation of data security governance is constantly strengthened

At present, cybersecurity threats continue to emerge, cyberattacks intensify, attacks on the supply chain occur frequently, and the overall integrity of cybersecurity remains under assault. China pursues a holistic approach to national security, accelerates the implementation of relevant laws and regulations, actively participates in the formulation of international standards on cybersecurity, solidly launches campaigns to tackle prominent problems on cybersecurity, promotes the aggregation and development of the cybersecurity industry, and facilitates the cultivation of cybersecurity talents and the publicity about cybersecurity.

Typical cyberattacks pose serious risks, and ransomware attacks target enterprises and steal data. High-traffic DDoS (Distributed Denial of Service) attacks increase significantly, and APT (Advanced Persistent Threat) attacks aim at critical information infrastructure and important information systems. The risk of data breaches has become prominent. According to statistics from the National Computer Virus Emergency Response Center at Tianjin, in the first quarter of 2023, data breaches mainly affected education, healthcare, finance and other industries, and personal information of citizens. In the face of multiple risks and challenges, China has steadily promoted data security governance and personal information protection, strengthened data security systems, solidified the construction of relevant systems on data-outbound-transfer security and personal information protection, accelerated the standardization of data security in an orderly way, carried out the management and governance of cybersecurity incidents, and regulated the illegal collection and use of personal information on apps. Simultaneously, China has severely cracked down on the illegal sale of citizens' online personal information , disposed of cybercrimes such as black industry in cyberspace, and promoted the Internet clean-up campaign 2022. China actively boosts the high-quality development of the cybersecurity industry and enhances the technological level and competitiveness of the cybersecurity industry. In 2022, the scale of the cybersecurity market in China totaled about 63.3 billion *yuan*, with a year-on-year increase of 3.1 percent. The demand for cybersecurity talent continues to grow. China actively conducts the training of cybersecurity personnel, and continuously promotes the construction of demonstration projects of first-class cybersecurity colleges, as well as the construction of national cybersecurity talent and innovation bases. China focuses on the idea of "Cybersecurity serves the people, Cybersecurity depends on the people," and continues to organize National Cybersecurity Publicity Week. In 2022, during National Cybersecurity Publicity Week, relevant topics were visited 3.86 billion times, 1.3 billion short public welfare messages were pushed out, and relevant short videos were played more than 500 million times. This created a strong atmosphere for safeguarding cybersecurity across the country and significantly enhanced the awareness of and capability in cybersecurity in the entire society.

1.6 The legal system in cyberspace is constantly improved, and law enforcement procedures are further standardized

China always upholds law-based Internet governance, constantly improves the legal system in cyberspace, thus ensuring the healthy development of the Internet. Over the past year, China continued to optimize relevant laws in key fields such as cybersecurity, data governance, and platform regulation. Great achievements were made in law-based governance of cyberspace, and law enforcement in cyberspace was deepened. In March 2023, the white paper *The Construction of Law-based Governance of Cyberspace in China in the New Era* was published, which systematically summarizes the ideas and practices of law-based governance of cyberspace since China's full-functional access to the international Internet in 1994; the paper contributes a Chinese solution and wisdom to international governance in cyberspace.

China has deepened the construction of cybersecurity systems, strengthened the protection systems for critical information infrastructure in key fields, and formulated special measures on cybersecurity management in key industries such as healthcare, electricity, and transportation. China continuously improves the management systems for cross-border data flow and releases departmental regulations and normative documents such as *Measures on Security Evaluation of Data Outbound Transfer*, *Measures on Standard Contract of Personal Information Outbound Transfer*, and *Announcement on Implementing Personal Information Protection and Certification*. The *Law on Combating Telecom and Online Fraud of the People's Republic of China*, a special law that punishes telecom and online fraud, has been officially implemented, providing comprehensive legal support for combating this type of fraud. The rules on digital economy continues to improve. *Twenty Articles on Data* determines the framework for basic data system. China has further optimized the requirements for data security management in key industries and strengthened the protection of intellectual property. Zhejiang, Beijing, and other regions first introduced the management measures on data intellectual property registration, and effectively protected the legitimate rights and interests of data processors. China thoroughly implements the governance of the Internet ecosystem and oversees the governance of cyber violence. The Supreme People's Court, the Supreme People's Procuratorate, and Ministry of Public Security jointly issued *Guiding Opinions on Punishing Cyber Violence and Cybercrimes in Accordance with the Law*, which regulates cyber slander, cyber insults, cyber manhunt, offline harassment, and other forms of cyber violence. China cements the protection of special groups such as women, minors, and the elderly in cyberspace, reviews and approves *Regulations on Protecting Minors in Cyberspace*, urges relevant parties to strictly implement the responsibility of protecting minors in cyberspace, and gives strong legal support for protecting minors in cyberspace. China continuously standardizes the governance of Internet information and content, and raises requirements for services such as Internet pop-up information push and Internet post comments. China bolsters the research on cutting-edge issues, accelerates legislation in emerging fields, and promotes the standardized development of new technologies and applications such as AI, algorithms, and deep synthesis. *Interim Measures on the Management of Generative Artificial Intelligence Services* stipulates the principles for the development and governance of generative artificial intelligence (GAI), and proposes specific measures to facilitate the development of GAI technology. Meanwhile, various provinces and cities have passed special laws to promote the healthy development of the AI industry. China reinforced the regulation of information security in deep synthesis technology by publishing *Regulations on the Management of Deep Synthesis in Internet Information Services*; it has clarified and optimized the application scenarios of deep synthesis technology, and determined the information security obligations of deep synthesis service providers and users. China has stepped up efforts in law enforcement in cyberspace. According to statistics, from January 2022 to the first half of 2023, national departments of cyberspace affairs summoned 14,126 website platforms for talks, warned 9,626 website platforms, fined 645 website platforms, suspended or updated 809 website platforms, and removed 540 mobile apps. Alongside administrative departments in charge of telecommunications, national departments of cyberspace affairs cancelled illegal website licenses or records, closed 32,937 illegal websites, and transferred 17,631 relevant case clues. The administrative law enforcement procedures have been gradually improved, and *Regulations on Administrative Law-Enforcement Procedures for Departments of Cyberspace Affairs* and *Regulations on Administrative Penalty Procedures for Industry and Information Technology* have been successively introduced. These regulations determine the scope of administrative law enforcement and provide a basis for the law enforcement of departments at all levels. Significant achievements have been made in the popularization of legal matters in cyberspace. China initiated a series of activities of "National Law Popularization in Cyberspace" in order to promote interest in the law among key groups such as minors. Simultaneously, the buildup of a smart judiciary such as smart courts and digital procuratorate has continuously improved. Relevant departments focus on personal information protection in public interest litigation, with a significant increase in the number of cases. Various departments have worked together and stepped up efforts to crack down on telecom and online fraud.

1.7 China extensively carries out international exchanges and cooperation in cyberspace and actively promotes building a community with a shared future in cyberspace

The report of the 20th CPC National Congress states that China actively participates in the reform and construction of a global governance system, practices the principle of extensive consultation, joint contributions, and shared benefits in global governance, upholds true multilateralism, promotes greater democracy in international relations, and makes global governance more just and equitable. Over the past year, guided by the idea of building a community with a shared future in cyberspace, China carried out international exchanges and cooperation in cyberspace, actively built platforms for international exchanges and cooperation in cyberspace, continuously deepened cooperation in cybersecurity and other fields, played a positive role in the formulation of international rules on the digital economy, strengthened the research and cooperation on hot topics in international governance in cyberspace, and worked to establish a global governance system on cyberspace that features openness and inclusiveness, justice and fairness, security and stability, vigor and vitality.

China actively has put forward proposals on international governance in cyberspace to help forge a global consensus. In November 2022, China released the white paper *Jointly Building a Community with a Shared Future in Cyberspace*, calling on the international community to engage in the information era and trends in human society, to respond to the risks and challenges in cyberspace, and to express China's sincere desire to strengthen cooperation with countries around the world on Internet development and governance. China actively participates in the UN cyberspace governance process and supports the formulation of global conventions under the UN framework. China constructively participates in the five formal negotiation meetings held by the Ad Hoc Committee for the Negotiation of *The United Nations Convention against Cybercrimes* and has achieved a series of positive results. China builds platforms for international exchange and cooperation in cyberspace, actively playing the role of a responsible major country and hosting the first annual conference since the founding of World Internet Conference International Organization, the WIC Nishan Dialogue on Digital Civilization. It continuously pools wisdom and consensus from all parties and deepens digital cooperation. China plays a positive role in international negotiations on digital economy issues, and deepens and expands bilateral and multilateral dialogue and cooperation in the digital economy through multilateral mechanisms such as the G20 and APEC (Asia-Pacific Economic Cooperation). China enthusiastically contributes to the formulation of standards in information technology by organizations such as the ISO (International Organization for Standardization) and ITU (International Telecommunication Union), undertakes and drafts hundreds of international standards that have been officially approved or published, and upgrades domestic innovative achievements to international standards.

2. Internet Development in Various Provinces, Autonomous Regions, and Municipalities Directly under the Central Government

Since 2017, the *China Internet Development Report* has released the China Internet Development Index. Guided by General Secretary Xi Jinping's important thoughts on building China into a country with strong cyber strength, the China Internet Development Index aims to conduct comprehensive evaluation of the achievements and levels of Internet development in various provinces, autonomous regions, and municipalities directly under the central government (excluding Hong Kong, Macao, and Taiwan) by building an objective, truthful, and accurate comprehensive evaluation index system. In this way, various regions can further clarify the strategic objectives and priorities for Internet development, accurately utilize comparative and regional advantages in Internet development, and promote the building of China into a country with cyber strength in the development of Internet and information technology.

The China Internet Development Index system covers six aspects, i.e., infrastructure construction, innovation capability, the development of a digital economy, the development of a digital society, cybersecurity, and cyberspace governance. It comprehensively showcases Internet development in thirty-one provinces, autonomous regions, and municipalities directly under the central government in China and provides a quantifiable reference for them in Internet development.

Grounded in the index system in 2022, the evaluation index in 2023 takes into consideration Internet development in various regions, widely solicits opinions from national departments, provinces, cities, think tanks on the Internet, and experts in relevant fields, and redesigns or improves the index system. On the premise of basically adopting original indicators, the China Internet Development Index in 2023 adjusted some indicators in line with new circumstances. Second-level indicators such as "Value of Data Elements" were added. Table 0-1 shows the China Internet Development Index System for 2023.

To ensure the authenticity, comprehensiveness, and accuracy of the data, the evaluation data of China Internet Development Index System for 2023 mainly stem from the statistical data of Office of the Central Cyberspace Affairs Commission, the National Bureau of Statistics, the General Office of the State Council, the Ministry of Industry and Information Technology, the Ministry of Science and Technology, other departments and institutions, and the statistical data of relevant cyberspace administration departments in various provinces, autonomous regions, and municipalities directly under the central government, as well as research reports published by relevant ministries and commissions or research institutions.

Table 0-1 China Internet Development Index System 2023

First-Level Indicator	Second-Level Indicator	Description
Infrastructure Construction Index	Broadband infrastructure	Per capita Internet broadband access port, the proportion of gigabit broadband users, average download rate of fixed broadband network, broadband network coverage in rural and remote areas, etc.
	Mobile infrastructure	Download rate of 5G network users, the proportion of 5G users, the proportion of the total number of 5G base stations, etc.
	Application infrastructure	Proportion of IPv6 active terminals, number of data centers, number of computing infrastructures, number of IoT terminals, coverage of the industrial Internet, etc.
Innovation Capability Index	Environment for innovation	The number of listed Internet and IT enterprises, the number of incubated enterprise per 10,000 people, etc.
	Innovation input	The proportion of R & D expenditure to GDP, the proportion of corporate R & D personnel, the proportion of governmental R & D investment to GDP, etc.
	Innovation output	The number of scientific research papers per 10,000 people, the number of national awards for scientific & technological achievements per 10,000 people, the number of invention patents per 10,000 people, etc.
Development of the Digital Economy Index	Basic data	The penetration rate of Internet, the total telecom business, the proportion of added value of software & IT service industries to GDP, etc.
	Value of data elements	Data resources, total factor productivity, etc.
	Industrial digitization	The numerical control rate of key processes, the application rate of industrial cloud platforms, the coverage rate of information-based agricultural production, the proportion of e-commerce consumption in final consumption expenditure, etc.
	Digital industrialization	The scale of digital core industries, the scale of e-commerce transactions, the scale of digital culture industry, the online sales of agricultural products, etc.
Development of the Digital Society Index	Development of public services	The coverage rate of telemedicine, the coverage rate of electronic social security card, the real-time forecast rate of bus/tram arrival information, etc.
	Construction of e-government	The online handling of government services, the WeChat communication index of provincial government services, the number of microblog-authentication accounts on government services per 100,000 people, etc.

Table 0-1 *(Continued)*

First-Level Indicator	Second-Level Indicator	Description
Cybersecurity Index	Environment for cybersecurity	The number of host IP addresses implanted with trojans or bots, the number of implanted backdoor websites and tampered websites, the proportion of infected hosts in the number of active IP addresses in one region, etc.
	Construction of cybersecurity Awareness	Cybersecurity search index, the number of participants in a series of Cybersecurity Week Activities, the proportion of the number of cultivated cybersecurity talents, etc.
	Development of the cybersecurity industry	The number of cybersecurity enterprises, the proportion of cybersecurity personnel, the number of cybersecurity industrial parks at the provincial level or above, etc.
Cyberspace Governance Index	Social collaboration	The number of Internet-related social organizations, the number of authorized cyberspace administration departments, the times of participation in international exchanges and cooperation, etc.
	Content governance	The number of campaigns in cyberspace, the governance of apps, the number of reports from Internet users, etc.
	Law-based governance of cyberspace	Cyberspace-related strategies, policies, regulations, and normative documents, the number of crackdowns on cybercrimes, the number of talks with Internet and IT enterprises, the number of Internet news information licenses, etc.

2.1 Comprehensive Ranking of China's Internet Development Index in 2023

Based on the China Internet Development Index System, *The Report* ranks Internet development indexes of 31 provinces, autonomous regions, and municipalities directly under the central government. In general, various provinces, autonomous regions, and municipalities directly under the central government comprehensively and thoroughly implement General Secretary Xi Jinping's important thoughts on building China into a country with cyber strength, earnestly act in accordance with the arrangements and requirements of the CPC Central Committee, give full play to their own advantages, and vigorously expedite the development process of the Internet based on regional advantages or local conditions. In the Comprehensive Rankings of China Internet Development Index in 2023, the top ten provinces and municipalities directly under the central government in Internet development were Guangdong, Beijing, Jiangsu, Zhejiang, Shandong, Shanghai, Fujian, Sichuan, Tianjin, and Hubei, as shown in Figure 0-1.

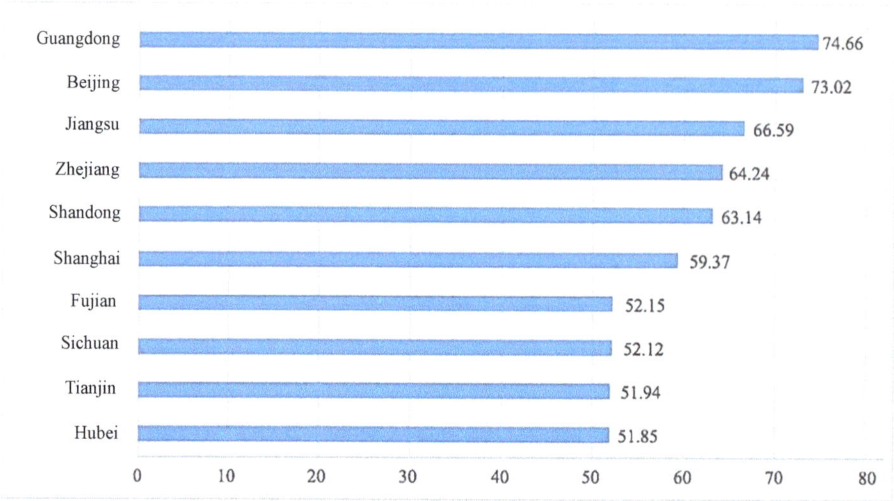

Figure 0-1 Top ten provinces and municipalities directly under the central government in comprehensive rankings of China Internet Development Index in 2023.

Guangdong coordinates and promotes the construction of a province with cyber strength and a "digital Guangdong." It accelerates the construction of technologically advanced and nationally leading network infrastructure, and builds a total of 232,000 5G base stations. 5G network achieves continuous outdoor coverage in urban areas of all counties (districts), and basic coverage in major areas of all towns. Guangdong ranks first in China, in the number of 5G base stations and the number of 5G users. It systematically promotes the layout of new computing power systems, quickly builds National Integrated Computing Power Network Guangdong-Hong Kong-Macao Greater Bay Area National Hub Node Shaoguan Data Center Cluster, and advances the construction of a number of major projects. It holds the First "East Data, West Computing" Guangdong-Hong Kong-Macao Greater Bay Area (Guangdong) Computing Power Industry Conference. Guangdong improves the overall level of application infrastructure, quickens the upgrading and transformation of service-oriented external governmental networks, optimizes more than 200 high-frequency certificates (about 200 million pieces), and provides identity authentication services for 1,666 government service systems in the province.

Beijing strengthens the innovation and application of new technologies, focuses on the construction of an international innovation center, deeply implements an innovation-driven development strategy, and conducts the research and development of key technologies such as blockchain, AI, and integrated circuits, and makes breakthroughs in a number of core technologies. Beijing continuously optimizes the layout of computing power and supports the surrounding areas. It vigorously cultivates digital economy enterprises, holds a high-level global digital economy conference, and focuses on the governance rules on the global digital economy. It established the Beijing International Digital Economy Governance Research Institute and prepared for the China Digital Economy Development and Governance Academic Annual Conference. Beijing innovates the integrated development model of "Internet + culture & tourism," and actively launches the construction of a smart culture and tourism platform and the research and promotion of Internet technological innovation and application in the culture and tourism industry. It organized the 2022 National Digital Literacy and Skills Enhancement Month to promote better use of digital products and services by citizens.

Jiangsu continuously consolidates the construction of Internet infrastructure. In 2022, Jiangsu promoted the construction and renovation of fiber to the home (FTTH), achieved large-scale deployment and application of IPv6, and built a provincial IPv6 development monitoring platform. In Jiangsu, the number of active IPv6 users exceeds 45 million, and the proportion of IPv6 traffic in mobile networks reached 46 percent. By March 2023, the number of IoT terminal users reached 240 million, ranking second in China. Jiangsu continuously strengthens the foundation of IoT and fosters the innovation in the entire chain of digital technology. By the end of 2022, Jiangsu had won a total of 190 national science and technology awards for general projects. Jiangsu accelerates the cultivation of innovation-based enterprise clusters in digital economy (mainly high-tech enterprises), selects innovation-based leading enterprises, supports leading enterprises to organize innovation consortia, and drives the innovation and development of the digital economy. Jiangsu boosts the digital transformation of education, improves digital medical and health services, optimizes the *Su Shi Yang Lao* elderly care service system, deepens the development of the "Smart Disabled Persons' Federation" information platform, vigorously develops new models for a digital countryside, solidly promotes the development of digital countryside construction projects, and tremendously enhances the efficiency of rural digital services.

In Zhejiang, the core industries of the digital economy developed rapidly in 2023. Zhejiang officially launched the construction of future industry pilot zones, focusing on key fields such as AI, future networks, and 3G semiconductors. It plans eight future industry pilot zones. Zhejiang actively promotes the innovation and development of AI. An entire industrial chain takes shape, from the R & D of core technologies and intelligent terminal manufacturing to industrial intelligent application. Zhejiang successfully develops quantum information platforms such as Megrez Post-Quantum Cryptography Platform and JanusQ Cloud. In terms of the platforms for digital technology innovation, Zhejiang Lab, Alibaba Damo Academy, and Yangtze Delta Region Institute of Tsinghua University continue to unleash their potential for technological innovation. Zhejiang actively follows the new trends that digital technologies fully integrate into social communication and daily life, quickens the development and application of digital society, promotes innovation in public services and social operation models, and builds a digital life accessible to all. Zhejiang takes efforts to build a digital "cultural brain," facilitates the development of an online audio-video industry, upgrades the "smart culture cloud," the *Shi Hua Zhe Jiang* and *Zhe Li Hao Wan* platforms, and promotes the deep integration of "Internet + culture & tourism."

Shandong continuously accelerates the construction of communication network infrastructure, vigorously improves the level of mobile communication network, expands the coverage of fiber-optic broadband, and deepens the deployment and application of IPv6. Shandong basically completes the network-side transformation of IPv6, and the proportion of IPv6 traffic in mobile network in the province has reached 47 percent. Shandong quickens the construction of satellite Internet, comprehensively builds independent and controllable remote-sensing satellite space infrastructure, and launched Qilu II and Qilu III into space. The in-orbit Qilu I satellite forms a network with Qilu II and Qilu III through intersatellite laser interconnection. Shandong built the first remote-sensing satellite constellation based on laser communication interconnections in China. The Jinan Supercomputing Center constructed a research and testing network for key technologies of the supercomputing Internet, with Jinan and Qingdao as two poles that cover the entire province. The 2G products of Sunway Blue Light were made, and the comprehensive computing power of Shanhe supercomputing platform is at the forefront of the world, achieving regional aggregation of supercomputing resources. Centering on the entire communication chain, Shandong Radio and TV Station explores "Five Intelligent Models" (i.e., intelligent cloud, intelligent product, intelligent communication, intelligent networks, and intelligent database), and accelerates the transformation from integrated media to intelligent media. Shandong held the 2022 Shandong Internet Civilization Week and organized the activity under the theme of "Good Internet Users in Shandong," covering 340 million people both online and offline.

Shanghai continuously promotes the construction of a "dual gigabit broadband city" and achieves basic coverage of 5G network throughout the city. It deepens the large-scale deployment and application of IPv6, and solidly advances the pilot work of technological innovation and integrated application of IPv6. Great breakthroughs have been made in AI. Eighteen scenarios, including the "East Sea Bridge Automatic Drive" (selected as one of the "100 typical application scenarios of AI" by the Ministry of Industry and Information Technology), puts Shanghai first in the total number in China. Shanghai builds several brands of data products, and continuously diversifies the data products of the Shanghai Data Exchange, covering multiple industries such as finance, transportation, industry, communications, shipping, science and technology innovation and energy, and promoting the transformation of data from resources to assets. Shanghai actively explores and improves standards and norms on data products and service rights, and continuously enhances the transformation of data elements into high-quality, knowledge-based, and brand-empowered data products.

Shanghai takes efforts to improve the digital commerce ecosystem and organizes various digital commerce activities. Shanghai continuously promotes the construction of smart transportation, smart elder care, and a digital countryside, empowers civil affairs with digital technologies, and comprehensively accelerates the construction of a digital society. The Office of the Shanghai Cyberspace Affairs Commission guides local platforms of audio-video, online literature, online socializing, and online live streaming to set up a "youth model" with high standards and strict requirements, establish exclusive content system in line with the model, and continuously increase the supply of positive energy content.

Fujian solidifies the foundation of digital infrastructure and promotes the large-scale deployment and application of IPv6. It quickly improves the pattern of new computing power network and continuously raises the utilization rate of data centers. Fujian quickens the high-quality development of the BDS industry and builds the "Beidou Town" industrial park. It continuously advances the aggregation and development of the blockchain industry, develops digital industrial clusters, and builds the first group of five provincial-level digital economy core industry clusters, involving IoT, AI, e-sports, and UHD video. Fujian accelerates the construction of digital society, and the coverage rate of urban management information platforms in built-up areas of designated cities has reached 99.7 percent. It fully mobilizes governments, enterprises, universities, and other parties, strengthens industry-university research cooperation, and promotes the construction of National Cybersecurity Education Technological and Industrial Integration Development Pilot Zone and Fujian Provincial Cybersecurity Industrial Demonstration Park.

Sichuan was selected as National Digital Economy Innovation and Development Pilot Zone, and Chengdu as National New Generation AI Innovation and Development Pilot Zone and National AI Innovation and Application Pilot Zone. Taking this opportunity, Sichuan continuously improves the creation of the industrial Internet system, promotes the construction of Industrial Internet Integrated Development National Demonstration Zone in Chengdu and Chongqing in an orderly way, seizes major strategic opportunity of "East Data, West Computing" Project, and coordinates the construction of an integrated big data center system throughout the province. With the help of modern information technology such as 5G, big data, and cloud computing, Sichuan optimizes urban management and intelligent services. It implements the "Dual Gigabit Town Connection" Project and achieves the access to 5G network and gigabit optical network in all towns in the province. It adheres to the effective integration of the construction of comprehensive Internet governance systems with the promotion of grassroots governance in urban and rural areas and urban social governance, as well as the construction of a "secure Sichuan." It effectively combines two reforms and supervision system, and empowers grassroots governance with the Internet and information technology.

Tianjin gives play to core industries of digital economy and focuses on strengthening technological research and innovation. It deepens the innovation and application of

"5G + specific industries" such as smart healthcare, smart port and ICV, and builds a complete industrial chain covering chips, operating systems, databases, computer systems, servers, and supercomputing. Represented by Phytium CPU and Kylin OS, the "PK" system has a market share of more than 80 percent. Tianjin builds a pilot zone for AI innovation and application in the Binhai New Area, and forms a pilot zone public service platform around the Tianjin Supercomputing Center, providing an integrated support environment for AI development with computing power, algorithms, data, and development tools. The Xinchuang Haihe Laboratory plays a leading role and has started nine major projects, including "Open Source Operating System for RISC-V Architecture" and "Unified Instruction Set and Its Supporting IP and Tool Chain." A number of key new products, including Brain Talker of Tianhe-3, the first brain-computer interface (BCI) chip in the world, have been successfully developed, reaching an advanced level internationally. Tianjin actively promotes the construction of the smart city, established 49 application scenarios of "city brain" such as "smart conflict solution," "direct access to polices benefiting people and agriculture," and *Hui Yan Shi Jin*, and promotes the in-depth development of smart public services.

Hubei empowers high-quality development within the digital economy and accelerates the construction of a "smart society." It comprehensively starts the construction of "gigabit city," implements Cloud-Network Foundation-Strengthening Action in small and medium-sized cities, promotes the integration and evolution of cloud networks in all county-level cities in the province, achieves the support of new generation information technology in county-level cities, and continuously improves the coverage of rural networks. Wuhan is officially approved to establish a national blockchain development pilot zone, and the first "Xinghuo Blockchain Network" backbone node in central China has been launched in Hanyang. Hubei promotes the aggregation of advantages and the upgrading of digital core industries. The Wuhan Optoelectronic Information Industry Cluster has been approved as a national advanced manufacturing industry cluster. Hubei continuously enhances cross-regional government services and improves integrated government services, which significantly raises the efficiency and convenience of handling government affairs. Hubei accelerates the cultivation of cybersecurity talents and strengthens the construction of first-class cybersecurity colleges. The Industrial Internet Industry Alliance Hubei Branch, the Artificial Intelligence Industry Alliance, and the Wuhan Artificial Intelligence Research Institute have been successively established, which continuously strengthen the intellectual support for digital Hubei.

2.2 Ranking of Second-Level Evaluation Indexes

In the China Internet Development Index System 2023, Table 0-2 shows the top ten provinces, autonomous regions, and municipalities directly under the central

Table 0-2 Top ten provinces, autonomous regions, and municipalities directly under the central government in the second-level evaluation indexes in 2023

Ranking	Infrastructure Construction Index	Innovation Capability Index	Development of Digital Economy Index	Development of Digital Society Index	Cybersecurity Index	Cyberspace Governance Index
1	Jiangsu	Beijing	Beijing	Jiangsu	Guangdong	Hebei
2	Beijing	Guangdong	Guangdong	Guangdong	Beijing	Shandong
3	Guangdong	Shanghai	Shanghai	Zhejiang	Shandong	Zhejiang
4	Tianjin	Jiangsu	Jiangsu	Shandong	Shanghai	Guangdong
5	Shandong	Zhejiang	Zhejiang	Henan	Zhejiang	Jiangsu
6	Zhejiang	Tianjin	Shandong	Anhui	Jiangsu	Fujian
7	Shanghai	Shandong	Hubei	Fujian	Fujian	Tibet
8	Henan	Hubei	Tianjin	Sichuan	Sichuan	Sichuan
9	Hubei	Fujian	Sichuan	Beijing	Hubei	Guangxi
10	Guangxi	Anhui	Henan	Hebei	Anhui	Liaoning

government from six aspects, i.e., infrastructure construction, innovation capability, the development of the digital economy, the development of the digital society, cybersecurity, and cyberspace governance.

1. Ranking of Infrastructure Construction Index

Various regions intensively deploy the construction of digital infrastructure, coordinate the construction of network infrastructure; computing power infrastructure, and application infrastructure; vigorously promote the systematic development and large-scale deployment of digital infrastructure; and enhance the integration of digital infrastructure. Specifically, Jiangsu, Beijing, Guangdong, Tianjin, Shandong, Zhejiang, Shanghai, Henan, Hubei, and Guangxi rank among the top ten in the infrastructure construction index. Jiangsu cultivates eight provincial-level industrial Internet logo innovation and application characteristic industrial demonstration zones and 22 industrial application solution service providers, and recommends 12 construction units for Industrial Internet Logo Registration Service Institution License, the largest number in China. Guangdong builds a total of 232,000 5G base stations. A 5G network achieves continuous outdoor coverage in urban areas of all counties (districts), and basic coverage in major areas of all towns. Guangdong ranks first in China in the scale of 5G base stations and the number of 5G users. Beijing deepens the deployment of IPv6 on a large scale. Among the top 200 commercial mobile Internet apps in China, the average proportion of IPv6 for 89 apps in Beijing reached 71.21 percent. Twelve apps account for over 90 percent of IPv6 traffic, a leading level.

2. Ranking of the Innovation Capability Index

Various regions continuously invest capital and manpower to support the innovation in digital technologies and make positive progress in the research and application of key digital technologies. Innovative achievements have been attained in integrated circuits, AI, high-performance computing, databases, operating systems, and other fields. Specifically, Beijing, Guangdong, Shanghai, Jiangsu, Zhejiang, Tianjin, Shandong, Hubei, Fujian, and Anhui rank among the top ten in the innovation capability index. Beijing builds a new-type AI infrastructure Super-large Scale Artificial Intelligence Model Training Platform (Jiuding Platform), with a computing power of 1,000 P. Beijing constructs an AI chip ecology laboratory that accelerates the ecological development of domestic AI chips. Guangdong firmly supports independent innovation in key digital technologies, and implements the key project "New Display and Strategic Electronic Materials" in the national key research and development plan in collaboration with relevant ministries. It promotes major scientific and technological projects such as "chips, software and computing," "blockchain and Fintech," and "intelligent robots," which makes breakthroughs in key technologies in the Internet and information technology. The Shanghai Artificial Intelligence Laboratory releases "OpenXLab" system and "Intern LM2," which further enhance universal visual ability and open-source efforts. Jiangsu fosters the innovation in the entire chain of digital technologies, supports Suzhou Industrial Park to build a core area of the National New Generation Artificial Intelligence Innovation and Development Pilot Zone, and develops 65 application scenarios of new-generation AI.

3. Ranking of the Development of Digital Economy Index

Various regions attach great importance to the development of the digital economy, focusing on digital industrialization and industrial digitization. They guide and support the construction of a number of characteristic digital industry clusters, continuously improve the governance system of the digital economy, and further enhance the scale and quality of core industries in the digital economy. Specifically, Beijing, Guangdong, Shanghai, Jiangsu, Zhejiang, Shandong, Hubei, Tianjin, Sichuan, and Henan rank among the top ten in the development of the digital economy index. In 2022, Beijing achieved an added value of 1.7 trillion *yuan* in the digital economy, accounting for 41.6 percent of regional GDP. The added value of core industries in the digital economy reached 995.83 billion *yuan*, accounting for 23.9 percent of regional GDP. In the field of digital industrialization, Beijing took the lead in the scale and performance of software and information service industry. Zhejiang implemented the "No. 1 Project" of the digital economy. In 2022, the added value of core industries in the digital economy reached 897.7 billion *yuan*, accounting for 11.6 percent of the regional GDP. The business revenue of core industries in digital economy reached

3.28 trillion *yuan*. Shandong centers on the steel, petrochemical, food, and other industries, determines the transformation goals and paths for "one industry, one policy," and comprehensively improves the digital level of enterprises. There are thirty-one national platform innovation and demonstration use cases, eleven typical mobile IoT use cases, four digital demonstration enterprises, and four pilot projects for empowering digital transformation and upgrading the new industrialization industrial demonstration base and platform.

4. Ranking of the Development of the Digital Society Index

Various regions solidly promote the construction of the digital society in various fields, quickening the sharing of high-quality service resources, significantly improving the digitization of key livelihood areas such as education, healthcare, employment, and elder care, and achieving significant results in making the digital society more accurate, inclusive, and convenient. Specifically, Jiangsu, Guangdong, Zhejiang, Shandong, Henan, Anhui, Fujian, Sichuan, Beijing, and Hebei rank among the top ten in the development of the digital society index. Jiangsu developed *Su Shi Yang Lao*, an elder care service applet, built a mobile platform for gathering elder care service information for society and the public, and provided more efficient and convenient elder care service information for the elderly in the provinces. Jiangsu forms an "Internet + elderly care" service platform ("virtual nursing home), which covers emergency rescue, housekeeping service, daily care, rehabilitation care, home appliances repair, spiritual comfort, the protection of legal rights, leisure and entertainment, and other services. Focusing on "Health Brain +," Zhejiang actively built a health service system for the public, and launched more than 70 digital apps in three subfields (i.e., smart healthcare, digital health management, and smart public health), serving more than 17 million people every day. Fujian enthusiastically promotes the pilot and demonstration of smart parking, expands ETC (Electronic Toll Collection) smart parking, smart refueling, and other applications, reduces traffic collisions, and takes multiple measures to ensure the safe travel of citizens. The ETC usage rate of highway buses in Fujian reaches 75.15 percent, ranking first in China.

5. Ranking of the Cybersecurity Index

Various regions continuously strengthen the strategic planning and top-level design of cybersecurity work, bolster the capability in safeguarding cybersecurity, organize various forms of cybersecurity publicity activities, and enhance the awareness of cybersecurity among the public. Cybersecurity technologies and industries have developed rapidly. Specifically, Guangdong, Beijing, Shandong, Shanghai,

Zhejiang, Jiangsu, Fujian, Sichuan, Hubei, and Anhui rank among the top ten in the cybersecurity index. Guangdong launched "Yue Dun-2022" Digital Government & Cybersecurity Attack-Defense Exercise and campaigns on data security and personal information protection in the fields of health, the medical insurance system, and the post and express delivery. It eliminates the risks and hidden dangers to security and improves the security protection system. Zhejiang solidly promotes the development of the Internet and data security technologies and industries, strengthens data security and personal information protection, introduced *Zhejiang Provincial Public Data Regulations*, the first local regulation in public data in China, as well as three local standards, and consolidates the monitoring and early warning of data security. Jiangsu implemented systems such as the *Classification and Grading Standards for Public Data in Jiangsu Province*, strengthens risk prevention and control of public data, focuses on protecting the government extranet, the government cloud, data and applications, and builds a security protection system that features one center and three-level protection and covers security management centers, regional boundaries, communication networks, and the computing environment.

6. Ranking of the Cyberspace Governance Index

Various regions attach great importance to cyberspace governance, vigorously promoting the creation of online content and the Internet, actively introducing laws and regulations on cyberspace governance, consolidating the foundation of cyberspace governance system, and continuously addressing problems on Internet ecology. Specifically, Hebei, Shandong, Zhejiang, Guangdong, Jiangsu, Fujian, Tibet, Sichuan, Guangxi, and Liaoning rank among the top ten in the cyberspace governance index. Hebei severely cracks down on various illegal activities in cyberspace and continuously improves citizens' Internet literacy. 1,134 websites that seriously disturb Internet information dissemination and harm Internet ecology have been shut down in accordance with the law. Hebei organized more than 220 promotional activities for the "Five Entries" of *Convention on Internet Ecology and Civilization in Hebei Province* in departments of cyberspace affairs in the province. Relevant departments come to residential communities, rural areas, campuses, enterprises, parks, and other places and guide Internet users to participate in the governance of Internet ecology by distributing brochures and conducting on-site explanations. Shandong organized 46 campaigns to purify the online environment, clearing more than 78,000 pieces of illegal information, and closing and punishing more than 750 illegal websites and more than 360 mobile apps, with remarkable achievements in the governance of Internet ecology. Guangdong takes the construction and evaluation of Internet civilization as an evaluation index of civilized cities, carrying out 630 "Good Internet Users in Guangdong" and other activities, and effectively constructing a concentric circle online and offline.

3. Outlook on the Trends of China's Internet Development

3.1 The digital economy sees high-quality development that deepens applications, optimizes structures, and delivers benefits to all

The digital economy has become an important factor that affects global resource allocation, industrial structures, and the international division of labor. In recent years, China has seen rapid development of its digital economy. In the total scale of the digital economy, China has ranked second in the world for several years. The digital economy plays a leading and supporting role in socioeconomic development. However, the digital economy in China is beset with the problem of "big but not strong, fast but not healthy." For example, the innovation capability in key fields such as high-end chips and basic materials remains weak, lower than the international advanced level. The digital development of traditional industries has slowed down. Some enterprises show low willingness or have difficulties with digital transformation.

In the future, China will accelerate the development of the digital economy, promote the deep integration of the digital economy and the traditional economy, cultivate a group of ecology-dominated enterprises with core competitiveness, quicken the construction of digital industry clusters with international competitiveness, and strengthen, optimize, and expand the digital economy. China continues to improve the level of "cloud service, data application and intelligence-based transformation," deepen the integration and development of new generation information technology with the primary, secondary, and tertiary industries, and supports the transformation of small and medium-sized enterprises. China expands the research and application of new technologies. AI widely penetrates into key fields such as agriculture, industry, finance, education, and healthcare. The application scenarios become diverse and catalyze new models of intelligent manufacturing. New technologies become a new engine for the development of the digital economy. China will improve the digital supply of public service resources and the level of Internet-based services, increase the supply of elder-friendly digital products, and raise the digital literacy and skills of the entire society.

3.2 Basic data system improves and fosters the sustainable development of the data element market

Currently, data, as a factor of production, receives more and more attention. Various regions extensively carry out the construction of the data element market, speed up the allocation of the data element market, and promote the construction of a competitive, orderly and complete data element market system. This not only follows national policies, but also meets the urgent needs of various market entities. Meanwhile, data elements feature replicability, nonstandardization, and complex ownership relationships, and face such problems as the risks to data security, isolated information islands, the lack of data standards, and the absence of trust among business entities.

In the future, China will accelerate the construction of a "1 + N" data element system, encourage pilot projects on the circulation and use of data elements in some regions and industries, and coordinate the construction of a multilevel, diversified, and on-site and off-site data element market system. China will improve the data element market trading system, optimize data trading market management systems, revitalize the national data trading market, build a collaborative and efficient data element trading platform, and fully stimulate the value of data elements. China will establish a complete data management system, break market barriers to data elements, achieve the circulation and sharing of data value, standardize the sharing, classification and grading and flow of data, and actively participate in the formulation of international standards in relevant fields. China will fully leverage the force of multiple parties in collaborative governance, ensure the legitimate and reasonable rights and interests of all data entities, determine the rights and obligations of market entities, continuously optimize the structure of the data element market, and improve the data element market ecosystem from the perspectives of the supply and circulation of data elements.

3.3 New technologies, applications, and business models continue to empower the creation of online content, and the construction of all-media communication systems accelerates

The report of the 20th CPC National Congress stresses that we will improve the communication system across all forms of media, create a new environment for mainstream public opinion, and foster a healthy online environment, raising new requirements for the construction and governance of online content. 2023 saw the tenth anniversary of General Secretary Xi Jinping's proposal for media integration and development. From 2013 to 2023, the integration of traditional media and new media accelerated, and the voice of the Party became the strongest voice in cyberspace. High-quality online content continued to emerge, and technologies such as big data, cloud computing, and AI deepened media integration. Simultaneously, the landscape of media and the ecology of public opinion underwent profound changes, posing new tasks and topics for the creation of online content. Problems such as hiring paid posters, malpractice in We Media and addiction to short videos occurred frequently, and hidden dangers such as regulatory blind spots and copyright disputes existed. New technologies, applications, and models not only empowered the production of online content, but also bred hidden risks such as false information dissemination and a lack of ideological security.

In the future, media integration will arrive at a new stage in which the construction of full media communication systems accelerates. Mainstream media will actively adapt to the trend of digital development, deepen the cultivation of high-quality content, and launch a group of excellent works with innovative form, vivid style, and rich meaning. China will innovate the channels of content dissemination, fully utilize diverse forms of information, and continuously improve the efficiency of content dissemination. China will see a new round of technological development and evolution, for example, AI. On the basis of technological innovation, China continues to promote the upgrading of media that will become more accurate, efficient, and intelligent in this critical period. As the artificial intelligence generated content (AIGC) industry grows rapidly, the commercial use of AIGC turns into reality, and the ecology of AIGC improves. Intelligent communication will revolutionize models of human information dissemination, which may trigger fundamental changes at various levels and in various areas of society.

Notably, the progress of digital and intelligent technologies will provide a larger space for the innovation and development of new applications, experiences, and consumption of digital culture. The supply capability of public cultural digital content continues to be strengthened, and new scenarios of digital cultural consumption will be immensely expanded. The misuse of digital technologies disrupts the digital cultural market. In response to malpractice in cyberspace, China will pool social forces, launch various campaigns, strengthen online regulation, enhance the protection of minors, and foster a positive, healthy, and upright environment for the digital culture ecosystem and online content supply.

3.4 Risks to data security: all of society works toward safeguarding data security

Presently, incidents of data security occur frequently, and risks to data security have become increasingly severe. Compared with typical cybersecurity threats, the threats to data security prove more complex and diverse. In particular, the emergence of new technologies like GAI intensifies the risks to data security. Illegal collection and use of personal information on apps, unclear data ownership, and other problems remain unsolved. The breach and abuse of data as well as attacks on data occur repeatedly, which attracts widespread attention among the whole society.

In the future, China will comprehensively strengthen cybersecurity, especially data security protection. China continues to optimize policies, regulations, and standards and to consolidate the work of data security governance. China will make efforts to address prominent issues in data security, continuously launching the campaign against the illegal collection and use of personal information on apps. Focusing on key fields, China will strengthen the protection of data and personal information and effectively enhance governance capabilities. China will solidify the research and development of key cybersecurity technologies, support regulatory requirements through technological means, and embed technological tests into the entire process of data protection, especially personal information protection. China will comprehensively analyze and judge, in a timely manner, the risks and hidden dangers from new technologies like AI and augment the ability to prevent and resolve risks. Simultaneously, driven by data compliance and corporate data protection, the demands for data security products and services in the market become more prominent. Data-centered security investment continues to grow, and the growth of the data security industry continues to expand. China continually organizes National Cybersecurity Promotion Week, which steadily heightens the awareness of cybersecurity protection among the public.

3.5 Various regions strengthen digital governance, continuously optimize domestic environment for digital development, and quicken the progress of international digital cooperation

Major economies around the world optimize digital governance systems, partake in the formulation of international rules on digital economy, and compete for the rights to speak. In digital development, China faces both domestic and international challenges. Domestically, China needs to continuously improve the digital governance system, introduce detailed rules for platform economy governance, and deepen the participation in international governance of the digital economy. Internationally, various countries have not reached a consensus on the governance of the digital economy or established effective governance models and complete governance systems. The politicization of digital technologies also poses big challenges to the development of the digital economy.

General Secretary Xi Jinping emphasizes that "[g]lobal digital economy is an open and close-knit entity. Win-win cooperation is the only right way forward, while a closed-door policy, exclusion, confrontation and division would only lead to a dead end." In the future, domestically, China will continue to improve the digital governance system, enhance the governance on data, algorithms, and other fields, regulate the competitive order in the economy, prevent vicious expansion of capital, optimize the business environment, achieve the integration of the digital economy and digital governance, and form a good environment for the standardized, orderly, and healthy development of the digital economy. Internationally, China will actively participate in negotiations and rulemaking in the digital field of international organizations, such as the United Nations, World Trade Organization (WTO), APEC, and BRICS (Brazil, Russia, India, China, and South Africa), and make suggestions and proposals based on the development of the digital economy in China. China will further improve and protect the bilateral and multilateral governance mechanisms of the digital economy, and actively provide public products for digital governance so as to strengthen the international governance system of the digital economy and lay open new ground for international cooperation in the digital economy. Meanwhile, China continues to enlarge exchanges and cooperation with various countries and regions, and promote building a community with a shared future in cyberspace.

10.2478/9788367405867-002

Chapter 1
Construction of Digital Infrastructure

Currently, a new technological revolution and industrial transformation is accelerating. Various countries around the world take the construction of digital infrastructure as an important driving force for achieving innovation and development, continuously invigorate new applications, expand new business formats, and create new models. But the global economy remains sluggish. Under such circumstances, digital infrastructure, as an important base, continues to support and lead new directions in economic development. General Secretary Xi Jinping has made arrangements to promote high-quality construction of digital infrastructure many times. At the beginning of 2023, when presiding over the second group study session of the Political Bureau of the CPC Central Committee, General Secretary Xi Jinping stressed that "We must appropriately deploy the construction of new infrastructure in advance, increase investment in high-tech industries and strategic emerging industries, and continue to stimulate the vitality of private investment." The CPC Central Committee and the State Council issued *Overall Layout and Planning for the Construction of Digital China*, which proposes to "unclog the main artery of digital infrastructure" and consolidate the foundation for the construction of a digital China.

Over the past year, China continuously promoted the systematic development and large-scale deployment of the digital infrastructure, and steadily advanced communication network infrastructure, computing power infrastructure, new technology infrastructure, and application infrastructure. By the end of June 2023, China had totally built and opened more than 2.937 million 5G base stations. 5G network covered all urban areas of prefecture-level cities and counties across the country. The number of 5G mobile phone users reached 676 million. One hundred ten gigabit cities had been built nationwide, with gigabit access users exceeding 100 million and IPv6 traffic on mobile networks exceeding 50 percent for the first time. The top-level design, such as *Overall Layout and Planning for the Construction of Digital China* and "East Data, West Computing" Project, continuously enlarges the demand for computing power. The construction of computing power infrastructure has reached a stage of rapid growth. In the list of top 500 supercomputers globally, China ranks first in the world, with 162 supercomputers. Quantum technology is developing rapidly, with positive progress made in quantum communication, quantum computing, and other fields. IoV, IoT, the industrial Internet, and other application infrastructures thrive, and industrial ecology keeps growing.

1.1 Construction of Communication Network Infrastructure Advances

In 2022, the scale of network connections such as 5G and gigabit optical networks continued to expand, and the revenue and scale of telecom services steadily increased. In the number of active IPv6 users, China ranks among the top in the world. Space-based network facilities play a significant role in empowering development and improving efficiency.

1.1.1 5G reaches a critical stage in large-scale application

The construction of a 5G network progresses in a stable fashion. In the four-year commercial use of 5G in China, 5G has been transformed from a model into reality, solving the digital problems faced by many industries and enterprises. By the end of June 2023, the total number of base stations for mobile phones in China had reached 11.29 million, with a net increase of 452,000 over the end of 2022. The number of 5G base stations totaled 2.937 million, accounting for 26 percent of mobile base stations. Three basic telecom enterprises had 1.71 billion mobile phone users. 5G users accounted for more than 30 percent of all users, reaching a leading level worldwide[1].

The application scenarios of 5G continue to deepen. 5G has been fully integrated into 52 major categories within the national economy and has been quickly applied in industry, healthcare, education, transportation, tourism, and other fields, with more than 50,000 use cases. In the field of energy, 5G has been continuously integrated and innovatively developed with the energy industry. In May 2023, the National Energy Administration and the Ministry of Industry and Information Technology edited *Compilation of Typical Cases of 5G Applications in the Energy Field in 2022*, which focuses on six directions, i.e., smart power plant + 5G, smart grid + 5G, smart coal + 5G, smart oil and gas +5G, comprehensive energy + 5G, and smart manufacturing and construction + 5G. The document selects 33 typical cases from among 198 cases. In the financial field, the People's Bank of China released *Development Plan for Fintech 2022–2025*, which clearly proposes the application of 5G to build a secure and ubiquitous financial network. In April 2023, the Bank of Communications, China Telecom, and Huawei jointly published the white paper *5G Financial Cloud Private Network Technology and Its Application*, which comprehensively summarizes the latest achievements of 5G Financial Cloud Private Network of Bank of Communications in technological architecture and application innovation. In the medical field, more than

1 "Economic Operation in the Communications Industry in the First Half of 2023." Accessed August 2023. https://www.miit.gov.cn/gxsj/tjfx/txy/art/2023/art_75d835da87d24c13aa5dc752b901aca7.html.

80 percent of pilot projects for "5G+ healthcare" applications have complete network coverage. China Mobile partners more than 2,000 medical institutions in China, including the Peking Union Medical College Hospital, to explore the construction of 5G smart hospitals, providing innovative applications in smart healthcare, smart service, and smart management, and promoting the digital and intelligent transformation of "integration of medical treatment, medical insurance and medicines supply."

The experiment on 5G air-to-ground communication technology expands new applications of 5G. In May 2023, the Ministry of Industry and Information Technology approved China Mobile's use of partial 5G frequency resources at 4.9 GHz to conduct the experiment on 5G air-to-ground (5G-ATG) communication technology. 5G-ATG is one of the important technological paths to achieve high-quality development of the aviation Internet. By setting special base stations and shaped beam antennas in line with international rules and domestic regulations, an air-to-ground communication link has been established between ground and aircraft cabin, enabling passengers to access the Internet through WLAN access in airplane cabins. The experiment further improves the spatial dimension of 5G network coverage, expands new applications and new business models of 5G in the field of aviation, and better meets the needs of aviation passengers for Internet access.

The exploration of 6G further deepens. The 14th Five-Year Plan (2021–2025) for National Economic and Social Development and the Long-Range Objectives Through the Year 2035 (The 14th Five-Year Plan) and The 14th Five-Year Plan for the Development of Digital Economy propose to proactively deploy 6G network technological reserves, enhance support for the R & D of 6G technology, and participate in promoting the international standardization of 6G. Presently, China has made significant progress in key technologies such as 6G ultralarge-scale multi-input and output, terahertz communication, integrated sensing and communications, endogenous AI communication, deterministic networks, and satellite to ground integrated networks. In March 2023, the 2023 Global 6G Conference was held in Nanjing, with the theme "Better Together, Better Future." It explored the technological transformation and innovation of 6G networks, enhanced international cooperation in 6G, promoted building a globally unified 6G standard and ecosystem, and injected new vitality and momentum into the development of 6G technology and industry in the future. The conference released Global Initiative for 6G International Cooperation and Collaborative Development, calling on participants to build a platform based on extensive consultation, joint contributions, and shared benefits, to pool global wisdom, and to implement a mechanism featuring complementary advantages, collaborative innovation, resource sharing, and mutual benefit.

1.1.2 Fiber-optic broadband network further expands

The number of fixed broadband access users continues to grow. One hundred ten gigabit cities have been built nationwide, with gigabit access users exceeding

100 million. The number of fixed broadband access users steadily increases. By the end of June 2023, three basic telecom enterprises had 614 million fixed broadband access users, with a net increase of 24.68 million over the end of 2022. Specifically, there were 579 million fixed broadband access users with an access rate of 100 Mbps and above, accounting for 94.2 percent of the total. There were 128 million fixed broadband access users with an access rate of 1,000 Mbps and above, accounting for 20.8 percent of the total, with a net increase of 36.12 million over the end of 2022.

The total length of optical cable lines steadily increases. By the end of June 2023, the total length of optical cable lines in China had reached 61.96 million kilometers, with a net increase of 2.38 million kilometers over the end of 2022, as shown in Figure 1-1. The proportions of access network optical cable, local network relay optical cable and long-distance optical cable were 62.6 percent, 35.7 percent, and 1.8 percent, respectively. The proportion of local network relay optical cable increased by 0.2 percent year over year.

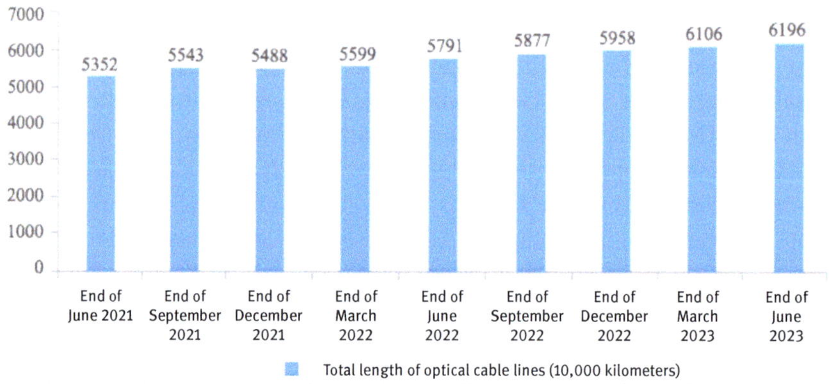

Figure 1-1 Total length of optical cable lines.

Source: Ministry of Industry an d Information Technology.

The service capability of the gigabit network continuously improves. By the end of June 2023, the number of broadband access ports in China had reached 1.11 billion, with a net increase of 34.57 million over the end of 2022, as shown in Figure 1-2. Specifically, the number of FTTH/O ports reached 1.06 billion, with a net increase of 38.55 million over the end of 2022, accounting for 96.2 percent of Internet broadband access ports. By the end of June 2023, the number of 10G PON ports with service capability of gigabit network had reached 20.29 million, with a net increase of 5.065 million over the end of 2022[2].

2 "Economic Operation in the Communications Industry in the First Half of 2023." Accessed August 2023. https://www.miit.gov.cn/gxsj/tjfx/txy/art/2023/art_75d835da87d24c13aa5dc752b901aca7.html.

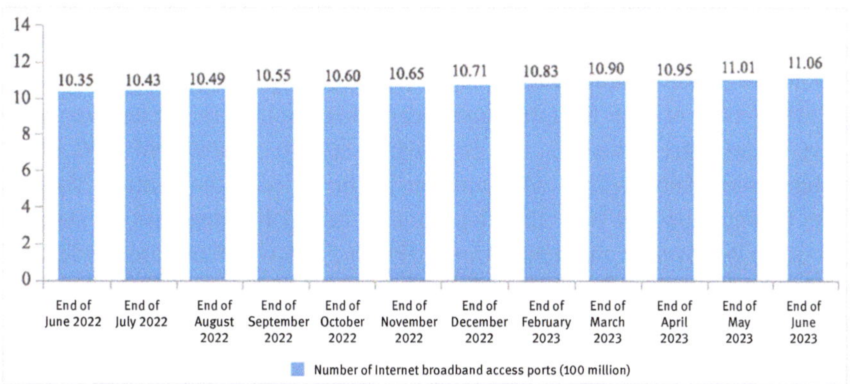

Figure 1-2 Number of Internet broadband access ports.

Source: Ministry of Industry and Information Technology.

1.1.3 Application of IPv6 is tremendously optimized

As the foundation for the development of next-generation Internet, IPv6 plays an important role in building China into a country with cyber strength. IPv6 provides an opportunity for China to utilize global Internet upgrades and evolution and to accelerate the upgrading of network infrastructures, the innovation of the technological industry, and the development of economy and society. At present, China has fully built an IPv6 network and optimized the application of IPv6. By the end of August 2023, the number of active IPv6 users had reached 762 million,[3] accounting for 71 percent of the total number of Internet users. IPv6 traffic outnumbered IPv4 traffic, marking a new milestone for China to promote the large-scale deployment and application of IPv6. China Mobile had 940 million active IPv6 connections nationwide, China Unicom basically possessed the capability to fully perform IPv6 services, and China Telecom mainly completed the transformation of end-to-end IPv6 cloud network.

In April 2023, the Ministry of Industry and Information Technology, the Office of the Central Cyberspace Affairs Commission, and the National Development and Reform Commission jointly issued *Implementation Opinions on Promoting IPv6 Technological Evolution, Application, Innovation and Development*, which clarifies that by the end of 2025, China will achieve remarkable results in IPv6 technological evolution, application and innovation, significantly enhance technological innovation of IPv6 network, further expand the application scope of innovative technologies like IPv6 +,

3 "National IPv6 Development Monitoring Platform." Accessed August 2023. https://m.china-ipv6.cn/complete/#/.

and tremendously improve the integrated application of IPv6 + in key industries. The *Implementation Opinions* deploys major tasks on building an IPv6 evolutionary technological system, strengthening the industrial foundation of IPv6, accelerating the development of IPv6 infrastructure, deepening the integration and application of IPv6 + and other industries, and improving security capability of IPv6, in a bid to achieve remarkable results. Simultaneously, the Office of the Central Cyberspace Affairs Commission and two other departments issued *Working Plan for Deepening Large-Scale Deployment and Application of IPv6 in 2023*, which outlines eleven major tasks, such as strengthening the carrying capacity of the IPv6 network, improving the supporting capacity of IPv6 terminals, optimizing the performance of IPv6 application facilities, continuously enhancing security protection, and solidly deepening large-scale deployment and application of IPv6.

1.1.4 Significant achievements are made in empowering and increasing the efficiency of space-based network infrastructure

1. The application of BeiDou Navigation Satellite System sees large-scale development

In a congratulatory letter to the First International Summit on BDS Applications, General Secretary Xi Jinping points out that global digital development is accelerating, and time-space information and positioning navigation services have become a new important infrastructure. As the BeiDou-3 Global Navigation Satellite System is comprehensively completed and launched, the large-scale application of BDS officially enters a new stage of market-oriented, industrial, and international development. Currently, there are a total of forty-five in-orbit BDS satellites, including fifteen BeiDou-2 and thirty BeiDou-3 satellites. Connected to the network, all satellites stay in orbit, provide services, and operate stably and smoothly. In basic navigation, positioning, and timing services, space signals remain stable. In the past two years, the indicators reached the one-meter level, the continuity of space signal exceeded 0.998 per hour, and the availability remained higher than 0.98. Characteristic services, such as global RDSS (Radio Determination Satellite System) communication, regional RDSS communication, international search and rescue, precise point position, satellite-based enhancement, and ground-based enhancement, operate stably and reliably, all meeting the requirements of indicators.

In November 2022, the State Council Information Office released the white paper *China's BeiDou Navigation Satellite System in the New Era*, which comprehensively reviews the development of BDS and showcases new service capabilities and industrial trends of BDS. Presently, BDS has been deeply integrated with emerging technologies such as big data, the IoT, and AI, which breeds new business models such as Beidou + and + Beidou, and has become an important technological force empowering the development of various industries in economy and society.

In the transportation industry, BDS is widely used in key transportation-process monitoring, highway infrastructure security monitoring, high-precision port dispatch monitoring, and other businesses. In 2022, more than 7.9 million road operating vehicles, more than 40,000 postal and express trunk vehicles, more than 47,000 ships, more than 13,000 water-assisted navigation devices, and about 500 general-purpose aircraft were equipped with BDS. This comprehensively improves the level of information-based transportation and significantly reduces the incidence of major traffic accidents.

In agriculture, forestry, animal husbandry, and fishery, there are more than 100,000 BDS-based auto-drive systems of agricultural machinery, more than 100,000 management terminals of BDS-based forestry integrated application and service platforms, more than 20,000 sets of positioning collars for BDS smart grazing, and more than 100,000 fishing vessels with BDS shipborne terminals. These raise the efficiency of operation management tremendously and improve the management level of the security of agriculture, forestry, animal husbandry, and fishery.

In the field of engineering construction, BDS, in combination with multisensors, the Internet, and other technologies, was widely used in the construction of the Chengdu-Kunming Railway, the Gansu S28 Expressway, the Shenzhen Mawan Cross-sea Channel, the Xinjiang Desert Highway, and other projects, which significantly improves the quality and efficiency of engineering construction and reduces labor and material costs.

In the field of mass consumption, BDS has become the standard device with positioning function for wearable devices such as smartphones and smartwatches. In 2022, the total shipment volume of smartphones supporting BDS reached 260 million units, accounting for 98.5 percent. In July 2022, the results of Beidou-3 RDSS communication service were released, achieving the integration of BDS RDSS communication into smartphones in a way that does not change cards or numbers and adds external devices. As BDS realizes the satellite communication capability of public smartphones for the first time worldwide, users in the Asia Pacific region can enjoy the Beidou-3 RDSS service. The lane-level navigation function based on BDS high-precision positioning has been successfully piloted in eight cities in China. Meanwhile, characteristic functions, such as location inquiry, green light navigation, and sharing locations to report safety, have been applied to public transportation.

Global application of BDS improves. In November 2022, China and four Cospas-Sarsat members (Canada, France, Russia, and the United States) signed a statement of intent for intergovernmental cooperation, officially becoming a space-segment provider of Cospas-Sarsat. Simultaneously, the 106th Session of IMO (International Maritime Organization) MSC (Maritime Safety Committee) passed the resolution that officially included BDS RDSS in Global Maritime Distress and Safety System (GMDSS), signaling that BDS RDSS became the third satellite communication system in the world recognized by IMO for GMDSS.

2. Application of satellite Internet speeds up

In the past three years, satellite Internet was officially incorporated into the construction of new infrastructure, and the construction of satellite Internet in China accelerated. The application of satellite Internet became more diverse, and the technology of satellite Internet reached a new level, developing from a single satellite to a networking constellation. The duration of satellite video calls also increased from three minutes to more than half an hour. In April 2023, the test and application of LEO satellite Internet were achieved in the field of power communication in remote areas for the first time. Without base stations for ground communication, the use of satellite signals can support power patrol inspection, emergency support, and other tasks. Satellite Internet terminals independently developed by Chinese enterprises can achieve automatic satellite alignment within two minutes, and accurately track satellites when vehicles are running at high speeds.

In recent years, many private enterprises in satellite manufacturing, rocket launch, and other fields have played an active role in the construction of satellite Internet, driving the satellite industry into a new development stage. The number of new registrations of Chinese satellite enterprises is growing rapidly, exceeding 30,000 for the first time in 2022. Simultaneously, relevant departments have successively released policies to vigorously promote the development of satellite Internet, aerospace information, and other industries. For example, Beijing introduces *Regulations on Promoting the Development of Digital Economy in Beijing*, proposing that satellite Internet is listed in the construction of key projects in information network infrastructure. Chongqing published *Opinions on Accelerating the High-Quality Development of the Aerospace Information Industry Led by Satellite Internet*. It plans to introduce and cultivate hundreds of enterprises that use special and sophisticated technologies to produce novel and unique products, and provide complete support for the upstream and downstream of the entire industrial chain.

3. Application of remote-sensing satellite comes to a stage of rapid development

Based on the satellite platform, remote-sensing technology carries various sensors to observe the earth surface, to obtain a series of conditions of ecological environment such as water, plants, land, and atmosphere on the ground. Simultaneously, in the case of emergencies and disasters, remote-sensing satellites can quickly form images and observe the situation at the affected locations. In recent years, the remote-sensing satellite has entered a period of rapid development in China, transforming from demonstration applications to business services in key industries such as agriculture, natural resources, ecological environment, water conservancy, and forestry. In the automation of remote-sensing technology, China has reached a leading level in global Earth observation satellite in both quantity and quality. According to the latest data of the China National Space Administration, China now has more than 300 satellites with a weight of more than 300 kilograms in orbit, ranking second in the world, as well as more than 200 in-orbit remote-sensing satellites, which achieve one-day global coverage of 16-meter-resolution satellite data and one-day global revisit of optical two-meter-resolution data. One-meter-resolution synthetic aperture radar (SAR) satellites can revisit any regions around the world in five hours. In 2022, the China National Space Administration opened the National Platform for Remote-Sensing Data and Application Services, which allows for easy access to China's remote-sensing data from 2012 to 2022.

1.2 Construction of Computing Power Infrastructure Enters a Period of Rapid Growth

The top-level design, such as *Overall Layout and Planning for the Construction of Digital China* and "East Data, West Computing" Project, tremendously enlarged the demand for computing power in China. In 2022, the revenue from cloud computing and big data services continued to grow in China, reaching 1,042.7 billion *yuan*, with a year-on-year increase of 8.7 percent, accounting for 14.9 percent of the revenue of information technology service. The construction of supercomputing centers steadily advanced, with several national supercomputing centers built and put into operation.

1.2.1 Construction of data center features green and intensive development

1. National policies encourage the construction of green and energy-saving data centers

From 2012 to 2022, the National Development and Reform Commission and other departments continued to release policies on data centers and propose requirements for the intensification of regional development and the use of green energy in the layout of data centers. In 2022, *The 14th Five-Year Plan for the Development of Digital Economy* proposed to accelerate the implementation of the "East Data, West Computing" Project. Over the past decade, national policies have focused on improving the cross-network and cross-regional data exchange capabilities of data centers, and promoting the construction of green data centers. In February 2023, the CPC Central Committee and the State Council issued *Overall Layout and Planning for the Construction of Digital China*, which proposes to promote the deep integration of digital technology with the "Five-sphere Integrated Plan" for progress in the economic, political, cultural, social, and eco-environmental fields, build a green and intelligent digital ecological civilization, accelerate coordinated digital and green transformation, and advocate for a green and intelligent lifestyle. Guided by a series of policies, data centers in China are developing toward energy-saving transformation and continuous improvement of the utilization of renewable energy.

The Ministry of Industry and Information Technology released *The Three-Year Action Plan for the Development of New Data Centers 2021–2023*, proposing that by the end of 2023, power usage effectiveness (PUE) of newly built large data centers would be reduced to below 1.3. The setting of hard indicators and timelines further accelerates the popularization of green data centers. In the List of National Green Data Centers in 2022 published by the Ministry of Industry and Information Technology and other departments, forty-three data centers were shortlisted, covering the fields of communications, the Internet, the public sector, energy, and finance. To date, China has built about 200 national green data centers.

2. The data center industry faces opportunities for development

The White Paper on Data Centers 2022[4] shows that in recent years, the number of data center racks in China has steadily increased, jumping from 1.24 million to 5.2 million from 2016 to 2021, with a CAGR (Compound Annual Growth Rate) of nearly 30 percent. In 2021, the number of data center racks with a capacity of over 2.5 kw in China reached 4.2 million, accounting for 80 percent of the total number. According to the data from the Press Conference on the Development of Industry and Information Technology in 2022, China has coordinated the layout of data and the construction of computing infrastructure. In the total scale of in-use data center racks, there are more than 6.5 million standard racks, with an average annual growth rate of more than 25 percent in computing power in the past five years. Affected by the policies on new infrastructure and digital transformation as well as market environment, the scale of the data center market in China shows a trend of high growth. As the International Data Corporation (IDC) predicts, by 2030, the scale of the data center industry in China will climb to 403.6 billion *yuan*. Servers, refrigeration systems, and power distribution systems rank among the top three in terms of scale and will become the largest market areas in the future. In addition, the compound growth rates of refrigeration systems and the power distribution system will reach 20 percent and 12 percent, respectively, with a large space for market growth, providing great opportunities for the development of enterprises.[5]

---

4 China Academy of Information and Communications Technology. *The White Paper on Data Centers 2022*. June 2022.

5 "East Data, West Computing Project Has Been Officially Launched, with a Comprehensive Interpretation of the Development Trends of the Data Center Industry." Accessed July 2023. https://m.thepaper.cn/newsDetail_forward_18016459.

1.2.2 Application of cloud computing slows down

The IDC report shows that the COVID-19 pandemic has impaired the development of the global IT market environment. In the global public cloud market, enterprise users face increasing instability. Upstream enterprises reduce budgets and continuously extend construction cycles, which blocks the development of the public cloud market. The public cloud service market remains stable, with a slight decline in China. According to the *China Quarterly Public Cloud Services Tracker* released by the IDC, in the second half of 2022, the total scale of public cloud service market in China reached 18.84 billion US dollars. Alibaba Cloud, Huawei Cloud, China Telecom e Cloud, Tencent Cloud, and Amazon are the top five markets, as shown in Figure 1-3. Specifically, the IaaS market grew by 15.7 percent year on year, and the PaaS market grew by 31.8 percent year on year. Yet, there was an obvious slowdown in the growth rates of the IaaS + PaaS markets, with a year-on-year growth of 19.0 percent in the second half of 2022, a year-on-year decrease of 23.9 percent over the second half of 2021, and a year-on-year decrease of 11.6 percent in the first half of 2022. According to the statistical data of Canalys, a market research firm, in the second quarter of 2023, the expenditure on cloud infrastructure services in China reached 8.7 billion US dollars, with a year-on-year increase of 19 percent.

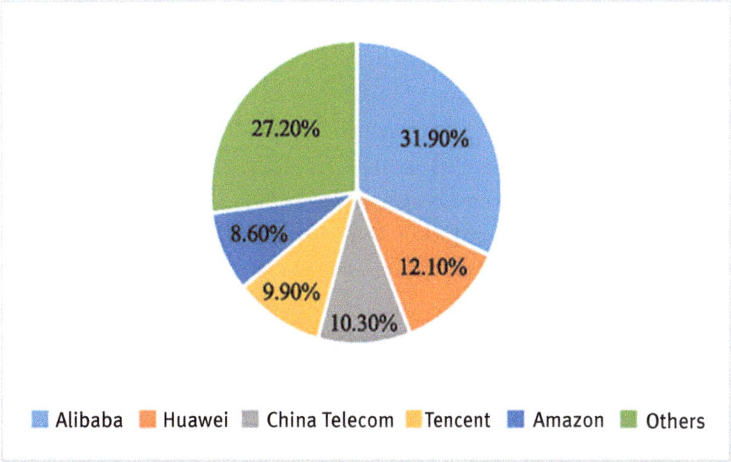

Figure 1-3 Market share of top five public cloud IaaS + PaaS manufacturers in China in the second half of 2022.

Source: International Data Corporation.

Since 2023, Chinese cloud manufacturers have expanded their overseas markets. Southeast Asia, Central Asia, Europe, and other regions have become popular destinations for overseas expansion. Alibaba Cloud announced that it will invest seven billion *yuan* in the next three years to expand the international ecosystem and add six overseas service centers in Europe, America, and Asia. Huawei Cloud has been deployed in 29 regions, covering more than 170 countries and regions worldwide. Tencent Cloud declared the establishment of the Overseas Ecological Alliance, providing strong support for localized operations for customers through operations in 26 regions across five continents worldwide. While Chinese cloud manufacturers go global, the domestic cloud market attracts a large number of overseas cloud manufacturers. According to the IDC report, if only Chinese enterprises that use overseas public cloud resources are included, and their businesses in China are accounted for, Amazon Web Services (AWS) has occupied nearly three-quarters of the market share.

Currently, cloud service evolves from an idea at the early stage to wide popularization and application. As a whole, despite the fact that domestic cloud computing market grew slowly in 2022, analysts take an optimistic view of the market prospects. IDC predicts that overall compound growth rate of cloud computing market in China will reach about 20 percent in the next five years.

1.2.3 Edge computing market grows rapidly

1. National strategy supports the development of edge computing

As the support for the integration of ICT and operation technology, edge computing faces an opportunity for significant industrial development. At the beginning of 2022, the State Council issued *The 14th Five-Year Plan for the Development of Digital Economy*, which clarifies the requirements for "strengthening edge computing capabilities for specific scenarios." The Ministry of Industry and Information Technology and the Ministry of Emergency Management released *Action Plan for Industrial Internet Safety Production 2021–2023*, which proposes that developing edge computing is one of the key tasks to build new capabilities in safety production based on the industrial Internet. Simultaneously, the Ministry of Industry and Information Technology and the National Development and Reform Commission successively established key projects in technological research and development, test and verification and demonstration-project construction related to edge computing. New-Generation Broadband Wireless Mobile Communication Network (National Science and Technology Major Project), Internet +, AI Innovation & Development, the Digital Economy Pilot, and other major projects support the development of the edge computing industry.

2. Edge computing market grows rapidly

According to the IDC report, in 2022, the edge computing server market in China maintained significant growth. The total shipment volume of edge-dedicated servers reached 34,000 units, with a year-on-year increase of 88 percent. The development of

5G and AI technologies promotes the growth of edge computing in China. Based on big data and AI/ML, edge intelligence is a major edge solution. The demands for edge computing in the fields of public services, telecom, IT services, government affairs, and energy have enlarged quickly. Internet service companies accelerate the use of specially designed servers to support the construction of edge infrastructure. As IDC predicts, the edge computing server market in China will reach 11.1 billion US dollars in 2027.[6]

1.2.4 Supercomputing centers provide more public computing services

TOP 500, a famous list of global supercomputers, was first published in 1993 by the international organization TOP 500; it is currently published every six months. On the latest *Top 500*, released in May 2023, China's Sunway Taihu Light and Tianhe-2 A ranked seventh and tenth, respectively. In the number of supercomputing systems on the list, China had 162, ranking first in the world, 31 and 36 more than the European Union and the United States, respectively. In total computing power, the United States accounted for 43.2 percent, ranking first. Japan accounted for 19.6 percent, ranking second. China accounted for 10.6 percent, ranking fourth.

By June 2023, China had built more than ten national supercomputing centers. In 2022, the construction project of the Taiyuan Advanced Computing Center received acceptance smoothly. The center relies on the advantages of strong computing power and efficient storage performance, attracts leading organizations in various industries and fields, builds an advanced computing service platform for industrial customers, explores the application scenarios of supercomputing, and provides integrated applications and services from resources supply to application for industrial customers. In August 2023, the construction project of the Xi'an Supercomputing Center successfully received acceptance. Based on advanced computing infrastructure, the center conducts cross-disciplinary research on advanced computing, provides public computing services, promotes the BRI in Shaanxi and northwestern China, supports technological innovation, and serves the digital economy.

1.3 Great Breakthroughs are Made in the Construction of New Technological Infrastructure

The integration and innovation of AI with digital technologies such as 5G, cloud computing, and big data have become new infrastructure that empowers the

6 IDC. *China Semiannual Edge Computing Tracker*, June 2023.

development of various industries, provides underlying support for the development of digital economy and the digital transformation of industries, and extends to multiple fields such as digital finance, IoT, intelligent manufacturing, supply chain management, and digital asset trading. Significant breakthroughs have been made in technologies such as quantum communication and quantum computing, which are expected to achieve large-scale applications in some industries.

1.3.1 Development of the AI industry accelerates

1. Various regions introduce policies to accelerate the development of the AI industry

Since 2023, many regions have intensively released favorable policies for AI and built new AI-led ecosystems for the digital economy. In May, Shanghai issued *Several Policies and Measures for Shanghai to Increase Efforts to Support the Development of Private Investment*, which fully leverages the guiding role of special projects on AI innovation and development and supports private enterprises to widely participate in the construction of AI infrastructure such as data and computing power. In the same month, Shenzhen released *Action Plan for Accelerating the High-Quality Development and High-Level Application of AI in Shenzhen 2023–2024*, which proposes construction plans to strengthen the supply of intelligent computing power clusters, enhancing key capabilities in the innovation on core technologies and products, and promoting the supply of data and talent factors. In addition, Beijing published two policies to promote the development of the AI industry. The first is *Implementation Plan for Accelerating the Construction of a Globally Influential AI Innovation Base in Beijing 2023–2025*, which proposes that by 2025, AI technological innovation and industrial development in Beijing will enter a new stage. The scale of the core AI industry will reach 300 billion *yuan* and the scale of related industries will exceed one trillion *yuan*. The second policy is *Several Measures on Promoting the Innovation and Development of General AI in Beijing*, which proposes twenty-one specific measures on five aspects: computing power, data, models, scenarios, and regulation. These policies will guide enterprises and markets to optimize the allocation of innovative resources and promote the transformation and upgrading of AI technologies and industries.

2. Generative AI has become a hot field for research and development

In November 2022, ChatGPT, developed by OpenAI, an American corporation, triggered a technological revolution in generative AI. The extensive application scenarios of ChatGPT in education, healthcare, design, and other fields have had a far-reaching impact on economy, politics, culture, society, ecology, and other fields. Domestic companies have embraced generative AI. Huawei and Tencent have launched products such as Pangu LM and Tencent Hunyuan. In February 2023, the Natural Language Processing Group, Fudan University, released the language model MOSS, inviting the public for internal testing. In March 2023, Baidu introduced ERNIE Bot, which has abilities in cross-modal cross-language deep semantic understanding and generation. Its key technologies include supervised fine-tuning, reinforcement learning from human feedback, knowledge enhancement, retrieval enhancement, and dialogue enhancement. ERNIE Bot has the function of multimodal generation, which can generate texts, pictures, audios, and videos. In July 2023, the Cyberspace Administration of China, alongside the National Development and Reform Commission, the Ministry of Education, the Ministry of Science and Technology, and other four departments issued *Interim Measures on the Management of Generative AI Services*, which is the first legal document in the world to regulate generative AI research and development and services. On August 31, the first group of eight large model products that passed the record were officially launched, including Yunque of Douyin, Knowledge Atlas ChatGLM (a Tsinghua AI company), and Zidong Taichu of the Chinese Academy of Sciences.

3. More AI computing centers are built

The AI computing center is an important infrastructure for building national new-generation AI innovation and development pilot zones, providing strong computing support for AI. In China, the construction of AI computing centers bolsters the development of technological innovation and the digital economy by expanding the scale and enhancing AI's capabilities. According to *Guidelines for the Innovation and Development of AI Computing Centers* jointly released by the State Information Center and relevant departments, more than thirty cities in China are currently constructing or proposing to build AI computing centers. Using the most advanced computing technologies and devices, these centers provide computing support and services in areas such as AI for various industries, as well as strong technological support and considerable computing resources for Chinese research institutes, enterprises, and governmental departments.

In December 2022, the China AI Computing Center, the first domestically-built AI computing service center in the Guangdong-Hong Kong-Macao Greater Bay Area, was officially launched, laying a solid foundation for building a trillion-*yuan*-output industrial cluster and the core engine for high-quality development of the Guangdong-Hong Kong-Macao Greater Bay Area. In December 2022, the Tianjin AI Computing Center Phase-I Project was successfully completed, and the computing device Atlas was put into trial operation. The project is located in Hebei District, Tianjin, with a total construction area of 15,700 square meters and a total investment of approximately 1.27 billion *yuan*. Atlas can provide a 300 P AI computing power system. In the construction of central computing rooms, a prefabricated modular scheme was adopted, which trains computing power via AI and efficiently serves the AI model training. In February 2023, the Hebei AI Computing Center Project entered the stage of device installation and debugging. With a total investment of 590 million *yuan* and a construction area of 12,000 square meters, it is the only AI computing center in Hebei Province. In the construction of the data center, a prefabricated modular scheme was used for computer rooms, and a prefabricated factory scheme was used for all devices. As planned, the computing power will reach 100 P, helping to incubate scenarios such as intelligent manufacturing, smart transportation, and smart healthcare.

1.3.2 Development of blockchain infrastructure quickens

1. Various regions introduce policies to strengthen the layout of blockchain

Governmental departments at all levels have successively published policies and documents on blockchain to spur the innovation and application of blockchain technology. *The 14th Five-Year Plan* regards blockchain as one of emerging digital industries and proposes the development of blockchain service platforms, as well as application solutions in fields such as Fintech, supply chain finance, and government services, with a focus on consortium blockchain. Afterwards, various ministries and commissions issued development plans for various industries and fields in *The 14th Five-Year Plan* and made strategic arrangements to promote high-quality economic and social development through the use of blockchain technology. According to *The White Paper on Blockchain 2022*,[7] by September 2022, twenty-nine provinces, regions, and cities included the development of blockchain technology in *The 14th Five-Year Plan* and released a total of 319 policies on the blockchain industry, covering multiple industries or fields, such as government data sharing, finance, supply chain and logistics, healthcare, and agriculture. Beijing proposes to use blockchain technology to accelerate government data sharing, improve administrative approval efficiency, and strengthen the application of cross-border financial blockchain service platforms. Shanghai proposes to develop blockchain applications, explore the research and development of Web 3.0 technology and ecology, build a blockchain-based healthcare platform, and formulate secure and trustworthy healthcare data-sharing solutions. Henan, Shandong, Sichuan, Yunnan, and Chongqing plan to foster the construction of blockchain infrastructure. Guangdong, Guizhou, Liaoning, Shandong, and Chongqing focus on exploring the application of blockchain in the financial industry.

7 China Academy of Information and Communications Technology. *The White Paper on Blockchain 2022*, December 2022.

2. Development of blockchain infrastructure accelerates

In February 2023, *Forbes* released *Global Blockchain Top 50 2023*. Six Chinese companies, including Ant Group, Baidu, China Construction Bank, Industrial and Commercial Bank of China, Tencent, and WeBank were on the list. In blockchain products, Tencent, Baidu, Ant Group, Huawei, and JD launched comprehensive blockchain products and services, such as consortium blockchain platforms, BaaS, open consortium blockchain, and industrial solutions. By November 2022, more than ten types of blockchain products and services emerged in China, including Chain Maker, BIF, Super Chain Open Network, Zhixin Chain Open Consortium Blockchain, Ant Open Consortium Blockchain, BSN Open Consortium Blockchain, ZXCLink, JD Chain Open Alliance Network, and VoneBaaS. The number continues to increase. The blockchain network is entering wider markets and providing users with more convenient services, with the number of users growing rapidly. In recent years, blockchain projects in China have mushroomed and shown an obvious upward trend. Since 2019, about 500 projects have been approved for filing by the Office of the Central Cyberspace Affairs Commission every year, with a total of more than 2,600 registered projects. In 2022, the number of announced filing projects reached 719, and more than 80 percent were applied for by small and medium-sized enterprises, which play an important role in the development of the blockchain industry in China.

1.3.3 Development of quantum technology picks up speed

As a key technology that ensures the security of social information, quantum technology is expected to achieve large-scale applications in multiple fields such as e-government, finance, e-commerce, e-healthcare, military affairs and national defense, and the power industry. In recent years, China has successively introduced supporting policies on quantum computing, forming a complete national-local system. *The 14th Five-Year Plan* clearly proposes to "focus on the cutting-edge fields of AI, quantum information and integrated circuit, and carry out a number of forward-looking and strategic national major scientific and technological projects." In 2022, the Central Economic Work Conference first proposed quantum computing and clarified the acceleration of the research and application of quantum computing. In 2022, provinces, autonomous regions, and municipalities directly under the central government, such as Shanghai, Beijing, Henan, Guangdong, Sichuan, and Jiangxi, all introduced supporting policies and plans. For example, in September 2022, Shanghai issued *Action Plan for Forging New Innovation Advantage of the Future Industry and Building and Developing Future Industrial Clusters in Shanghai*, which proposes the goal of deploying and building future industrial clusters. While building future intelligent industrial clusters, the *Action Plan* emphasizes that Shanghai will actively cultivate the quantum technology industry centering on quantum computing, quantum communication, and quantum measurement, and promote the application of quantum technology in finance, big data computing, healthcare, resources and environment, and other areas. In October 2022, Beijing released *Several Measures on Accelerating the Construction of High-quality Entrepreneurial Investment Clusters*, which clarifies strengthening the interaction with the Beijing Science and Technology Innovation Fund and jointly initiating entrepreneurial investment funds to support cutting-edge technologies such as AI, life sciences, and quantum computing.

In terms of quantum communication, China has launched the world's first quantum satellite, Micius, and successfully achieved quantum communication between satellites, laying a foundation for the construction of quantum key distribution (QKD) and a quantum communication network. In May 2022, China's Micius satellite made a new record of 1,200-km surface quantum-state transmission. Currently, China plays a leading role in implementing a road map for wide-area quantum secure communication technology internationally, and makes positive progress in international standardization. Since 2022, the quantum communication industry has developed rapidly and the market scale has expanded. Three major domestic operators have accelerated the deployment of quantum communication. China Telecom launched a VoLTE encrypted communication product based on quantum information technology, Tianyi Quantum High-Definition Secret Voice. The product adopts three-level protection, i.e., domestically customized mobile phones, quantum security SIM cards, and national security algorithms. Based on ensuring the support to native terminals and VoLTE high-definition communication, it provides users with integrated connection-end-chip security protection and brings a new experience of technology, fashion, and security as well as convenience in confidential communication. China Mobile and Origin Quantum signed a cooperation agreement for the first time to explore the solutions to quantum algorithms to break the bottlenecks in computing power faced by 5G and 6G. Simultaneously, China Mobile announced the launch of quantum encrypted communication services to provide secure quantum communication services. China Unicom released *The White Paper on Quantum Communication Technology in the Cloud Era*, exploring the integration, development, and application of quantum communication technology and traditional information communication technology. In 2022, the team led by academician Guo Guangcan from the University of Science and Technology of China made significant progress in the research on QKD networking. The research team achieved a nontrustworthy-node QKD network that is resistant to environmental interference, which comprehensively improves the security, availability and reliability of QKD network and signals an important step toward a next-generation quantum network. In May 2023, the University of Science and Technology of China, working with Tsinghua University, Jinan Institute of Quantum Technology, and Shanghai Institute of Microsystem and Information Technology, Chinese Academy of Sciences, realized 1,002-km point-to-point remote QKD in optical fibers by developing technologies such as low cross talk phase-reference signal control and an extremely low-noise single-photon detector. This not only sets a world record for the distance of repeaterless QKD in optical fibers, but also provides a solution for high-speed backbone links in intercity quantum communication.

With regard to quantum computing, the R & D of hardware systems has stayed in the stage of parallel development of multiple technological paths, covering superconductors, photons, ion traps, etc. In the field of the software for compilation and development and algorithmic applications, the competition becomes fierce. There are both open-source communities and ecosystems built by technological giants. According to incomplete statistics, by September 2022, global investment in quantum technology totaled 16 billion US dollars. In particular, Chinese startups in quantum information attracted wide attention from the market and received considerable financial support through equity investment from social capital and the IPO financing in the security market, with a trend of explosive growth in the past two years. In January 2023, Taihu Quantum Artificial Intelligence Computing Center, the first quantum AI computing center in China, was unveiled in Binhu District, Wuxi. The center was built by Wuxi Photonic Chip Joint Research Center, Shanghai Jiaotong University, and Shanghai TuringQ Technology Co., Ltd. Based on the technological strength of the National Supercomputing Center in Wuxi, Taihu Quantum Artificial Intelligence Computing Center built a quantum-classical hybrid architecture platform, providing a new public computing infrastructure required by quantum AI applications, such as computing, data, and algorithmic services, and created a new benchmark for domestic computing infrastructure.

Concerning quantum measurement, quantum precision measurement demonstrates a trend in the evolution and development of measurement technology. Presently, the application and development of quantum measurement technology center on timing and positioning based on quantum time frequency standard, autonomous state control, and navigation based on the quantum gyroscope, and metal target detection or biological magnetic signal imaging based on quantum weak magnetic field measurement. Multiple types of quantum measurement prototypes and products have been explored and applied in fields such as aerospace, national defense, medical treatment, environmental protection, and scientific research. In the number of patent declarations for quantum measurement technology, China ranks first in the world, accounting for 49 percent. The United States accounts for 32 percent[8]. In September 2023, with the theme of "Collaborative Innovation for a Quantum Future," the 2023 Quantum Industry Conference was held in Hefei, Anhui Province. The innovative achievement of "A Quantum Precision Measurement Solution for Power System Current" released by the State Grid Anhui Electric Power Research Institute can be widely applied in various scenarios, such as ultrahigh voltage AC/DC power grid, a flexible DC power grid, power distribution network, new energy

8 China Academy of Information and Communications Technology. *Report on the Development and Application of Quantum Information Technology 2022*, January 2023.

generation, electric vehicles, and traceability of measurement standards, promoting the innovation of current measurement technology in power systems.

1.4 Application Infrastructure Develops Vigorously

Driven by the formulation of national policies and the deployment of new infrastructure strategies, the IoV industry in China has basically completed electrical transformation, taking the lead worldwide in technological innovation, application and demonstration, and the industrial ecosystem. As a critical infrastructure that supports the digital economy, the IoT is applied in various aspects of social and economic life, including industry, agriculture, environment, transportation, logistics, security, home furnishings, healthcare, education, finance, tourism, etc. As the product of the deep integration of new-generation information technology and the manufacturing industry, the industrial Internet is a critical information infrastructure for the digital and intelligent transformation of the manufacturing industry. By connecting people, machines, and things in an all-round way, the industrial Internet has built a new production, manufacturing, and service system that features total factors, entire industrial chains, and entire value chains.

1.4.1 IoV faces an important period for establishing a new pattern

1. The scale of IoV users continues to expand

According to the data from the Ministry of Industry and Information Technology, in 2022, the sales volume of new ICV equipped with an auxiliary auto-drive system in China reached seven million, with a year-on-year growth of 45.6 percent. The proportion of new energy vehicles equipped with auxiliary auto-drive systems reached 48 percent. According to *The White Paper on Internet of Vehicles* released by the China Academy of Information and Communications Technology, the scale of the intelligent vehicles market in China will approximate one trillion *yuan* by 2025, as predicted. More automobile manufacturers have incorporated IoV technology into their product development and marketing strategies. For example, domestic automobile brands such as Gac Motor and BYD made remarkable progress in the field of IoV and strengthened their layout. The intelligent vehicle is an important field for the application of IoV technology. By the end of 2022, the scale of the intelligent vehicles market reached about 270 billion *yuan*. By 2025, the penetration rate of the IoV industry will exceed 75 percent, and the scale of IoV users will exceed 380 million, as estimated.

2. Deployment of IoV demonstration and pilot zone enlarges

In April 2023, in addition to Wuxi, Changsha, Tianjin, and Chongqing Liangjiang New Area, the Ministry of Industry and Information Technology released national-level IoV pilot zones in Xiangyang, Deqing, and Liuzhou, and determined their major tasks and goals. As approved, there are seven national-level IoV pilot zones in China. Currently, more than 9,000-km test roads have been opened, and more than 1,900 test licenses have been issued nationwide.

3. IoV technology advances

Presently, China has made breakthroughs in ICV products, IoV wireless communication technology, and roadside system and application service platforms, and explored various paths for technological industrialization. The L2-level autonomous driving technology has matured and become popular in the market, and the industrialization of LTE-V2X has accelerated, forming a complete chain that covers chip module, terminal, the whole vehicle, security, testing and verification, high-precision positioning, and map service. The testing and evaluation system for a roadside perception system has been continuously improved, and the multilevel (edge-region-center) IoV architecture platform is widely recognized by the industry. In terms of key components, breakthroughs have been made in key technologies such as new-generation electronic and electrical architecture, automotive operating systems, high-computing-power computing chips, and laser radar. With multiple technological advantages, ICV went viral in the market. At the 2023 Automobile Shanghai, major automobile companies scrambled to display their latest R & D achievements and technological trends in the future, attracting the attention of numerous consumers. Noticeably, ICV, autonomous driving cabin and immersive experience allow people to understand the unique charm of technology in life. ICV, which integrates multiple innovative technologies such as IoT, cloud computing, big data, and AI, has become a common goal for the global automotive market.

1.4.2 IoT maintains a high speed of development

1. The number of mobile IoT connections continues to grow

In August 2022, mobile IoT connections outnumbered mobile phone users for the first time in China, making China the first country among major global economies that realized "things beyond human." According to data from the Ministry of Industry and Information Technology, by the end of 2022, the number of mobile IoT connections increased to 1.845 billion households, with a net increase of 447 million households over the end of 2021, accounting for 70 percent of the global total. According to statistical data from the Ministry of Industry and Information Technology, by the end of June 2023, three basic telecom corporations, i.e., China Telecom, China Mobile, and China Unicom, had 2.12 billion cellular IoT terminal users, with a net increase of 279 million over the end of 2022, accounting for 55.4 percent of the total number of mobile network terminal connections (including mobile phone users and cellular IoT terminal users). As the China Academy of Information and Communications Technology predicts, by 2030, the number of mobile IoT connections in China will reach more than ten billion. According to *Mobile Internet of Things Development Report 2022,*[9] China has initially formed a pattern of coordinated development of NB-IoT, 4G, and 5G, which continuously improves network coverage and stimulates innovation and application.

2. IoT industrial ecology continuously expands

At present, China has formed a complete mobile IoT industrial chain that covers chips, modules, terminals, software, platforms, and service. In the market structure of the mobile IoT chip module, Chinese suppliers make continuous efforts. In the third quarter of 2022, the top five IoT module suppliers all came from China, i.e., Quectel, Fibocom, Sunsea AIoT, China Mobile, and MeiG Smart.[10] Spurred by policies and technologies, the number of smart terminals that serve public services, such as smart water meters, electricity meters, and gas meters, has shot up, at a growth rate of 19.2 percent. Narrowband IoT has formed four ten-million-level applications, including water meters, gas meters, smoke detectors and tracking, as well as seven million-level applications, including white goods, streetlights, parking, agriculture, etc. The scale of mobile IoT terminals applied in public services, IoV, smart retail, smart home, and other fields reach 496 million households, 375 million households, 250 million households, and 192 million households, respectively. Industrial application continuously expands into intelligent manufacturing, smart agriculture, intelligent transportation, intelligent logistics, consumer IoT, and other fields.[11] Digital technologies, such as 5G, cloud computing, and AI, accelerate the process of the Internet of Everything (IoE). In the future, the focus of mobile network connection will shift from humans to things.

---

9 China Academy of Information and Communications Technology. *Mobile Internet of Things Development Report 2022*, November 2022.

10 China Academy of Industrial Internet. Report on the Innovation and Development of Industrial Internet Platforms in China, May 2023.

11 "Mobile IoT Connections in China Account for 70% of the World". Accessed July 2023. http://paper.people.com.cn/rmrbhwb/html/2023-01/31/content_25962190.htm.

1.4.3 Industrial Internet has broad prospects for development

1. Policies and measures are continually introduced

As an important part of new infrastructure, the industrial Internet plays a key role in promoting the deep integration of the digital economy and the traditional economy. To boost the development of the industrial Internet industry, relevant national departments have successively issued a series of policies and documents. For example, *Report on the Work of the Government 2023* proposes to "support the development of industrial Internet and effectively promote the digitalization and intelligentization of the manufacturing industry." *The 14th Five-Year Plan for the Development of Digital Economy, The 14th Five-Year Plan for the Development of Intelligent Manufacturing, The 14th Five-Year Plan for the Deep Integration of Information and Industrialization, Outline of the Strategic Plan for Expanding Domestic Demand 2022–2035*, and other documents propose to deepen the implementation of the strategies on the innovation and development of the industrial Internet, promote the aggregation of production factors such as data, personnel, and technologies in traditional industries, and accelerate the digital transformation of enterprises.

The Ministry of Industry and Information Technology continues to implement the *Three-Year Action Plan for the Innovation and Development of Industrial Internet 2021–2023*, research and formulate policies and measures to promote the large-scale development of the industrial Internet, improve the top-level design, fully utilize financial and fiscal policies, strengthen industry-finance cooperation and industry-education integration, and create a favorable environment for the development of the industrial Internet. The Ministry of Industry and Information Technology bolsters technological innovation, implements projects on the innovation and development of the industrial Internet, surmounts the obstacles that restrict large-scale development, and improves standard systems. It deepens industrial innovation, supports various market entities such as telecom enterprises, Internet platform enterprises, and industrial enterprises to leverage their advantages, strengthens linkage and collaboration, cultivates leading industrial Internet enterprises and small and medium-sized enterprises that use special and sophisticated technologies to produce novel and unique products, develops industry alliances on the industrial Internet, and builds a healthy and sustainable industrial ecosystem. The Ministry of Industry and Information Technology promotes the cultivation of advanced factories, encourages enterprises to actively utilize technologies like 5G for the digital transformation of factories, and enlarges the wide application of new technologies, scenarios, and models. It accelerates the upgrading of industrial clusters, carries out "Industrial Internet Hundred Cities and Thousand Parks Activity," summarizes and promotes successful cases, and fosters the digital and green development of industrial parks.

2. Standard systems improve

As the industrial Internet deeply develops, various industries establish corresponding technical specifications and industrial standards, promote industrial standardization, and improve the overall level of the industry. In May 2023, the State Administration for Market Regulation (Standardization Administration) issued *National Standards Announcement of the People's Republic of China (2023, No. 2)*, and formally approved *Requirements for the Selection of Industrial Internet Platforms*, *Microservice Reference Frameworks for Industrial Internet Platforms*, and *Functional Requirements for Open Application and Compilation Interfaces of Industrial Internet Platforms*. The publication of these standards plays a significant role in improving the standards for industrial Internet platforms, enhancing the supply capability of diverse industrial Internet platforms, and fostering the high-quality development of industrial Internet platforms. *Requirements for the Selection of Industrial Internet Platforms* provides a basis for platform demanders and helps enterprises to evaluate the empowering capability of industrial Internet platforms and choose industrial Internet platforms meeting their needs. *Microservice Reference Frameworks for Industrial Internet Platforms* and *Functional Requirements for Open Application and Compilation Interfaces of Industrial Internet Platforms* provide guidance for platform providers, guide enterprises to develop industrial microservice and application interfaces, accelerate the modeling accumulation of industrial knowledge and the interconnection of platforms, and lay a foundation for the construction of the ecologies of industrial Internet platforms.

3. Industrial Internet empowers various industries in an efficient way

The industrial Internet serves as a strategic infrastructure for new industrialization and a key base for the deep integration of the digital economy and the traditional economy. With the development of 5G, AI, edge computing, and other emerging technologies, the industrial Internet extends from the manufacturing industry to various fields of the traditional economy. Simultaneously, the development of the industrial Internet promotes the collaboration of industrial chains. By connecting suppliers, manufacturers, and retailers, the industrial Internet achieves the collaboration of supply chain and value chain, and facilitates industrial integration and optimization. By the end of February 2023, the industrial Internet had covered forty-five major categories and 166 medium categories of national economy, and more than 85 percent of industrial categories. In manufacturing, energy, transportation, medical care, finance, and other industries, more enterprises started to implement industrial Internet plans to raise production efficiency, reduce costs, and improve the customer experience. In the first quarter of 2023, the Ministry of Industry and Information Technology released 218 industrial Internet pilot and demonstration projects, such as 5G factory, industrial Internet parks, and public service platforms, aiming to build a group of application models, guide factories and parks to "know and use industrial Internet, and achieve the transformation to industrial Internet," and accelerate digital transformation. According to statistics on industrial development from the National Development and Reform Commission, in 2022, the Industrial Internet Platform Development Index increased by 17.23 percent over 2021, up by more than 15 percent for four consecutive years. According to the data released by the 2023 Industrial Internet Conference, the scale of the industrial Internet industry in China has exceeded 1.2 trillion *yuan*, with more than 240 influential industrial Internet platforms and more than 260,000 enterprises.

10.2478/9788367405867-003

Chapter 2
Development of the Digital Economy

Developing a digital economy means a strategic choice to seize new opportunities of a new round of technological revolution and industrial transformation. The report of the 20th CPC National Congress stresses that "We will accelerate the development of digital economy, further integrate it with real economy, build internationally competitive digital industrial clusters, and promote digital trade." As the top-level design is continuously optimized and improved, the digital economy becomes an important force for China to build a new development landscape, foster the construction of a modern economic system, and forge national competitiveness.

Over the past year, under the impact of global turbulence and the pandemic, the digital economy in China has achieved sustainable innovation and developed steadily. In 2022, the scale of the digital economy in China expanded to 50.2 trillion *yuan*, with a year-on-year nominal growth of 10.3 percent, accounting for 41.5 percent of the GDP.[1] The digital economy plays a prominent role in leading and supporting economic and social development and becomes an important engine for stable growth and transformation. The data element market system improves, which effectively drives the innovation and development of the digital economy. The scale of data continues to expand, and the data trading market develops in an orderly manner. The innovation capability of the digital industry is steadily enhanced, and the innovation and application are accelerated. Industrial digitalization has a multiplier effect, ensures the stable growth of the national economy, and quickens the digital transformation of traditional industries. New technologies, such as big data and AI, penetrate all aspects of social development, and play an increasingly important role in enriching digital life, transforming production and governance approaches, breeding new business models, stimulating consumption, and driving investment.

2.1 Policy System of Digital Economy Improves

At the 20th CPC National Congress, General Secretary Xi Jinping emphasized that "We will build a modern industrial system. In pursuing economic growth, we must

1 China Academy of Information and Communications Technology. *Research Report on the Development of Digital Economy in China 2023*, April 2023.

continue to focus on real economy. We will advance new industrialization and move faster to boost China's strength in manufacturing, product quality, aerospace, transportation, cyberspace, and digital development." As the top-level design and overall layout of the digital economy advance, a series of institutional measures are introduced. Various ministries and commissions and local governments work together to boost the development of the digital economy.

2.1.1 Top-level design is continuously optimized

In February 2023, the CPC Central Committee and the State Council issued *Overall Layout and Planning for the Construction of Digital China*, which clearly proposes to strengthen, optimize, and expand the digital economy, cultivate and develop core industries of the digital economy, research and formulate measures to promote high-quality development of digital industries, and build internationally competitive digital industry clusters. In December 2022, the CPC Central Committee and the State Council issued *Outline of the Strategic Plan for Expanding Domestic Demand 2022–2035*, urging the acceleration of digital industrialization and industrial digitization. Relevant regions should establish and improve cross-departmental and cross-regional data resource circulation and application mechanisms, strengthen the capabilities in data security protection, and optimize the environment for data element circulation. Relevant regions should promote the development and utilization of data resources and the construction of institutional norms, build digital industrial clusters with international competitiveness, and make digital technologies better empower small and medium-sized enterprises, especially those in the manufacturing industry. Relevant regions should actively participate in the formulation of international rules and standards in the digital field, follow the trend of a new round of technological revolution and industrial transformation, lead and create new demands based on innovation-driven development and high-quality supply, and achieve a virtuous cycle of supply and demand at a higher level.

2.1.2 Various regions formulate policies on the digital economy

Guided by national top-level design, the digital economy plays a leading role in high-quality economic development. In order to seize the opportunities of digital-economy development and serve the high-quality development of local economy and society, various regions actively deploy the tasks and clarify the goals for the development of the digital economy. By April 2023, thirty-one provinces, autonomous regions, and municipalities directly under the central government had issued policies on the digital economy, including five-year plans, three-year action plans, implementation plans, development guidelines, and action plans. Shanxi, Henan,

Guangdong, Yunnan, Beijing, and other provinces and cities published *Key Working Points for Digital Economy in 2023* and *Regulations on Promoting Digital Economy in 2023* to guide the development of the digital economy in 2023. Zhejiang introduces *Implementation Plan for the "No. 1 Development Project" of Improving the Innovation and Quality of Digital Economy in Zhejiang Province*, which proposes that by 2027, the added value of the digital economy and core industries in the province will reach seven trillion *yuan* and 1.6 trillion *yuan*, respectively, with 100 future factories and 1,200 intelligent factories (digital workshops) to be built. Hebei issues *Action Plan for Accelerating the Construction of Digital Hebei 2023–2027*, proposing that by 2027, the digital economy in Hebei will enter a period of expansion in an all-round way, with the added value of core industries reaching 330 billion *yuan*, with the digital economy accounting for more than 42 percent of the provincial GDP. Heibei will build Beijing-Tianjin-Hebei Industrial Internet Collaborative Development Demonstration Zone, as well as a number of demonstration zones for the innovation and development of modern ecological agriculture. Guangdong releases *Key Working Points for Digital Economy in Guangdong in 2023*, proposing to focus on key cities and segmented industries, accelerate the cultivation of industrial Internet platforms in specific fields and industries, drive the overall digital transformation of small and medium-sized enterprises in the industrial chain and supply chain, and promote the digital transformation of more than 5,000 industrial enterprises and 100,000 small and medium-sized enterprises. Yunnan published *Key Working Points for Digital Economy in Yunnan in 2023*, which clarified that by 2023, the investment to digital economy would reach 30 billion *yuan* and the revenue of core industries in digital economy would increase by more than 20 percent. Yunnan plans to build the Yunnan Provincial Software Industry Park, develop the Yunnan Provincial Digital Economy Park, and introduce more than ten leading enterprises in the digital economy.

2.1.3 Various regions introduce policies on the digital transformation of traditional industries

Overall Layout and Planning for the Construction of Digital China stresses that in the construction of a digital China, China will take a holistic, systematic, and coordinated approach to promote the deep integration of the digital economy and the traditional economy, and accelerate the innovation and application of digital technologies in key areas such as agriculture, industry, finance, education, healthcare, transportation, and energy.

In agriculture, in January 2023, the CPC Central Committee and the State Council issued *Opinions on Comprehensively Promoting the Key Work of Rural Revitalization in 2023*, proposing to deepen the implementation of digital rural development plans, promote the research and development of digital application scenarios, accelerate the application of big data in agriculture and rural areas, and foster the development of smart agriculture. In February 2023, the Ministry of Agriculture and Rural Affairs issued *Opinions on Implementing the Deployment of the CPC Central Committee and the State Council on the Key Work in Comprehensively Promoting Rural Revitalization in 2023*, further clarifying the need to strengthen agricultural technology and equipment support, lay a foundation for building a strong agriculture, vigorously develop smart agriculture and a digital countryside, deepen data integration and digital technology innovation, implement projects on digital agriculture, build a number of digital agriculture innovation centers and digital agriculture innovation and application bases, and work together to promote the research and development of key and core technologies in smart agriculture. In April 2023, the Office of the Central Cyberspace Affairs Commission, the Ministry of Agriculture and Rural Affairs, the National Development and Reform Commission, the Ministry of Industry and Information Technology, and the National Rural Revitalization Administration jointly issued *Key Working Points for Digital Countryside in 2023*, which proposes to develop smart agriculture according to local conditions, accelerate the digital transformation of the entire agricultural industry chain, and strengthen agricultural technology and intelligent equipment support. By the end of 2023, phased progress had been made in the development of the digital countryside, with the information rate of agricultural production reaching 26.5 percent.

In industry, in November 2022, the Ministry of Industry and Information Technology released *Guidelines for Digital Transformation of Small and Medium-sized Enterprises*, guiding promoting the scientific and efficient digital transformation of small and medium-sized enterprises in three ways, i.e., enhancing the capability in transformation, improving the level of supply, and increasing the support of polices. Meanwhile, the Ministry of Industry and Information Technology, the National Development and Reform Commission, and the State-owned Assets Supervision and Administration Commission of the State Council jointly issued *Notice on Consolidating the Trend of Recovery and Boosting Industrial Economy*, requiring the implementation of intelligent manufacturing projects, carrying out demonstration actions for the pilot of intelligent manufacturing, accelerating the digitization of equipment, selecting and publishing a new group of service-oriented demonstration zones for the manufacturing industry, and promoting a intelligent, green, and service-oriented transformation. Various regions implement industrial Internet innovation and development projects as well as "Ten-Hundred-Thousand" Project of 5G industrial application, deepen the integration and application of "5G + industrial Internet," accelerate the construction of 5G fully connected factories, and promote the high-quality construction of industrial Internet demonstration zones and "5G + industrial Internet" integration and application pilot zones around the country. In December 2022, Central Economic Work Conference stressed the need to accelerate the construction of a modern industrial systems, focus on key industry chains of manufacturing, determine the weaknesses in key core technologies and components, pool high-quality resources to tackle major problems, build a modern industrial system that is independent, controllable, safe, and reliable, and ensure smooth circulation within the national economy. The NPC (National People's Congress) and CPPCC (Chinese People's Political Consultative Conference) in 2023 issued the *Report on the Work of the Government* and reaffirmed that China will give priority to the manufacturing industry in the development of the traditional economy, deepen the integration of the digital economy and the traditional economy, support the development of the industrial Internet, and effectively promote the digital and intelligent transformation of the manufacturing industry.

In the service industry, in August 2022, the General Office of the CPC Central Committee and General Office of the State Council issued *The 14th Five-Year Plan for Cultural Development*, which proposes to raise the digital level of public culture, connect various levels of public cultural digital platforms, create a public cultural digital resources library group, and establish a national cultural big data system, to combine the expansion of domestic demands with the deepening of supply-side structural reform, improve industrial planning and policies, strengthen innovation-driven development, implement digital strategies, accelerate the upgrading of the industrial foundation and the modernization of industrial chain, and foster the sustainable and healthy development of the cultural industry. In December 2022, the General Office of the State Council issued *The 14th Five-Year Plan for the Development of Modern Logistics*, requiring the acceleration of the digital transformation of logistics; the *Plan* will utilize modern information technology to promote the network and data-driven development of logistic elements, develop diverse application scenarios, and achieve online and offline connection of logistic resources. In April 2023, the Ministry of Industry and Information Technology and Ministry of Culture and Tourism issued *Notice on Strengthening Collaborative Innovation and Development of 5G+ Smart Tourism*, proposing that by 2025, the construction of a 5G network in tourist venues will be basically improved, the level of 5G integrated application and development will be significantly raised, and industrial innovation capability will be continuously enhanced. 5G+ smart tourism will prosper and develop in scale.

2.1.4 Platform economy comes into a new stage of healthy development

Since 2020, China has launched several campaigns on the governance of the platform economy from various aspects such as personal information protection, anti-monopoly, fair competition, and the regulation of recommendation algorithms, aiming to promote the rule-based operation and healthy development of platforms. The platform economy enters a new stage of healthy development.

In July 2022, the meeting of the Political Bureau of the CPC Central Committee proposed to "promote the standardized, healthy and sustainable development of platform economy, complete the reform of platform economy, and implement regular regulation of platform economy." In October 2022, at the 37th meeting of the Standing Committee of the 13th National People's Congress, in *Report on the Development of Digital Economy*, the National Development and Reform Commission further clarified that China will encourage platform enterprises to utilize market, technology, data, and other advantages to empower the traditional economy; support platform enterprises to continuously improve the level of international development; give play to public service platforms (e.g., digital collaboration platforms); lead in empowering economic development; promote and guide the standardized, healthy, and sustainable development of platform economy; complete the reform of the platform economy; implement regulation of the platform economy; and publish a group of "green light" investment cases. In December 2022, the Central Economic Work Conference underscored that China will vigorously develop the digital economy, enhance the level of regulation, and support platform enterprises to play their role in leading development, promoting employment, and participating in international competition. *Overall Layout and Planning for the Construction of Digital China* points out that China supports the development and growth of digital enterprises, improves the integration and innovation mechanisms of large, medium, and small enterprises, gives play to the guiding role of "green light" investment cases, and boosts the standardized and healthy development of platform enterprises.

2.2 Ecology of Data Element Market Improves

In 2022, the construction of a data element market system in China advanced in an orderly way, signaling a new path for developing digital productivity, providing a basis for accelerating the release of the value of data elements, and stimulating the potential of data elements. With the continuous expansion of the scale of data, the data element market system improves, and the data trading market develops in an orderly manner. Simultaneously, China further accelerates the construction of national public data opening system and continuously optimizes a public data opening platform. The number of government data opening platforms at or above the prefecture level continues to increase. The multiplying effect of platforms continually enhances public support capabilities, and the construction of the ecology of data element market progresses steadily.

2.2.1 The data element market system improves

Data elements serve as a leverage for the innovation and development of digital economy. At the national level, a series of policies have been introduced to promote the development of the data element market. *Overall Layout and Planning for the*

Construction of Digital China proposes to unclog the circulation of data resources, establish a national data management system and mechanism, and improve the institutions for data coordination and management at various levels. In December 2022, the CPC Central Committee and the State Council issued *Twenty Articles on Data*. As stated, data, as a new type of production factor, profoundly alters the models of production, lifestyle, and social governance. The construction of basic data system relates to national development and security. *Twenty Articles on Data* also lists twenty specific policies or measures from the aspects of data property rights, data element circulation and trading, data element income distribution, and data element security governance, forming multiple pillars of basic data system in China. In August 2023, the Ministry of Finance issued *Provisional Regulations on Accounting Treatment of Corporate Data Resources*, which would take effect on January 1, 2024, so as to standardize accounting treatment of corporate data resources, strengthen the disclosure of accounting information, and serve for the construction of a digital economy governance system.

2.2.2 Data trading market displays great vitality

Data constitutes the foundation of the data element market. China has formed large-scale data production and storage. According to the statistics and calculations of the Chinese Academy of Cyberspace Studies and the China Academy of Information and Communications Technology, in 2022, data production in China reached 8.1 ZB, with a year-on-year increase of 22.7 percent, accounting for 10.5 percent of global data production, ranking second in the world. Data storage in China reached 724.5 EB, with a year-on-year increase of 21.1 percent, accounting for 14.4 percent of global data storage. The scale of the big data industry reached 1.57 trillion *yuan*, with a year-on-year increase of 18 percent.[2] The China Data Element Marketization Index shows that, from 2021 to 2022, the index of the eastern region was significantly higher than that in the central and western regions. Data element enterprises are mainly distributed in economically developed regions, such as Guangdong, Shanghai, Jiangsu, Shandong, Sichuan, and Beijing.[3]

As the data element market system improves, the data trading market develops in an orderly way. In 2022, the scale of data transactions in China exceeded 70 billion *yuan*, and would exceed an estimated 220 billion *yuan* by 2025.[4] The data property

2 "Cyberspace Administration of China Releases *Digital China Development Report 2022*." Accessed July 2023. http://www.cac.gov.cn/2023-05/22/c_1686402318492248.htm.

3 National Industrial Information Security Development Research Center. *Report on the Development of the Data Element Market in China 2021-2022*, November 2022.

4 "Data Transactions See a New Round of Development, Projected to Exceed 220 Billion *Yuan* by 2025." Accessed July 2023. https://www.chinanews.com.cn/cj/2023/04-15/9990465.shtml

rights system receives more attention. Various data trading platforms establish models of rights authentication, such as data registration and data rights use based on technological empowerment, to promote data circulation. This not only recognizes the ownership of original data producers over the data but also facilitates the development and utilization of data value by relevant parties. Based on protecting users' privacy and rights, the data property rights system fully unleashes the value of data. Simultaneously, the types of data involved in transactions enlarge. New demands for data are distributed in medical care, transportation, industrial electricity, and other fields. The upstream and downstream industrial chains of data transactions take initial shape.

2.2.3 Data opening and sharing are promoted in an orderly way

In 2022, China accelerated the construction of a national public data opening system, and continuously optimized public data opening platforms. The number of government data opening platforms at the prefecture level and above continued to grow. According to the 2022 China Open Data Index and *China Local Government Data Openness Report 2022* jointly released by the Lab for Digital & Mobile Governance, the Fudan University, and the Digital China Research Institute, State Information Center, by October 2022, local governments in 208 provinces and cities in China had launched government data opening platforms, twenty-one provincial-level platforms (including provinces and autonomous regions, excluding municipalities directly under the central government and Hong Kong, Macao, and Taiwan), 187 municipal-level platforms (including municipalities directly under the central government, subprovincial cities and prefecture-level administrative regions). *Vis-à-vis* the second half of 2021, the total number of platforms increased by about 8 percent.

The multiplier effect of data sharing platforms becomes prominent, and the public-supporting capability of data sharing platforms constantly improves. According to *Guidelines for the Construction of National Integrated Government Big Data System* released by the General Office of the State Council in October 2022, the National Integrated Government Data Sharing Hub has been connected to 5,951 governmental departments at various levels, sharing 13,500 types of data resources from 53 departments of the State Council, and supporting more than 400 billion national sharing calls in total. National platforms have provided e-certificate sharing services for local departmental platforms 7.95 billion times and identity authentication and verification services 6.74 billion times. By the end of 2022, the National Government Service Platform had collected more than 900 types of e-certificates and licenses from 32 regions and 26 departments of the State Council, shared 5.672 billion pieces of directory information, and provided a total of 7.9 billion e-certificate sharing and application services.

In terms of regional data, data opening systems in various regions improve. The Green and Digital Development Research Center, the Shanghai Academy of Social Sciences, and the Shanghai Data Exchange Research Institute jointly released *Open*

Data Index for Major Cities Worldwide 2022. As it shows, the level of data opening in Chinese cities is above the average globally. Among the thirty shortlisted cities, Shanghai, Shenzhen, Guiyang, Guangzhou, and Qingdao ranked in the top ten, ranking fourth, fifth, sixth, eighth, and ninth, respectively.[5]

2.3 Innovation Capability in Digital Industrialization Steadily Improves

Over the past year, in China's electronic information manufacturing, production recovered, with a comeback of efficiency and growth in investment. Yet, there was a downward trend in exports. The software and IT service industry continued to improve, with rapid growth of business revenue and sustainable development of specific fields. The revenue from the Internet and related services industry rebounded slightly, and the total profit grew quickly.

2.3.1 Electronic information manufacturing industry remains stable

In China's electronic information manufacturing, production recovers, the export continues to decline, and the total profit declines slowly. From January to June 2023, the added value of the industry above a designated size reached the same level over the corresponding period (from January to May), up by 0.3 percent in growth rate, down by 3.8 percent in industry, and 1.7 percent in high-tech manufacturing. In exports, affected by continuous trade restrictions caused by the pandemic, the export delivery value of electronic information manufacturing above a designated size fell by 9.2 percent year on year (4.8 percent in the last year), up by 0.9 percent over the corresponding period (from January to May). With the recovery of production, efficiency continuously improves, and investment steadily increases, which boosts industrial development. From January to June 2023, the industry achieved a revenue of 6.78 trillion *yuan*, with a year-on-year decrease of 4.2 percent, the same from January to May in 2022. The total profit reached 241.8 billion *yuan*, with a year-on-year decrease of 25.2 percent, 24 percent lower than from January to May in 2022. Fixed-asset investment increased by 9.4 percent year-on-year, 0.5 percent higher than industrial investment in the corresponding period a year before. Figure 2-1 shows the cumulative growth rate of added value in the electronic information manufacturing industry from January 2022 to June 2023.

---

5 Shanghai Academy of Social Sciences. *Open Data Index for Major Cities Worldwide 2022*, November 2022.

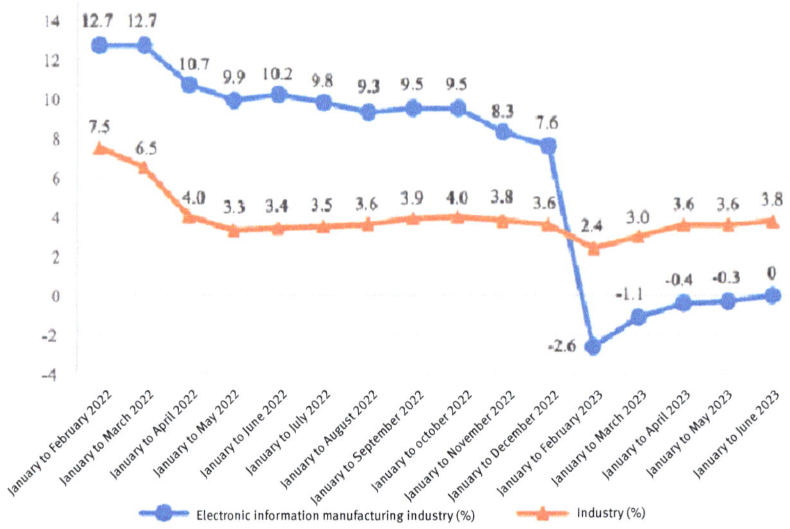

Figure 2-1 Cumulative growth rate of added value in the electronic information manufacturing industry from January 2022 to June 2023.

Source: Ministry of Industry and Information Technology.

In mainstream products, the production of mobile phones, microcomputers, and integrated circuits continues to decline. From January to June 2023, the production of mobile phones reached 686 million units, with a year-on-year decrease of 3.1 percent. Specifically, the production of smartphones reached 507 million units, with a year-on-year decrease of 9.1 percent. The production of microcomputer devices reached 162 million units, with a year-on-year decrease of 25 percent. The production of integrated circuits reached 165.7 billion units, with a year-on-year decrease of 3 percent.

As an emerging industry that develops quickly, energy electronics combines electronic information technology with the demand for the integration and innovation of new energy. In January 2023, the Ministry of Industry and Information Technology, the Ministry of Education, the Ministry of Science and Technology, the People's Bank of China, the China Banking and Insurance Regulatory Commission, and the National Energy Administration jointly issued *Guiding Opinions on Promoting the Development of the Energy Electronics Industry*, setting short-term and medium and long-term development goals for the industry by 2025 and 2030. From March to April 2023, the photovoltaic industry in China operated well, with new highs in output. Intelligent photovoltaic applications continued to advance, and the production of polycrystalline silicon and silicon wafer links increased by 72.1 percent and 79.8 percent year on year, respectively. Tthe production of crystalline silicon batteries and crystalline components increased by 81.6 percent and 92.5 percent year on year, respectively.

The lithium-ion battery industry in China maintains a trend of growth. According to data from the Ministry of Industry and Information Technology, in the first half of 2023, the lithium-ion battery industry in China kept growing. According to the announcements from industrial standards, corporate information, and industrial associations, in the first half of 2023, the production of lithium batteries exceeded 400 GWh, with a year-on-year increase of more than 43 percent. The revenue of the entire lithium battery industry reached 600 billion *yuan*, and the export value of lithium battery products rose by 69 percent year on year.

2.3.2 Software and information technology service industry continues to improve

The software and information technology service industry in China continues to improve, and the business revenue and total profit from software grow rapidly. From January to June 2023, the business revenue of the industry achieved 5,517 billion *yuan*, with a year-on-year increase of 14.2 percent; profits reached 617 billion *yuan*, with a year-on-year increase of 10.4 percent. The decline in software exports narrowed, reaching 24.18 billion US dollars, with a year-on-year decrease of 2 percent. The exports of software outsourcing services grew by 8.2 percent year on year. Figure 2-2 shows the revenue, total profits, and export growth of the software and information technology service industry from January 2022 to June 2023.

Figure 2-2 Revenues, total profits, and export growth of the software and information technology service industry from January 2022 to June 2023.

Source: Ministry of Industry and Information Technology.

In various fields, information technology services achieved a revenue of 3,668.7 billion *yuan*, with a year-on-year increase of 15.3 percent, accounting for 66.5 percent of total revenues. To be specific, cloud computing and big data services achieved a total revenue of 551.5 billion *yuan*, with a year-on-year increase of 16.5 percent, accounting for 15 percent of the revenue of information technology services. Integrated circuit design realized a revenue of 134.9 billion *yuan*, with a year-on-year increase of 3.7 percent. Technological services of e-commerce platforms realized a revenue of 476.2 billion *yuan*, with a year-on-year increase of 6.1 percent. The revenue of software products reached 1,295.9 billion *yuan*, with a year-on-year increase of 11.7 percent, accounting for 23.5 percent of total revenues. The revenue from embedded system software reached 466.7 billion *yuan*, with a year-on-year increase of 14 percent, accounting for 8.5 percent of total revenues. The revenue from information security products and services reached 85.6 billion *yuan*, with a year-on-year increase of 10.8 percent, accounting for 1.6 percent of total revenues.

Regionally, from January to June 2023, the eastern region saw a rapid growth in the revenues from the software and information technology service industry in China; the central region took the lead. Eastern, central, western, and northeastern regions accounted for 82.9 percent, 5 percent, 10.1 percent and 2 percent of total revenues, respectively. The revenues from five major software provinces (cities), i.e., Beijing, Guangdong, Jiangsu, Shandong, and Shanghai, accounted for 70.3 percent of total revenues, up by 0.9 percent compared to the corresponding period in the previous year. In the software business, 15 subprovincial cities and central cities achieved a revenue of 2,743.1 billion *yuan*, with a year-on-year increase of 11.6 percent, accounting for 49.7 percent of total revenues, down by 1.2 percent compared to the corresponding period during the previous year.

2.3.3 Internet and related service industries develop smoothly

In China, the revenues from the Internet and related service industries experienced a steady comeback total profits grew quickly, but investment in research and development continued to decline. From January to June 2023, in Internet business, enterprises above a designated size achieved a revenue of 643.3 billion *yuan*, with a year-on-year increase of 2.6 percent, and a total profit of 63.96 billion *yuan*, with a year-on-year increase of 27.6 percent. The total R & D investment reached 30.54 billion *yuan*, with a year-on-year decrease of 6.8 percent (5.9 percent from January to May in 2022).

Regionally, the business revenue in the eastern region further increased, with positive growth in the Internet business in some regions. From January to June 2023, the eastern region achieved a revenue of 598.6 billion *yuan*, with a year-on-year increase of 3.8 percent, accounting for 93.1 percent of the total. In fourteen provinces, autonomous regions, and municipalities directly under the central government, there was a positive growth in the revenue from the Internet business. Beijing, Shanghai,

Zhejiang, Guangdong, and Tianjin ranked among the top five; their cumulative revenue totaled 564 billion *yuan*, accounting for 87.7 percent of the total (excluding cross-regional enterprises). Figure 2-3 shows the cumulative growth rate of the revenue from Internet business from January 2022 to June 2023.

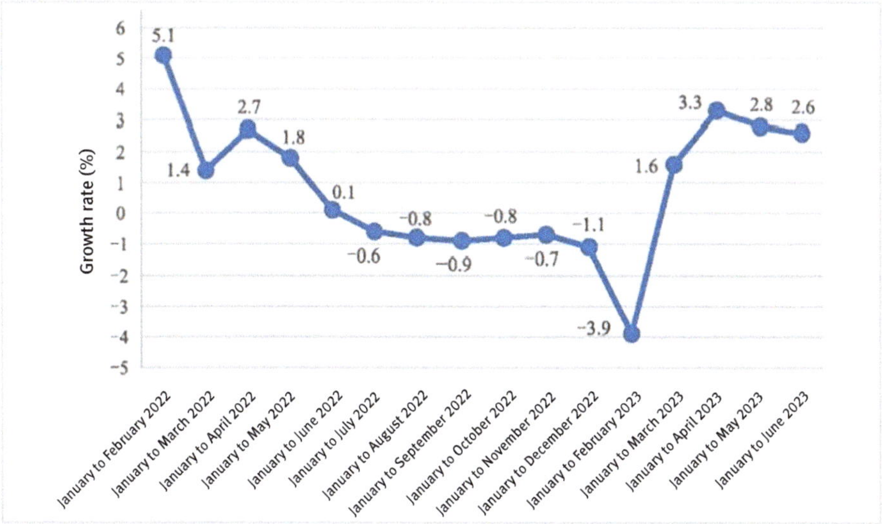

Figure 2-3 Cumulative growth rate of the revenues from Internet businesses from January 2022 to June 2023.

Source: Ministry of Industry and Information Technology.

In the first half of 2023, the application of the Internet expanded continuously, and the number of users of various applications grew remarkably. Specifically, instant messaging ranked first, accounting for 97.1 percent of user numbers. Online video (including short video), online payments, and online shopping accounted for more than 80 percent of the user numbers. In user numbers, online ride-hailing, online travel booking, and online literature grew fastest, increasing by 34.92 million, 30.91 million, and 35.92 million, respectively, compared to December 2022, with a growth rate of 8 percent, 7.3 percent, and 7.3 percent, respectively.[6]

In online ride-hailing, the aggregation model creates opportunities for the development of the online ride-hailing industry, and helps small ride-hailing platforms reach more users. The General Office of the Ministry of Transport and four other departments jointly issued *Notice on Effectively Standardizing the Management of Ride-hailing Aggregation Platforms* and *Working Plan for Promoting Platform Enterprises*

---

6 CNNIC. The 52nd Statistical Report on China Internet Development, August 2023.

in New Forms of Transport to Reduce Excessive Commissions in 2023. These industrial regulations effectively improve the standardization of the online ride-hailing industry. By June 2023, the number of online ride-hailing users in China reached 472 million, accounting for 43.8 percent of the total number of Internet users,[7] as shown in Figure 2-4.

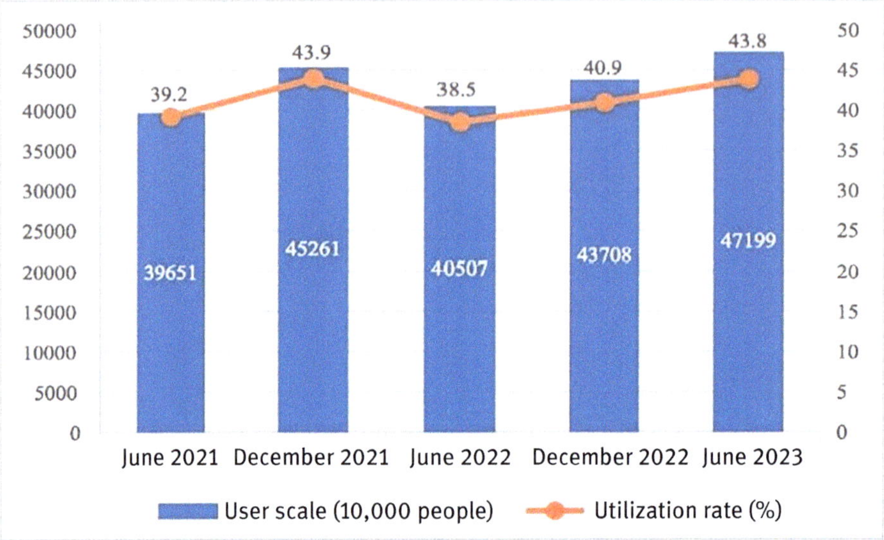

Figure 2-4 Scale and utilization rate of online ride-hailing users from June 2021 to June 2023.

Source: The 52nd Statistical Report on China Internet Development.

In online travel booking, the travel booking market in China displayed a strong recovery. Online booking enterprises, such a Ctrip, Ly, and Fliggy, achieved significant growth in business. While diversifying product and service supply, online travel booking experienced continuous growth in user numbers. By June 2023, the number of online travel booking users in China reached 454 million, accounting for 42.1 percent of the total number of Internet users.[8] In the second quarter of 2023, the average number of monthly active users of Ly reached 280 million,[9] as shown in Figure 2-5.

In online literature, the ecosystem of the copyright for online literature continues to improve. On the one hand, the deep integration of online literature and the video industry further strengthens the ability in content creation of video platforms. On the other hand, the adaptation of online literature in comics, games, and other fields

7 CNNIC. The 52nd Statistical Report on China Internet Development, August 2023.
8 CNNIC. The 52nd Statistical Report on China Internet Development, August 2023.
9 "Ly Releases Q2 2023 Financial Report." Accessed October 2023. https://finance.cnr.cn/zghq/20230822/t20230822_526391160.shtml

stimulates more commercial potential. By June 2023, the number of online literature users in China reached 528 million, accounting for 49 percent of the total number of Internet users,[10] as shown in Figure 2-6.

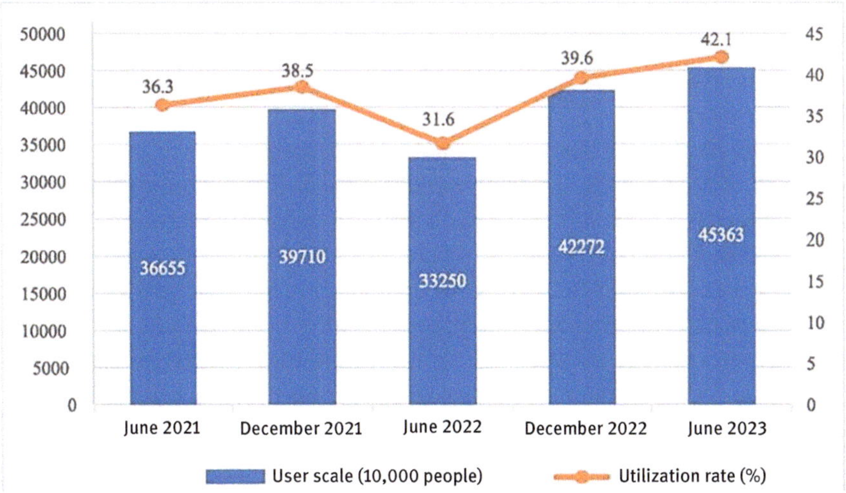

Figure 2-5 Scale and utilization rate of online travel booking users from June 2021 to June 2023.

Source: The 52nd Statistical Report on China Internet Development.

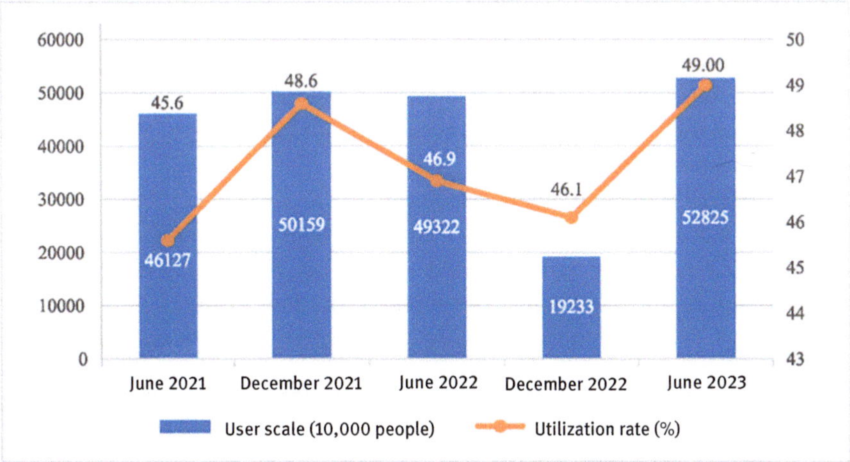

Figure 2-6 Scale and utilization rate of online literature users from June 2021 to June 2023.

Source: The 52nd Statistical Report on China Internet Development.

10 CNNIC. The 52nd Statistical Report on China Internet Development, August 2023.

2.3.4 Internet industry shows sound development

As the prevention and control measures on the pandemic are optimized and adjusted, the national economy improves steadily and boosts market confidence. Under such circumstances, The Internet ecosystem in China is gradually upgraded. Traditional businesses recover and grow stably, and innovation-based businesses achieve positive progress, with a better business environment for enterprises and an upward trend for development.

The market value and business revenue of listed Internet enterprises rally steadily. By the end of March 2023, the total market value of listed Internet enterprises in China had reached 11.1 trillion *yuan*, with a month-on-month increase of 7.8 percent over the fourth quarter of 2022. In particular, the market value of the top ten Internet enterprises accounted for 76.1 percent of the total.[11] In the first quarter of 2023, the total revenue of listed Internet enterprises in China reached 1,081.5 billion *yuan*, up by 6.3 percent year on year. The total revenue of e-commerce, games, social platforms, and online communities accounted for 80 percent, with an increase of 1 percent over the fourth quarter of 2022. The software tool and healthcare sectors saw rapid growth, up by 17.3 percent and 19.9 percent year on year, respectively. The business revenue of the top ten Internet enterprises accounted for 87.8 percent, up by 7.2 percent, higher than the growth rate of the total revenue of listed Internet enterprises.

Regionally, by December 2022, among listed Internet enterprises at home and abroad, most of them were registered in Beijing and Shanghai, accounting for 33.3 percent and 19.5 percent, respectively, followed by Shenzhen, Hangzhou, and Guangzhou, accounting for 10.7 percent, 10.7 percent, and 5.0 percent, respectively. In the types of enterprises, online games, e-commerce, and cultural and entertainment enterprises had the highest proportion, accounting for 20.8 percent, 15.1 percent, and 15.1 percent, respectively.

In the business environment for enterprises, the investment and financing of the Internet industry in China remain sluggish. According to the report *Internet Investment and Financing in the Second Quarter of 2023* released by the China Academy of Information and Communications Technology in July 2023, in the second quarter of 2023, the total number of Internet investment and financing in China was 223, down by 30.5 percent month on month and by 60.9 percent year on year. The total amount of Internet investment and financing disclosed by enterprises reached 1.01 billion US dollars, down by 40.4 percent month on month and 69.8 percent year on year. The investment and financing market in Internet-related fields continued to develop. The proportion of early rounds of financing remained high, especially in

---

11 China Academy of Information and Communications Technology. *Operation of Internet Listed Enterprises in China in the First Quarter of 2023*, June 2023.

core areas. In 2022, the number and amount of investment and financing events in Internet-related fields accounted for 23.0 percent and 14.8 percent of all investment and financing events in all fields, respectively. In the distribution of rounds of financing, the number of seed rounds, angel rounds, and A rounds in Internet-related fields accounted for 63.0 percent of the total number of investment and financing events, with an increase of 7.7 percent over 2021. In the amount of investment and financing, the number of events in Internet-related fields with 110 billion *yuan* accounted for 3.0 percent of the total number, reaching the same level in 2021. In regional distribution, Beijing, Shanghai, Guangdong, Zhejiang, and Jiangsu ranked among the top five in the investment and financing in Internet-related fields in China, with the number of events accounting for 79.5 percent of the total, and the amount accounting for 85 percent of the total.[12]

The innovation capability in digital industries has significantly enhanced, which establishes a solid economic foundation for the information-based innovation industry. In 2022, the information-based innovation industry in China continued to deepen, and the procurement of information-based innovation services by the Party and governmental departments significantly increased. Accordingly, the demand for information-based innovation products such as middleware, databases, and operating systems continue to rise. Hap Academy, the China Software Industry Association, and soft6 jointly released *Market Research on China Information-Based Innovation Ecology and Selection Evaluation Report 2022*. As shown, in 2022, the core market scale of the information-based innovation industry, composed of IT infrastructure and basic software core products, reached 239.28 billion *yuan*, accounting for 26.0 percent. The noncore market scale of the information-based innovation industry, composed of platform software, application software, and IT security noncore products, reached 682.74 billion *yuan*, accounting for 74.0 percent. According to *The White Paper on the Development of the Information-Based Innovation Industry in China in 2023* released by iiMedia Research, in 2023, the scale of the information-based innovation industry reached 2,096.19 billion *yuan*.

2.4 Industrial Digital Transformation Accelerates in an All-Round Way

With the upgrading and development of digital economy and the implementation of innovation and application, the digital transformation of traditional industries acceleratedin an all-round way. The advent of smart agriculture produced remarkable progress, with a focus on smart farms and rural e-commerce platforms. The scale

12 CNNIC. *The 52nd Statistical Report on China Internet Development*, August 2023.

of the industrial Internet continues to expand. With the help of 5G, the digital transformation of the manufacturing industry quickens and moves toward a new stage of high-end, intelligent, and green development. New digital models of service industries, such as online consumption, online retail, mobile payment, online ride-hailing, and online food delivery, show growth.

2.4.1 Significant achievements are made in smart agriculture

1. Smart farms help to save costs and improve efficiency in agricultural production

In 2022, China stepped up efforts to improve the digital level of agricultural production and build up strength in agriculture based on the dual drives of technology and reform. Digital technology was adopted to alter the production modes of traditional agriculture and achieve the improvement of agricultural quality and efficiency. Intelligent farmland management systems, intelligent irrigation systems, precision seeding, variable-rate-based fertilization, environmental control, unmanned transplanting machines, unmanned plant protection machines, unmanned reapers, and other technologies and devices started to be widely applied, which tremendously reduced labor costs and raised the efficiency of agricultural production. According to *China Digital Countryside Development Report 2022*, the use of technology in field planting in China has reached 21.8 percent, with the rate of production in wheat, rice, and corn exceeding 39.6 percent, 37.7 percent, and 26.9 percent, respectively. In the spring sowing of Great Northern Wilderness in Heilongjiang Province, there are already six large-scale unmanned farms with domestically produced machinery, reducing field labor by more than 70 percent and improving work efficiency by more than 30 percent. Water conservation, fertilizer conservation, and pesticide reduction exceed 20 percent, 50 percent, and 30 percent, respectively, and the demonstration zone increased production by more than 10 percent.[13]

2. Various platforms provide support for the digital governance of agriculture and rural areas

To break down data barriers and revitalize agricultural and rural data resources, various agricultural and rural digital platforms have been constructed and developed. By integrating data resources, strengthening data analysis, providing

13 "Building an Agricultural Power and Promoting the Development of Smart Agriculture: A Group of Smart Farms for Grain Crops Emerging in Various Regions."Accessed July 2023. https:/news.cctv.com/2022/12/27/ARTIbwuSDt5Ifqyck7qCRNoR221227.shtml.

precise services, and assisting decision-making management, the models of digital regulation and governance of agriculture are continually being innovated in China. Currently, geographic information public service platforms, government data sharing platforms, and agricultural and rural big data platforms of the Ministry of Agriculture and Rural Affairs have been established, which enrich agricultural and rural data resources. “One Map” for National Digital Farmland Construction, National Third Soil Survey Platform and National Farmland Comprehensive Monitoring and Regulation Platform have all been built. The pilot construction of big data in the entire industrial chain of fifteen varieties and eight categories, including soybean and apple, steadily advances. Information data platforms for live pig products have been launched and operated, which publishes data for the entire industrial chain of live pigs. The National Agricultural Products Quality and Safety Traceability and Management Information Platform achieves integration and connection with thirty-one provincial-level platforms and agricultural reclamation platforms, which comprehensively improves the capability in the information technology-based regulation of agricultural green production. Simultaneously, the platform injects new momentum into poverty alleviation in China. According to *China Digital Countryside Development Report 2022*, by the end of 2022, online sales platforms for agricultural and sideline products in poverty-stricken areas (“832 Platform”) attracted more than 20,000 suppliers from poverty-stricken areas, with a transaction volume of more than 13.65 billion *yuan* in 2022, with a year-on-year increase of 20 percent.

3. New business forms and models of rural digital economy continue to emerge

In the rural digital economy, rural e-commerce plays a leading role. China continuously promotes the Digital Commerce for Rural Revitalization Project, encourages e-commerce platforms for agricultural products to adopt the models of direct procurement and customized production, builds e-commerce live streaming bases for agricultural and sideline products, and revitalizes agriculture with digital commerce. The Digital Commerce for Rural Revitalization Project drives the construction of new infrastructure in rural areas, and connects the “first mile” for the sales of agricultural products by improving rural logistical systems. In 2022, Douyin e-commerce helped to sell 2.83 billion orders of agricultural products and specialties, and the number of new farmers on the platform increased by 252 percent year on year. Kuaishou e-commerce live streaming helped to sell 560 million orders of agricultural products as well.

In January 2023, the Ministry of Agriculture and Rural Affairs announced the List of Key Counties for National Leisure Agriculture in 2022, actively developing various agricultural functions via the “agriculture-tourism dual chain” model, exploring the diverse value of rural areas, and assisting in the modernization of agriculture and rural areas. In the pilot zones of the digital countryside in China, new application scenarios for rural digital development, such as "transparent service system in rural areas," a "digital flower market," and "e-commerce + Internet celebrities," have been formed, which provide an idea for comprehensively promoting the construction of a digital countryside.

2.4.2 Industrial Internet empowers the digitization of the manufacturing industry

1. The digital transformation of the manufacturing industry accelerates

The manufacturing industry becomes a main battlefield for the digital economy, and serves as a major direction and starting point for promoting the integration and development of the digital economy and the traditional economy. China implements projects on intelligent manufacturing, fosters the digital transformation of industries, and steadily improves the digitization of enterprises and the digitization rate of devices. Many typical applications, such as remote device control, machine vision inspection, unmanned intelligent inspection, flexible production and manufacturing, and personalized customization, have been put into practice. Digitization extends from device management, production-process control, and other links to product R & D and design, and manufacturing and process optimization. By the end of 2022, the CNC rate of key processes in industrial enterprises nationwide reached 58.6 percent, and the popularization rate of digital R & D and design tools reached 77.0 percent,[14] which greatly reduced costs and improved efficiency in the manufacturing industry.

2. Industrial scale of the industrial Internet continues to expand

As a new strategic infrastructure for industrialization, the industrial Internet becomes a core means for industrial enterprises to develop the digital economy. China implements projects on the innovation and development of the industrial Internet. The scale of the industrial Internet keeps expanding. Three functional systems of the industrial Internet, i.e., networks, platforms, and security, take shape. The number of industrial Internet platforms continues to increase. According to the "2022 Industrial Internet Platform Development Index" released by the Ministry of Industry and

14 "Ministry of Industry and Information Technology. Promoting the Transformation in Six Aspects to Build Green New Energy." Accessed July 2023. http://www.news.cn/fortune/2023-06/15/c_1129695638.htm.

Information Technology, in 2022, the index reached 251, with a year-on-year increase of 17 percent, more than 15 percent for four consecutive years.

3. Innovation and development of "5G + industrial Internet" enter the fast lane

"5G + industrial Internet" has evolved from initial exploration to large-scale development. 5G features high speed, wide connections, and low delays. China actively gives play to the technological characteristics of 5G, deploys the construction of a new digital infrastructure from a high starting point, and explores a new path for technological upgrades in traditional industries. "5G + industrial Internet" shores up high-end, intelligent, and green development of the manufacturing industry. In November 2022, the China Academy of Information and Communications Technology released *Evaluation Report on the Development of "5G + Industrial Internet" in 2022.* As the report states, China has completed the "5G + Industrial Internet" 512 Project with high quality. The number of "5G + industrial Internet" projects invested and constructed nationwide exceeds 4,000, covering ten key industries such as electronic equipment manufacturing, steel, and power, and forty-one major categories of the national economy. Twenty typical application scenarios have been formed, including collaborative R & D and design, remote device control, machine vision inspection, unmanned intelligent inspection, all-sector logistics inspection, and production energy efficiency control. Among the seed projects of 5G fully connected factories, the projects with more than 60 percent of industrial equipment connected to 5G account for more than 50 percent of all the seed projects. 5G is deeply integrated with various industries. On this basis, 5G has quickly penetrated various industries and fields such as healthcare, transportation, and education. New technologies such as AI, AR/VR and 8K have matured, and new business models like IoV thrive.

2.4.3 Integrated development is realized in the digital economy and modern service industry

The development of the digital economy effectively promotes innovation in the service industry. The modern service industry is developing rapidly. Based on networks, platforms, and intelligence, the modern service industry serves as an important force that boosts industrial transformation and coordinated development. In 2022, the revenue from the strategic emerging service industry continued to expand. According to data from the National Bureau of Statistics, the revenue of enterprises above a designated size in the service industry in China increased by 2.7 percent compared to 2021. In particular, the revenue from enterprises in the strategic emerging service industry increased by 4.8 percent compared to 2021.

1. New forms and models of online retail show great vitality

In 2022, online retail in China maintained a trend of growth and played an important role in promoting consumption expansion. By June 2023, the number of online shopping users in China reached 884 million, accounting for 82 percent of the total number of Internet users.[15] Additionally, customs data show that the imports and exports of cross-border e-commerce in China reached 2.11 trillion *yuan*, with a year-on-year increase of 9.8 percent.

Online retail has demonstrated a new vitality. In 2022, the Chinese e-commerce live streaming market displayed enormous potential and vitality. On major monitored e-commerce platforms, more than 120 million live streams were reported, with more than 1.1 trillion views (more than 95 million types of products, and about 1.1 million active streamers). In addition, as urban logistics and distribution networks and new commercial infrastructure improve, real-time retail business has grown rapidly, covering a wider range of industries and products, and becoming an emerging field in new retail markets.

2. Digitization drives innovation in mobile payment in the financial industry

Mobile payment is most deeply affected by the digital transformation of the financial industry. In 2022, the mobile payment market in China developed steadily. Furthermore, with the development of biometric technology, biometric technologies such as fingerprint identification and facial recognition are used more widely. Payments have become disintermediated. According to the *Report on Overall Operation of the Payment System in 2022* released by the People's Bank of China, in 2022, Chinese banks processed a total of 278.965 billion electronic payment transactions, with a total amount of 3,110.13 trillion *yuan*, with a year-on-year increase of 1.45 percent and 4.50 percent, respectively. Specifically, there were 102.126 billion online payment transactions, with a year-on-year decrease of 0.15 percent. There were 158.507 billion mobile payment transactions, with a year-on-year increase of 4.81 percent. Simultaneously, in response to new trends of financial payment, the People's Bank of China accelerated the process of e-CNY (Chinese *Yuan*), further promoting the transformation of payment models. By December 2022, e-CNY had been piloted in twenty-six regions in seventeen provinces in China.[16] The pilot scenarios in various regions covered multiple fields, such as wholesale and retail, catering, culture and

15 CNNIC. *The 52nd Statistical Report on China Internet Development*, August 2023.

16 "The Pilot of e-CNY Expands: Fully Covering Guangdong, Jiangsu, Hebei and Sichuan Provinces, with Five Newly-Added Cities." Accessed July 2023. https:/news.cctv.com/2022/12/17/ARTIQPRMBqzneb3RzWIzOQ70221217.shtml.

tourism, and government payments. According to statistical data from the People's Bank of China, the stock of e-CNY in circulation has reached 13.61 billion *yuan*.[17]

3. Digitization of the consumer service industry quickens

With the advancement of digital technology and the upgrading of consumer structure, the proportion of service-oriented consumption has expanded. By June 2023, the number of online ride-hailing users in China reached 472 million, accounting for 43.8 percent of the total number of Internet users.[18] In technological application, Robotaxi has become a hot area in the development of Internet travel platforms. In August 2022, Baidu officially launched the commercial operation of fully automated robotaxis. Wuhan and Chongqing are the first two cities to obtain the permission to operate fully automated robotaxis on urban public roads, bringing a new experience to residents' travels.

The online food delivery market is developing rapidly. The market scale keeps expanding with the digitization of platforms. Online food delivery covers diverse types of products, from catering and food to supermarkets, fresh fruits and vegetables, maternal and child products, etc. Meanwhile, platform services have been optimized. Based on the use of digital technology, precision marketing and multiscenario services improve the matching efficiency between merchants and consumers, thus increasing user loyalty and promoting the digital development of the online food delivery market.

2.5 AI Spurs the Development of the Digital Economy

In July 2022, the Ministry of Science and Technology and five other departments jointly issued Guiding Opinions on Accelerating the Innovation in Application Scenarios and Promoting High-quality Economic Development through High-level Application of Artificial Intelligence, providing policy guidance for the development of AI in China. It stresses that the innovation in the application scenarios of AI is guided by creative application of new technologies and is realized by the supply-demand linkage, which promotes iterative upgrading of new technologies and achieves rapid growth in industries. In recent years, AI, as a cutting-edge technology in the innovation

17 "The People's Bank of China: The Stock of e-CNY in Circulation Reaching 13.61 Billion *Yuan*." Accessed July 2023. http://www.news.cn/fortune/2023-01/13/c_1129282672.htm.
18 CNNIC. *The 52nd Statistical Report on China Internet Development*, August 2023.

and development of the digital economy, has been integrated with the traditional economy. This spurs the transformation and upgrading of platform economy and catalyzes new products, models, and forms, thus becoming an important engine for economic and social development. As the Ministry of Industry and Information Technology estimates, in 2022, the scale of the core AI industry in China reached 508 billion yuan in 2022, with a year-on-year increase of 18 percent. There were 4,227 AI enterprises, accounting for 16 percent of the total number of global AI enterprises.

2.5.1 Intelligent decision-making boosts a green industrial transformation

AI technology can achieve data-driven intelligent decision-making through deep analysis and comprehensively optimizing the allocation of industrial chain resources. The AI + IoT-based IoE model aims to achieve optimal efficiency, empower a green industrial transformation, and accelerate carbon neutrality. China's launch of the first year of action towards the "dual carbon" goal promotes the application of energy-saving and carbon-reduction technologies, improves the efficiency of energy utilization, and fosters the green and low-carbon transformation of industries. In August 2022, the Ministry of Industry and Information Technology, the National Development and Reform Commission, and the Ministry of Ecology and Environment jointly issued *Implementation Plan for Carbon Peaking in the Industrial Sector*, which requires the transition to digital, smart, and green development driven by innovation. One important task is to utilize new-generation information technology, including AI, to upgrade and transform process flow and devices with a green and low-carbon approach, strengthen the connection between enterprise demand and information service supply, and accelerate the application and promotion of digital low-carbon solutions.

In practice, AI can be applied to various industrial scenarios by predicting, monitoring, and reducing emissions. For example, in smart homes, centralized management of residential devices can be achieved through automation, computer control, and other technologies, with optimal energy consumption. In the field of green transportation, self-adaptive air conditioning technology can be applied to wind-water linkage control systems, taking the ventilation and air conditioning systems at the subway station as the overall unit. Through a real-time dynamic and active optimization control algorithm, the operating condition parameters with the lowest energy consumption and highest energy efficiency can be determined, achieving an overall energy-savings rate of more than 30 percent for ventilation and air conditioning systems.[19] In the construction industry, in January 2023, the

19 *2023 Rail Transit Green Intelligent Construction Technology Development Summit Forum*, April 2023.

China National Institute of Standardization and other organizations launched the "100 Billion Green Steel Initiative," which advocates for using digital methods for standard certification and procurement grading of green and low-carbon steel, and achieving large-scale transactions. As predicted, in the 14th Five-Year Plan, about 25 million tons and 100 billion *yuan* of green steel transactions will be completed, reducing a total of more than 2.5 million tons of the emission of carbon dioxide. By 2030, a total of 150 million tons of green steel will be traded, with a transaction amount of 600 billion *yuan*, as well as a cumulative reduction of more than 15 million tons of the emission of carbon dioxide.

2.5.2 AI triggers new application scenarios and business models

Currently, the rapid development of the digital economy creates favorable development conditions and a technological environment for the entire AI industry. As a key new technology, AI becomes an important driving force or engine that makes breakthroughs in technological development, promotes industrial optimization and upgrading, improves overall productivity, and boosts the development of the traditional economy. According to the *14th Five-Year Plan for the Development of Digital Economy* issued by the State Council in 2022, the added value of core industries in the digital economy, including AI algorithms and computing power, will reach 13.8 trillion *yuan* by 2025. This will accelerate the digital transformation of various industries, facilitate deep integration of digital technology and the traditional economy, and make the digital economy a new economic form that promotes fairness and efficiency. In April 2023, the meeting of the Political Bureau of the CPC Central Committee proposed highlighting the development of general AI, creating an innovative ecosystem, and preventing risks.

In technological development, the algorithms, computing power, and data that drive the development of AI showed considerable progress.[20] In terms of algorithms, super large-scale pretrained models stirred wide attention; knowledge-driven AI signals an important direction for improving cognitive ability. In July 2023, at HDC Cloud 2023, Pangu LM 3.0, positioned as "born for the industry," was officially released, which can be used for precise weather forecast in megacities. In terms of basic computing power, single-point computing power continues to improve, and customized and diversified computing power became an important trend. In terms of data, as the demand for massive labeled data increases, data services are optimized and customized, with more knowledge sets constructed and utilized.

---

20 China Academy of Information and Communications Technology. *The White Paper on Artificial Intelligence 2022*, April 2022.

In various industries, manufacturing, energy, transportation, and other industries promote the application of AI technology. In the field of energy, the Huawei remote intelligent inspection solution combines AI with technologies such as automatic control and the IoT, which significantly raises the security and accuracy of inspection and reduces the risks of erroneous operations. In the field of intelligent transportation, Tencent implements intelligent signal control in cities based on a vehicle-road-cloud-map digital base, creating a holographic perception intelligent intersection solution, and providing an overall experience of intelligent traffic management. In the medical industry, a series of intelligent medical imaging innovative products, such as intelligent biomimetic minimally invasive intervention systems, global AI-empowered CT, and dual-navigation surgical vision systems, emerge rapidly, which effectively solves the shortage of doctors and the imbalance of medical resources in the field of traditional medical imaging. In May 2023, the Shanghai Computing Power Network Digital Medical Innovation Laboratory released the "Uni-talk" medical computing network LM, successfully achieving the integration of general AI into the field of medical AI.

Major cities contend for the leading position in the new round of AI development. In Beijing, AI large model companies are densely distributed at Zhongguancun. In September 2023, the construction of the Zhongguancun Artificial Intelligence Large Model Industry Cluster Zone was started. Four AI industrial parks at Wudaokou, Beida West Gate, Zhongguancun West District, and Tsinghua Science and Technology Park are listed in the first group, promoting the application of large model scenarios. The *Implementation Plan for General Artificial Intelligence Innovation-Led Development in Zhongguancun Science City 2023–2025* proposes building globally influential AI innovation-led zones and industrial cluster zones by 2025, with the scale of core AI industry exceeding 230 billion *yuan* and more than 100 large model enterprises and institutions. In Shanghai, AI large models are developed by SenseTime, Fudan University, and others. In July 2023, SenseTime released SenseNova 2.0. Shenzhen possesses great strength in AI large models. In the Futian District, Shenzhen, IDEA (International Digital Economy Academy) launched the open-source universal large model "Jiang Ziya" series, which has 13 billion parameters and performs pretraining at the level of more than 100 billion tokens.

10.2478/9788367405867-004

Chapter 3
Creation of Online Content

At present, the Internet has become a new space for forging consensus, a new field for gathering positive energy, and a new battlefield for steering public opinion. Over the past year, the creation of online content was promoted with high quality. While highlighting the central theme, guiding the direction, pooling efforts, innovating forms to follow the laws of communication, updating communication concepts, creating a communication atmosphere, and enriching communication patterns, China ensures that mainstream values prevail and advance with the times, and that cyberspace becomes a powerful source of inspiration to work closely and build the Chinese dream together.

2023 is the first year to fully implement the guiding principles of the 20th CPC National Congress. At the 20th CPC National Congress, the National People's Congress (NPC), and the Chinese People's Political Consultative Conference (CPPCC), major themes and topics tally with the core ideas of propaganda campaigns, maintain the right tone in public communication, and spread positive energy based on the instruction of "upholding fundamental principles and breaking new ground." The mainstream public opinion in cyberspace is consolidated and developed, the Party's innovative theories are deeply rooted and firmly planted among the public, and a beautiful picture of Internet civilization is unfolding. In international communication, a new pattern of multiple parties, diverse contexts, and different perspectives has been established. The creativity, attraction, credibility, and influence of China are continuously improved, and Chinese discourse in the world and its efficiency in international communication in cyberspace are comprehensively enhanced. In the production and supply of online content, China prioritizes content-centered production, fully meets public demands, strengthens technological support, adopts targeted supply, and deepens emotional effect, maximizing social consensus and improving the quality and efficiency of communication.

The comprehensive governance system of cyberspace has been basically established, and the capability in cyberspace governance has been fully enhanced. The ecosystem in cyberspace continues to improve. The comprehensive governance of cyberspace has become more law-based and scientific, with more extensive public participation. The protection of minors in cyberspace, elder-friendly transformation and barrier-free information construction promote the inclusive development of a digital society. The integrated development of media advances solidly, and the construction of full-media communication systems accelerates. County-level integrated media report local news, participate in grassroots governance, and serve rural revitalization. Government's new media strengthens the interpretation of and response to social issues, deepens government-citizen interaction, and innovates social governance. Cutting-edge technologies, such as big data, metaverse, and AI, quickly penetrate the media field, empower the intelligent transformation of news media, and drive the upgrading and integration of media.

3.1 Promoting High-Quality Construction of Online Content, Consolidating Mainstream Public Opinion in Cyberspace

The Internet provides massive amounts of social information. Billions of Internet users obtain and exchange information via the Internet. The dissemination of online content has a great impact on people's thinking models, values, and ideologies. Over the past year, progress has been made in the high-quality creation of online content. Joint efforts were taken to propagate major themes and topics. New advances were achieved in the construction of Internet civilization, and the efficiency of international communication in cyberspace was comprehensively improved. The supply of online content closely met the needs of the public. Online and offline media, TV, and mobile phones were coordinated and integrated. Mainstream public opinion in cyberspace was consolidated and developed.

3.1.1 Mainstream values prevail and forge consensus

In the past year, major mainstream media and websites centered on the online propaganda in the spirit of the 20th CPC National Congress, which focused on the planning and dissemination of major themes, coordinated communication resources, and innovated communication methods. In these works, positive energy and mainstream values prevail, which showcase the historic achievements made by the Party and the country, present a vivid picture of the whole Party and all Chinese people making contributions in the new era, and forge consensus and stimulate a powerful impetus in cyberspace.

1. Firmly upholding central themes and promoting integration and innovation: The online propaganda of the spirit of the 20th CPC National Congress is deeply rooted among the public

The 20th CPC National Congress was successfully held in October 2022, which was broadcast in real time on various website platforms, TV stations, and mobile phones.

New media works, such as *Together with the People*, *Micro Records of Current Affairs: The Successful Convening of the 20th CPC National Congress*, *New Members of the Standing Committee of the Political Bureau of the CPC Central Committee Meeting with Chinese and Foreign Journalists* (short videos of current affairs), and *A Quick Look at the Report of the 20th CPC National Congress in One Picture* ranked at the top for a long time, vividly demonstrating the leadership style, political wisdom, and love for the Chinese people of General Secretary Xi Jinping. The propaganda of major themes of the 20th CPC National Congress has become the strongest voice that guides public opinion in cyberspace. On October 12 through the 24th, the online coverage of the 20th CPC National Congress exceeded 4.5 million, with more than 88.7 billion clicks and more than 590 million discussions. Mainstream media, such as Xinhua News Agency, the *People's Daily*, and the China Media Group, focused on the five major themes, i.e., "Steering a Steady Course,", "Extraordinary Ten Years," "My Suggestions for the 20th CPC National Congress," "New Pictures of China," and "Embarking on a New Journey and Making Achievements in the New Era," innovated the content, approach, and methods of full-media coverage, and continuously launched a series of high-quality down-to-earth news works with insights and creativity, via online communication channels such as WeChat, Weibo, news client-ends, and short video platforms. Excellent full-media works, *Follow General Secretary to Watch China*, *Close Shots: Warm Moments*, *Decoding the Last Decade*, *Amazing Chinese Counties*, *The Great Rejuvenation on a New Journey*, and *Road*, followed the inspection footprints and recorded the touching stories of General Secretary Xi Jinping, showcased the tremendous changes in Chinese society in the form of a series of short videos, interpreted the "Chinese Code" of the ten-year changes through the reporting method of "satellite perspective + big data investigation + news stories," and incorporated popular rap elements into news reports to present the development achievements of Chinese counties. With simple, story-based, and multi-angle news reporting, these works interpreted major themes with small things, attracted the public with people-oriented styles, and expanded the dissemination of new media products. While enhancing the dissemination effect and strengthening ideological guidance, these works better delivered the spirit of the 20th CPC National Congress to the public. In 2022, the online themed promotion activity of "Devoting the Splendor of Youth on the Land of the Motherland" for ideological and political course was continuously conducted, which invited representatives of the 20th CPC National Congress, astronaut heroes, and youth models to meet with young people via the cloud and learn the spirit of the 20th CPC National Congress online and offline. In "Starting Again with Youth," college teachers and students were organized to participate in online themed propaganda, and young people were led to keep pace with the times and society in the widespread practice of implementing the spirit of the 20th CPC National Congress in various regions and departments. In a series of activities of "Internet Celebrities Investigating National Conditions," Internet celebrities were organized to visit Xinjiang, Guangxi, Heilongjiang, and other regions and introduce development achievements of these regions and the spirit of the cadres and masses through various forms of online content. Relevant topics were read 1.02 billion times in total. The online selection activity of "Discovering the Most Beautiful Scenery in China" closely followed major themes and staged many activities in Anhui, Shaanxi, Fujian, and other regions. With relevant topics read more than 1.8 billion times in total, the activity helped to create a strong atmosphere of "linking the Party and the people, and welcoming the grand event among billions of Internet users." The themed event of "Ten-Year Tour of New Era and New Achievements" gathered strong spiritual strength to welcome the successful convening of the 20th CPC National Congress and realize the Second Centenary Goal.

2. Presenting in an all-round way and using innovative methods: Full-media coverage of the National People's Congress (NPC) and the Chinese People's Political Consultative Conference (CPPCC)

In 2023, the first year to fully implement the guiding principles of the 20th CPC National Congress, NPC and CPPCC were held, which attracted worldwide attention and possessed great significance. Taking this opportunity, mainstream media, websites, and new media fully leveraged the advantages of the full-media communication system, and integrated newspapers, magazines, websites, client ends, social media, and TV so as to present a panoramic view of the grand events and deepen the promotion of major themes. Xinhua News Agency produced the micro video *Close Shots of Xi Jinping at the Two Sessions* to represent the scenes and voices of General Secretary Xi Jinping attending events and delivering speeches. The *People's Daily Online* launched special reports of *Shi Xi Zhi: Xi Jinping's Concerns at the Two Sessions* and *Xi Jinping's Schedules at the Two Sessions*. *Guangming Daily* produced a series of short videos entitled *Warm Moments in the Two Sessions* on the Douyin platform, which focused on General Secretary Xi Jinping's talks with delegates and members about people's livelihood, and showed his concern for people's livelihood at the micro-level, with total views of hundreds of millions. Important documents were finalized with the innovation in the expressions of the coverage of NPC and CPPCC. New media of the *People's Daily* first released a simplified version of *Report on the Work of the Government* in 700 words, and launched various forms of interactive products such as questions and answers and dictionaries, organically combining timeliness, succinctness, and fun. The China Media Group used live streaming and short videos to conduct on-site coverage and clarify key points of the report, enhancing the publicity about the report with audiovisual elements.[1] In addition, the coverage of NPC and CPPCC

1 Zeng Xiangmin, Zou Jiyu, and Hu Haiyue: "Multidimensional Aggregation and Deep Embedding: An Analysis of the Innovative Coverage of Integrated Media on the Two Sessions in 2023," *Media*, 2023 (8): 9–13.

included delegates and members. Guangming Net established multimedia columns such as “Guangxiaoming’s Cultural Seminar on the Two Sessions,” “A Channel for Voices,” and “Delegates and Members from the Grassroots” so as to provide channels for delegates and members to offer suggestions directly. The *People’s Daily Online* produced online video interviews such as “Observation on the Two Sessions” and “Evening Interviews on the Two Sessions,” which invited delegates and members to exchange ideas and interpret trends with experts, scholars, and front-line workers, so that Internet users easily understood the views of the Two Sessions.

3. The Party’s innovative theories are deeply rooted and firmly planted among the public through the Internet, and new ideas are widely accepted by the masses

Over the past year, various websites and platforms vigorously developed new forms, channels, and languages for online promotion and interpretation of the Party’s innovative theories. Vivid cases and expressions sparked wide ideological response and value recognition among Internet users. Central news websites and theoretical websites launched learning columns in such forms as short videos, micro-animation, and cloud salons in an innovative way. For example, brand columns, such as *Xue Xi Lu Shang* of *People’s Daily Online*, *Xue Xi Jin Xing Shi* of Xinhua Net, *Xue Xi Bi Ji* of QSTHEORY.CN, *Tian Tian Xue Xi* of CCTV.com, and *Li Xiang Zhong Guo* of Guangming Net, focused on visual presentation and interactive communication, continuously innovated the languages of publicity and the forms of presentation, comprehensively interpreted the profound principles, theories, and philosophies contained in the latest achievements of adapting Marxism to the Chinese context and the times, continually expanded the number of Internet users for positive publicity, spread the voice of the Party to the masses, and guided billions of Internet users to follow the Party’s leadership and its footsteps.

Online media strengthen the interpretation of major theoretical and practical issues like Chinese path to modernization. Xinhua News Agency releases *Magnificent Prospects of Chinese Path to Modernization from Ten Dimensions* in full-media channels, and depicts the vivid practice of China’s striving for modernization. *Economic Daily* publishes a series of special articles on the in-depth analysis of Chinese path to modernization, deeply explores the spirit and engine of Chinese path to modernization, and on this basis, produces innovative media products such as *What Is Chinese Path to Modernization*. CCTV News launches large-scale multimedia activity, “The Revitalization of Counties,” in the forms of micro-video, visits, selling goods through live streaming, and H5. Internet users are invited to visit famous counties and unveil the secret of the development of county-level economy as well as rural revitalization. The activity vividly presents the new appearance of county governance in China in the new era and mirrors the road of Chinese path to modernization by observing the development of counties. Relevant websites and platforms are guided to plan and organize multimedia projects such as "Weibo-based interview of Internet celebrities," "heavyweights say," and "views of influencers" to propagate and interpret the Party's innovative theories. Internet celebrities are encouraged and guided to create and disseminate high-quality content based on major themes and social issues, convey positive values to Internet users, continuously consolidate mainstream public opinion, and help to build a clean and upright cyberspace. In the activity of "Praising the New Era, Making Achievements on the New Journey," Internet celebrities are invited to visit the grassroots, witness the achievements of rural revitalization, share what they see and feel with Internet users in their special styles, display the vivid practice of high-quality development, and tell the story of the Chinese path to modernization, based on their influence on Internet.

3.1.2 Primary platforms strengthen the creation of an Internet civilization and promote new lieas

As a major component of social etiquette and civility under new circumstances, Internet civilization is a key area of enhancing China's strength in cyberspace. Over the past year, the creation of an Internet civilization remained in full swing and built a strong momentum. New trends in Internet culture were continuously fostered, new practices of Internet civilization were enriched, and primary platforms for online propaganda were consolidated. Cyberspace was purified and shaped with new trends of the times, and built into a beautiful spiritual home with value identification, humanistic care, and emotional belonging, to effectively enhance the sense of gain, happiness, and security of billions of people in cyberspace.

1. The top-level design continues to be strengthened, and the creation of an Internet civilization continues to be promoted

In recent years, the Office of the Central Cyberspace Affairs Commission regarded the creation of an Internet civilization as an important task that can enhance China's strength in cyberspace, made efforts in both construction and governance, promoted the comprehensive creation of Internet civilization, and achieved positive progress and significant results. The Office of the Central Cyberspace Affairs Commission organized the National Conference on Promoting the Construction of Internet Civilization, issued *Implementation Plan for Strengthening the Construction of Internet Civilization*, made overall arrangements to strengthen the construction of Internet civilization under new circumstances, and cooperated with various departments. In July 2023, under the theme of "Gathering Forces through the Internet and Embarking on the Great Journey," the China Internet Civilization Conference was successfully held in Xiamen. At the main forum of the conference, *Report on the Development of Internet Civilization in China 2023*, as well as the results of "Excellent Works in Four

Fields Contest" based on online selection, was released. Twelve subforums focused on topics such as the Internet and the creation of an Internet civilization, the publication of online content, the construction of an Internet ecosystem, social participation in the creation of an Internet civilization, the governance of algorithms, law-based governance of cyberspace, rumor-refutation in cyberspace, international exchanges and mutual learning of Internet civilization, the development of digital charity, the development of digital culture and tourism, data security and personal information protection, and the construction of Internet literacy of teenagers across the Taiwan Straits. The conference comprehensively demonstrated fruitful achievements in the creation of an Internet civilization in the new era and provided many vivid cases and insightful ideas for building an Internet civilization in which everyone participates and benefits. The Forum on Developing Integrity in Cyberspace centered on hot topics like integrity in cyberspace and released constructive achievements such as "Ten Major Events of Integrity in Cyberspace in China in 2022" and *Development Report on Integrity in Cyberspace in China in 2023*, which comprehensively reflected new progress and achievements in developing integrity in cyberspace in China and guided Internet users to practice integrity in cyberspace.

2. With brand projects deeply implemented, online reading and online science popularization help to promote the creation of an Internet civilization

The Good Internet Users in China Project has been implemented. In 2023, a series of activities of "Good Internet Users of Students, Financial Staff, Workers, the Youth and Women Railway Workers" were widely carried out, making the brand effect more prominent and publicizing the idea of civilized Internet users among the public. Excellent stories of the sixth "Young Good Internet Users in China" were published, covering five categories: promoting new trends of the times, creating high-quality online products, promoting cultural activities, guarding online platforms, and assisting in Internet governance. By combining online live streaming and on-site storytelling, the activity sparked warm discussions and widespread attention among Internet users. More than ten million people from various channels and platforms liked the stories of candidates. At the end of March 2023, under the theme "Sparks of Talents Are Coming Together," the "Good Online Reviews Competition" was launched in Changsha, leading more Internet users to understand the power of online reviews and participate in the creation of online reviews. Internet users expressed their sincere praise and deep respect for China, deepened their patriotism in new forms, and drew the inclusive circle of struggle and progress. In 2022, 100 accounts with outstanding achievements in implementing online products were commended, which effectively encouraged all departments and Party members and cadres to hear people's voices, act on their needs, and solve their concerns through the Internet so as to better organize the masses, publicize policies among the masses, rally the masses, and serve the masses. The "Stories of Chinese People" online selection tool was continuously published, earnestly telling the stories of the Party, the new era, and young people, and uniting young Internet users to undertake responsibility for the times with self-confidence and self-improvement. The Office of the Central Cyberspace Affairs Commission extensively carried out online publicity of models and their deeds such as model workers, role models of the times, models with moral excellence, and good neighbors, built online brand columns such as "sunshine of the masses," "power of ordinary people," and "sparks of the public," implemented online public welfare projects, closely followed the principle of benefiting the public, strengthened the coverage of typical public welfare projects, contributed wisdom to building a healthy and civilized new ecology of digital public welfare and charity, and promoted the formation of an environment for Internet civilization in which people would act in a good and virtuous manner and emulate paragons of virtue.

As a key carrier of the construction of spiritual civilization in the new era, the National Reading Campaign plays a significant role in promoting the prosperity of national culture, fostering the development of the knowledge economy, and accelerating the popularization of knowledge and the inheritance of culture. In recent years, with the advancement of media technology, reading has shifted to online platforms. Digital reading platforms provide comfortable environments and diverse resources for the public and further enhance public participation in reading. In addition, the popularization of knowledge serves as an important approach to improving the level of Internet civilization. Digital platforms of Innovation China and China Science Communication are national-level platforms and resource libraries that promote technological innovation and scientific dissemination. By March 2023, on the digital platform of Innovation China, the content had been disseminated 1.939 billion times. On the digital platform of China Science Communication, there were 28,500 original videos, 230,000 texts with pictures, and a total of 66.9899 million users. Relevant topics were disseminated 169.572 billion times in total. These platforms play an important role in improving scientific literacy of citizens and promoting the creation of an Internet civilization.

3. Activities on the Internet civilization are extensively carried out, and new trends of the times are widely propagated

In January 2023, the "Online China Festivals Spring Festival" themed event was officially held, with special columns and interactive topics. Various forms of multimedia products were launched to report touching stories and heartwarming moments of ordinary people in the festival, and spread the spring festival through the Internet. Before the Qingming Festival, *Notice on Standardizing the Order of Online Sweeping and Advocating New Civilized Trends* was issued, requiring online sweeping platforms to attach great importance to the historical inheritance and cultural value of traditional festivals, actively promote good folk customs, prohibit publishing illegal information such as distorting history and defaming martyrs, and guide Internet users to express their grief for their deceased loved ones through online sweeping.

3.1.3 Online international communication integrates multiple languages and enhances global influence

At present, online international communication faces a series of new challenges, such as technological iteration and upgrading. Strengthening international communication channels and building global digital platforms meet the requirements of the times to improve international communication capabilities. Based on the ideas of strategic communication, various websites take root in excellent Chinese culture and strive to enhance the efficiency of international communication.[2] Various websites propose new concepts, contexts, and expressions that integrate Chinese and foreign styles. They tell the story of China well and spread the voice of China well through the Internet, presenting a trustworthy, lovely, and respectable image of China.

1. Themed reports show the image of a big country, and innovative discourse enhances the appeal of the concept of building a community with a shared future for mankind in cyberspace

In the second half of 2022, President Xi Jinping visited Saudi Arabia. Heads of state of China and the United States met face-to-face in Bali. The CPC in Dialogue with World Political Parties High-level Meeting was staged. President Xi Jinping paid a state visit to Russia. Leaders of Spain, Malaysia, Singapore, France, Brazil, and other countries visited China. A series of head-of-state diplomacy achieved fruitful results and attracted great attention from domestic and foreign online media. Xinhua Net successively published in-depth reports, such as *Writing a New Chapter on Major-Country Diplomacy with Chinese Characteristics: A Review of China's Head-of-State Diplomacy in 2022*, and *Pursuing the Just Cause Together: A Chronicle of China's Head-of-State Diplomacy in Spring 2023*, which profoundly interpreted President Xi Jinping's major concepts of diplomacy and marked new interactions between China and the world.

Central news websites produce projects on online international communication, such as Why Red Stars Shine in China, Steering a Steady Course in the New Era of China, and Quest: Twenty Questions on the 20th CPC National Congress. These websites make short videos, illustrations, posters, and other multimedia products, carry out online

2 Chen Hong and Qin Jing. "Framework for Constructing an International Communication Strategy System with Chinese Characteristics." *Modern Communication*, 2023 (1):55–59.

international communication through multiple languages, platforms, and channels, and thoroughly publicize the spirit of the 20th CPC National Congress to the world, vividly presenting the development history, governing philosophy, and governing achievements of the Communist Party of China, and effectively displaying an image of the Communist Party of China that is democratic, pragmatic, open, and confident. China.com enhances its initiative in online international communication, and carries out regional, targeted, and multigroup international communication based on the reading interests of audiences in different languages and countries. For example, the Famous Sentences in Reports Series covers seven languages, including English, German, and Japanese. China.com has launched multilingual poster products, such as The 20th CPC National Congress and China's Diplomacy, China's Approaches to World Problems, and The CPC in the Eyes of Foreigners, which use visual means to introduce China's plans and achievements in participating in global governance.

Mainstream media and news websites attach great importance to building capabilities in online international communication, updating expression strategies and enriching dialogue channels, and have achieved remarkable results. The new media platform of *People's Daily* launches *CPC*, and *PRC*, online promotional videos of the Communist Party of China and China, as well as their online versions in twelve foreign languages. In 2022, "Chinese Buzzwords" released a forty-episode short video, with total views of more than fifty-two million at home and abroad, which effectively responded to the concerns of overseas Internet users about China and showcased China's new development and changes to the world. Central news websites plan and implement projects such as *A Community with a Shared Future for Mankind*, *Impressions on 100 BRI Countries Short Video Contest*, *In the New Era, I Am in China*, and *Multiple Perspectives of High-quality Development*. Central news websites create a series of original, down-to-earth, influential, and attractive multimedia products, widely promote the development achievements of the Chinese path to modernization through the Internet, and interpret the connotation and value of a community with a shared future for mankind. These websites help dissolve barriers with the self-shaping ability of international communication, allowing overseas audiences to understand China truly and objectively, and spreading more Chinese stories globally.

2. Key issues amplify the voice of China and strengthen the guidance on international public opinion

In today's world, changes unseen in a century are unfolding at a faster pace, the geopolitical environment remains tense, multiple crises are intertwined, and the S2IS-D-24-00031 international landscape changes dramatically. On key global issues, such as the Ukrainian crisis, Nancy Pelosi's visit to Taiwan, and Saudi-Iran reconciliation in Beijing, mainstream media and news websites firmly upheld their positions, kept their bottom line, expressed China's positions, explained China's philosophies, and spread China's voice. Central news websites promptly released the document of the Ministry of Foreign Affairs of China, *China's Position on the Political Settlement of the Ukraine Crisis*. On Pelosi's visit to Taiwan, Xinhua Net published news comments such as *Six Crimes of Pelosi's Visiting Taiwan* and *Some Facts of Pelosi's Visiting Taiwan. People's Daily Online* published news reports such as *International Community Strongly Condemns Pelosi's Visit to Taiwan of China* and *On Pelosi's Visit to Taiwan, Our Counterattack Will Continue*, which clearly expressed China's firm position. In March 2023, China, Saudi Arabia, and Iran issued a three-party joint statement, announcing the resumption of diplomatic relations between Saudi Arabia and Iran. Mainstream media and websites followed up in a timely manner and interpreted the important significance of the event. A series of reports on China.com, such as *Century Reconciliation: The Meaning and Inspiration of Saudi Arabia and Iran's Handshake and Peace*, highlighted China's unremitting pursuit of regional and global peace as a responsible major country.

Additionally, CCTV's new media account uses "anchor Vlog" to showcase major country diplomacy. As narrators, anchors deeply analyze the connotation and extension of China's diplomacy in a friendly way, express China's efforts and attempts as a major country in international diplomacy, expand China's domestic and international influence, and build China's image as a major country. Numerous Internet users widely share news and information from the Ministry of Foreign Affairs on social media platforms such as Weibo, Bilibili, and Twitter at home and abroad, and spontaneously engage in secondary creation, effectively spreading the voice of China to the world.

3. Roles of "Generation Z" and "foreign Internet celebrities" become prominent, and the path to innovation comprehensively improves the efficiency of online international communication

Generation Z was born in the years from 1995 to 2009. Foreign Internet celebrities come to China or live in China. With comprehensive abilities in cross-cultural communication, content production and new media dissemination as well as social influence, foreign Internet celebrities play an increasingly important role in online international communication. Chengdu combines traditional culture with the Internet and creates a short video IP "Crazy for Folk Music" for Generation Z. In the form of "folk music art + urban culture," the IP revolutionizes traditional performance scene of folk music, produces more than 100 music short videos in line with the rules of online overseas communication, and obtains more than 1.2 million fans on social platforms at home and abroad, including Douyin, YouTube, Instagram, and Facebook. The website of *China Daily* launches the video program *China Surprises Me* for international students, which tells the life of foreign students studying in China and targets overseas Generation Z, promoting mutual understanding between Chinese and foreign youth. China.com plans micro-videos such as *Dialogue with China* and *Vlogger in China* for overseas Generation Z, which invite foreign students studying in China as guests to focus on hot topics in China from an international perspective and improve the inclusiveness of online international communication.

Xinhua Net launches a series of short videos *Foreign Journalists Observing China: I Am Full of Confidence in China's New Journey*, which highlight impressive photos of various regions of China taken by foreign journalists who have been working and living in China over the past ten years, and interpret the report of the 20th CPC National Congress for overseas audiences. China.com produces a multilingual feature film *Finding Answers in China*, which invites eleven foreign anchors to visit the regions where General Secretary Xi Jinping inspected, introduced China's practices, analyzed China's solutions, and interpreted China's wisdom, in eight languages such as English, French, Spanish, Japanese, and Russian, in the form of personal interviews and comments from Chinese and foreign scholars, focusing on key issues such as common prosperity and rural revitalization. In activities such as *An Invitation from China: Understanding the Communist Party of China with a 100-Year History* and *Coming to China: The Most Beautiful Landmark*, foreign friends living in China and understanding China and foreign bloggers are organized to visit Tianjin, Jilin, Inner Mongolia, Shanxi, and other regions to conduct interviews and reports on historic achievements made in economic construction, ecological civilization construction, social construction and other aspects since the 18th CPC National Congress. They personally witness the beautiful life Chinese people long for, and promote online international dissemination of Chinese culture in eight languages, including English, Korean, and Russian, with a total of 2.66 billion views in China and the world.

3.1.4 Supply of online content closely follows new demands and arouses wide public response

Despite the evolution of media form and the change of technological support, content remains the foundation of Internet media. In the digital era, the abundant supply of high-quality content plays an important role in a complex cyberspace. In the production of online content, Internet media should closely meet and the demands of Internet users, achieve targeted supply via the creation and dissemination of high-quality content, expand the scope of online dissemination, arouse public response, and enhance cultural recognition.

1. Enhancing empathetic interaction with new language styles

In the environment for new media, mobile Internet, social media, short videos, and other forms of communication develop rapidly. Efforts should be made to achieve innovation in the language of expression, accurately analyze the empathy of users, make a communication link between media and users, and truly attract users with high-quality content. The official account of Zhejiang Publicity considers and analyzes social issues and problems from the perspective of ordinary people, and expresses views and standpoints clearly and directly. Articles such as "History Sees Pelosi's visit to Taiwan" and "The Trap of Public Opinion Behind the Slap on High-speed Railway Event" are popular on mobile media. These articles are short and to the point, with rational views and public appeal. Among massive information on the Internet, these articles attract readers, making them deeply understand the power of persuasive arguments. With the slogan of "the most reliable science popularization, the most interesting soul," the official account of the Shenzhen Municipal Health Commission is committed to building an authoritative and user-friendly new media government account of medical and health affairs. The cover page of the official account often takes the form of "emojis + titles + one-sentence summary," flexibly adopts down-to-earth communication methods such as vertical comics and short videos, makes "hard science popularization" with high-quality original content more interesting with the unique language style of the youth, and quickly brings users closer with approachable expressions.

2. Creating an immersive experience with new technologies

Technological revolution has become a key driving force for media transformation and integration, and the application of advanced technology provides strong support for the creation and dissemination of content. Over the past year, news media and their websites vigorously strengthened technology-based empowerment in the coverage of major themes, launched many popular programs based on technological innovation, and allowed the public to experience news products rather than just know them. In 2023, in NPC and CPPCC, the client-end of Xinhua News Agency focused on a series of reports on "Metaverse: New Career Experience," told the stories of many delegates with cutting-edge technology of metaverse, created an interactive metaverse space of "person + field" with "digital twin + high-simulation digital human" technology, and allowed users to personally experience news through a scenario blending the virtual and the real. This enhanced audience experience, participation, and immersion, and augmented their sense of acquisition and recognition of the content.[3] CCTV.com and Douyin jointly launched *Glory in the Last Decade*, which comprehensively used interactive games, hand-drawn Chinese-style animation and other expressions

3 Qi Huijie, Hu Guoxiang, Tang Haochen, Kong Weiqian, and Qiu Shijie. "Innovation in the Coverage of Major Themes Empowered by New Technology: Taking 'Metaverse New Career Experience' in the Coverage of the Two Sessions of Xinhua News Agency as an Example." *The Press*, 2023 (8): 66–68.

suitable for youth, enabled users to play five types of roles such as astronaut, athlete, and new farmer via AI face-swapping technology and experience experiments in the space station, figure skating in a skating gym, selling goods through live streaming in rural areas, and other scenarios, and gave full play to the positive effect of scenario-based communication.

3. Stimulating users' emotions and recognition with creativity

By June 2023, in China, the number of short video users reached 1.026 billion, the number of online live streaming users reached 765 million, the number of online music users reached 725 million, and the number of online game users reached 549 million, with the application level continuing to improve.[4] As users choose online reading and change their habits while using the Internet, short videos become an important channel for information acquisition and knowledge dissemination. The number of short video users continues to increase, injecting vitality into the production and dissemination of creative content. Thirteen retired teachers who taught knowledge through the Internet won Touching China Awards 2022. They creatively used short videos and live streaming platforms on the Internet as classes, which broke the boundaries of knowledge in time and space, and gave everyone fond of learning equal access to high-quality resources. In the field of online live streaming, the combination of selling goods through live streaming and public service communication became a highlight. Golden Eagle Broadcasting System organically combines three elements of "selling goods through live streaming + variety show + supporting farmers and agriculture," launches "Mango TV Supporting Farmers and Agriculture among the Youth" live streaming public-service activity, organizes the youth to advertise good products in various regions of China, and comprehensively presents a new appearance of rural areas.

In online music, concerts can be staged on the Internet in addition to traditional venues, which tremendously expands the viewing space. Online concerts provide audiovisual feasts for the public. High-quality music programs, such as *Everlasting Charm of Music: Hong Kong Music Season* and *Everlasting Charm of Music: Taiwan Music Season*, are widely broadcast on the Internet. With such large influence, the programs strengthen the friendship between the audiences in the Chinese mainland and Hong Kong and Taiwan and enhance their national identity. In online games, traditional culture and famous historical and cultural sites are innovatively presented in digital form, allowing users to experience a combination of games and culture. For example, "Honor of Kings," in collaboration with the China Aerospace Science and Technology

4 CNNIC (China Internet Network Information Center). *The 52nd Statistical Report on China Internet Development*, August 2023.

Corporation and the China Agricultural Museum, launches "Aerospace Dream" and "An Abundant Harvest," which vividly reflect the great journey of China's aerospace industry as well as the beautiful wish of Chinese agricultural culture for a bountiful harvest. "Call Me the Boss," an ancient-style game, delves into the combination of traditional cultural elements and game products, and integrates lines, facial makeup, and other elements in classic Peking Opera such as *The Big Disturbance in the Heavenly Palace* and *Bailiang Pass* into the game, allowing players to understand the charm of Chinese culture anytime, anywhere in a relaxing atmosphere.

3.2 A Comprehensive Internet Governance System takes Initial Shape, which Tremendously Enhances the Capability in Cyberspace Governance

Currently, the Internet has become a primary platform for ideological struggle, a new space for cultural prosperity and development, and a new home for the spiritual life of millions of people. From the 19th CPC National Congress to the Fourth Plenary Session of the 19th CPC Central Committee and the 20th CPC National Congress, China transitioned from "establishing a comprehensive Internet governance system" to "establishing and improving a comprehensive Internet governance system" and "improving a comprehensive Internet governance system and promoting the formation of a good Internet ecosystem," which deepens and consolidates the comprehensive Internet governance system in China. In recent years, departments of cyberspace affairs in China have implemented systematic planning, comprehensive governance, and coordinated development, established a comprehensive Internet governance pattern that follows the leadership of the Party Committee at various levels, requires the cooperation of multiple departments and combines various approaches, and continuously promotes the transformation of Internet governance to collaborative governance. A comprehensive Internet governance system takes initial shape, which tremendously enhances the capability in cyberspace governance.

3.2.1 Upholding systematic planning and comprehensive governance and promoting the scientific development of cyberspace governance

In the past year, departments of cyberspace affairs in China actively took the modernization of the national governance system and governance capability as a benchmark, planned and promoted the construction of an Internet governance system at a higher starting point, improved the laws and regulations on Internet governance, launched regular governance campaigns, deepened the construction of six systems (i.e., leadership in Internet management, the dissemination of positive energy, the control of online content, collaborative governance in society, law-based governance of cyberspace, and technology-based Internet governance), made Internet governance more law-based, professional, and scientific, and promoted the fundamental transformation from "management" to "governance."

1. Improving the laws and regulations on Internet governance, and jointly building the foundation for cyberspace governance

It is a global consensus to use legal strategies and approaches to promote Internet development and governance. Over the past year, departments of cyberspace affairs in China gave priority to establishing and improving a comprehensive Internet governance system, strengthened overall coordination, highlighted major themes, solved practical problems, implemented the tracking and efficiency evaluation system, and steadily enhanced the level of Internet management. In the second half of 2022, the Cyberspace Administration of China successively issued departmental rules or normative documents, such as *Regulations on the Management of Internet User Account Information*, *Regulations on the Management of Internet Pop-up Information Push Service*, and *Regulations on the Management of Mobile Internet App Information Service*. These clarify the regulations on the registration, use, and management of account information, add the requirements such as displaying account IP addresses and the regulations such as accountability for violations, establish and improve the requirements for managing pop-up information content, strengthen the standardized management and ecological governance of pop-up information push service, and comprehensively cement the responsibilities for managing information content on distribution platforms such as app stores, applets, and app centers. In February 2023, the Cyberspace Administration of China issued *Measures on Standard Contract of Personal Information Outbound Transfer* in the form of a departmental rule that details the cross-border transfer system of personal information by concluding standard contracts with overseas recipients and innovates comprehensive mechanism of cyberspace governance. In March 2023, the Cyberspace Administration of China issued *Regulations on Administrative Law-Enforcement Procedures for Departments of Cyberspace Affairs*, which aims to standardize and ensure that departments of cyberspace affairs perform their duties according to the law, protect the legitimate rights and interests of citizens, legal persons, and other organizations, comprehensively promote strict, standardized, fair, and civilized law enforcement, and make facts clear, evidence conclusive, the basis accurate, and procedures legal. In July 2023, the Secretariat of Office of the Central Cyberspace Affairs Commission issued *Notice on Strengthening the Management of We Media*, which focuses on labeling information sources and cutting off the chain of interest, effectively solves deep-seated problems such as distorted information content and wrong operational behaviors of We Media, tightens the responsibilities of website platforms, warns We Media about self-management, and promotes the formation of a good ecosystem for online public opinion.

In terms of AI governance, in November 2022, the Office of the Central Cyberspace Affairs Commission, the Ministry of Industry and Information Technology, and the Ministry of Public Security jointly released *Regulations on the Management of Deep Synthesis in Internet Information Services*, which specifies that no organizations or individuals shall use deep synthesis services to produce, copy, publish, and disseminate information prohibited by laws and administrative regulations, requiring deep synthesis service providers to establish and improve the rumor-refutation mechanism. In July 2023, the Office of the Central Cyberspace Affairs Commission, in collaboration with the National Development and Reform Commission, the Ministry of Education, the Ministry of Science and Technology, the Ministry of Industry and Information Technology, the Ministry of Public Security, and the National Radio and Television Administration released *Interim Measures on the Management of Generative Artificial Intelligence Services*, which states that China adheres to the principles of balancing development and security, promoting innovation and combining legal governance, takes effective measures to boost the innovation and development of generative AI, and formulates specific measures to accelerate the development of generative AI technology.

2. Launching regular governance campaigns, ensuring long-term governance, and addressing both symptoms and root causes

It is hard to eradicate maladies in one move. Internet governance requires organically combining law-based governance, centralized governance, and normalized governance, adhering to the principle of addressing both the symptoms and root causes, improving the long-term governance mechanism, investigating and eliminating illegal actions in cyberspace, and making the Internet operate healthily on the right track. In combating cyber violence, the Office of the Central Cyberspace Affairs Commission launched "Clean up: Nationwide Campaign to Combat Cyber Violence" and issued *Notice on Effectively Strengthening the Governance of Cyber Violence* in November 2022. By taking measures such as monitoring and identification, real-time protection, intervention and disposal, tracing and accountability, publicity and exposure, 28.75 million pieces of information on cyber violence were intercepted and cleared, and more than 22,000 perpetrators were severely punished. Relevant departments took an unequivocal stance toward cyber violence and effectively safeguarded the legitimate rights and interests of Internet users. In the fields of online live streaming and short videos, the Office of the Central Cyberspace Affairs

Commission launched "Clean up: Nationwide Campaign to Combat the Malpractice in Online Live Streaming and Short Videos," which focused on the presentation of information content, optimized ranking settings, effectively addressed the problem of inappropriate rewards for live streamers, strengthened the management of accounts of Internet celebrities, and consolidated the responsibilities of MCN institutions for the management of information content. *Opinions on Further Regulating the Profit-Making Behaviors on Online Live Stream Platforms to Promote the Healthy Development of the Industry* was issued to establish a long-term regulatory mechanism for departmental collaboration and strengthen the standardized guidance of profit-making behaviors on online live streaming platforms. From December 2022 to February 2023, the Office of the Central Cyberspace Affairs Commission launched "Clean up: Nationwide Campaign to Combat the Disorder in the Field of Mobile Internet Applications," which focused on the standardized management of app distribution platforms, tackled prominent problems reported by Internet users, strengthened the monitoring and supervision of information content on apps, strictly punished illegal apps, and guided local departments of cyberspace affairs to follow *Regulations on the Management of Mobile Internet App Information Services* in the filing work according to laws and regulations, and effectively purified the Internet ecosystem in the field of app distribution. In 2022, the Office of the Central Cyberspace Affairs Commission organized thirteen "Clean up" campaigns, cleared more than 54.3 million pieces of illegal and harmful information, disposed of more than 6.8 million accounts, removed more than 2,890 apps and applets, disbanded and closed 260,000 groups and forums, and closed more than 7,300 websites. These campaigns resolutely and accurately combated various illegal issues and continuously improved the efficiency of cyberspace governance. In 2023, the Office of the Central Cyberspace Affairs Commission focused on the concerns of Internet users, solved various problems, and innovated governance models. Taking "promoting the formation of a good Internet ecosystem" as a goal, the Office focused on new problems and bottlenecks, and carried out ten campaigns, including optimizing the Internet environment in the spring festival, standardizing We Media, combating the manipulation of information content by an online water army, regulating the communication order of major traffic links, improving the online environment for business, protecting the legitimate rights and interests of enterprises, correcting wrong information content on life service platforms, guiding the information content in short videos, purifying the online environment for minors on summer vacation, and combating cyber violence. In "Clean up: Nationwide Campaign to Optimize the Internet Environment in Spring Festival" in 2023, relevant departments strictly investigated and controlled prominent issues such as provoking conflicts, fabricating false information, spreading vulgar information, and inducing minors to be addicted to the Internet. More than 1.19 million pieces of illegal and harmful information were intercepted and cleared, and more than 160,000 illegal accounts and groups were punished. In "Clean up: Nationwide Campaign to Strictly Combat the Disorder in We Media," departments of cyberspace affairs at various levels addressed prominent problems such as making and spreading rumors, creating fake accounts, and illegal profit-making according to laws and regulations. On major platforms, more than 1.4109 million pieces of illegal information were cleared, more than 927,600 illegal accounts were punished, and more than 66,600 accounts were permanently closed.

Simultaneously, the Office of the Central Cyberspace Affairs Commission carefully organized "Online Campaign against Pornography and Illegal Publications," thoroughly investigated and addressed prominent problems of online pornography and illegal publications, focused on key areas such as the home pages, hot search lists, hot topics, push pop-ups, and pages with important information content of website platforms, cleaned up illegal and harmful information such as obscenity, vulgarity, violence, terror and horror, creating a clean cyberspace. According to statistics, in 2022, national departments of cyberspace affairs summoned 8,606 website platforms for talks, warned 6,767 website platforms, fined 512 website platforms, temporarily suspended or rectified 621 website platforms, removed 420 mobile apps, canceled the licenses or records of illegal websites with administrative departments in charge of telecom, closed 25,233 illegal websites, and transferred 11,229 related case leads. To optimize the online environment for business, the Office of the Central Cyberspace Affairs Commission organized "Campaign to Optimize the Online Environment for Business and Protect the Legitimate Rights and Interests of Enterprises," which focused on combating online activities such as false information about enterprises and entrepreneurs, malicious damage to the reputation of enterprises and entrepreneurs, and seeking illegal benefits. In the campaign, about 148,000 reports on the information about enterprises were received, about 86,000 effective reports were addressed, about 37,500 illegal accounts were punished, 214 websites were closed and blocked, and 25 mobile apps were removed. The Center of Office of the Central Cyberspace Affairs Commission launched a pilot project among "planned listed enterprises," unclogged the channels for addressing offline reporting and acceptance concerning the infringements of enterprises in a timely manner, cleaned up false information that harmed the legitimate rights and interests of "planned listed enterprises" according to laws and regulations, and actively created a good environment for online public opinion for the healthy and standardized development of enterprises. In December 2022, the Secretariat of the Office of the Central Cyberspace Affairs Commission and the General Office of the China Securities Regulatory Commission issued *Working Plan for the Governance of Online Information Content in Illegal Securities Activities*, which aims to minimize illegal news on stock and illegal recommendation of stock and effectively ensure a clean cyberspace as well as social harmony and stability. Additionally, the Office of the Central Cyberspace Affairs Commission strengthened the management of financial information services, severely cracked down on financial online fraud, enhanced the management of the staff in Internet information content service organizations, and actively worked with relevant departments to step up efforts in promoting anti-monopoly supervision and preventing the disorderly expansion of capital in the field of the Internet, optimized the environment for the development of platform economy, maintained the order of fair market competition, and fostered high-quality development on the Internet.

The Office of the Central Cyberspace Affairs Commission comprehensively promotes the supervision and management of the staff in the online content industry, strengthens their training , holds training courses for the editors in central Internet platforms and online training courses for the staff in central news websites, and guides local departments of cyberspace affairs to carry out the training for local websites and platforms. In 2022, more than 50,000 professionals were registered and managed in the staff management information system. By the end of June 2023, press cards were issued to sixteen central news websites and fifty-three local news websites, or to more than 6,500 people.

The Office of the Central Cyberspace Affairs Commission solidly combats telecom and online fraud, strengthens the review of key links such as account nicknames, private messages and groups, detects information on suspected fraud and click farming by robots, identifies and handles accounts with fraud risks, and thoroughly cleans up harmful information related to fraud. By the end of 2022, more than 2.72 million fraud-related websites, 180,000 fraud-related apps, and 87,000 fraud-related phone calls were discovered. The Office established an early warning mechanism with mobile phone manufacturers. In total, more than 7.1 billion warnings and dissuasions were conducted, involving nearly 300 million mobile phone terminals. In 2022, the Office and Ministry of Public Security co-developed the National Anti-Fraud Center APP, with a total of more than 530 million registered users, publishing 350 million warnings. Since its founding, the National Anti-Fraud Big Data Platform has supported the Ministry of Public Security in publishing 174 million warnings through the platform.

3.2.2 Innovating social collaborative governance and building a healthy Internet ecosystem

In Internet governance, governments cannot solve all the problems in Internet development. Multiple parties, including Internet enterprises, social organizations, and Internet users, are required to pool resources, jointly undertake governance responsibilities, build the foundation for cybersecurity, and ensure the effectiveness of comprehensive Internet governance.

1. Internet enterprises enhance their awareness of responsibilities and perform their responsibilities with practical actions

Currently, website platforms have become an important carrier for the production and dissemination of information content with social and public characteristics.

Website platforms play an indispensable role in upholding correct values, ensuring the security of online content, and safeguarding the legitimate rights and interests of Internet users. It is an important and urgent task to enhance the awareness of responsibilities of Internet enterprises. The newly revised *Regulations on the Management of Internet Post Comment Services* specifies that post comment service providers should regulate and standardize post comment service users and public account operators according to user service agreements. Many Internet platforms innovate the automatic filtering, screening, and identification system of posts by technological means to assist manual review, and improve the efficiency, depth, and accuracy of posted comment review from underlying algorithms and review rules to the experience of review editors. Douyin releases *Platform Standards and Industrial Initiative on AIGC*, which clarifies the standards for behaviors on the platform for the first time, including AI-generated videos, pictures, and live streaming by virtual humans derived from AI. Publishers should significantly identify AIGC, virtual humans must be controlled by real people for real-time interaction, and the use of generative AI technology is prohibited from creating and publishing infringing content.

Additionally, Internet enterprises focus on both old and young users. First, Internet platforms enhance their awareness of the protection of minors, actively embed the protection of minors into product design and content management, and build a complete system for minors' protection on the Internet. Tencent Growth Guidance Platform is committed to helping teenagers cultivate healthy gaming and entertainment habits through parent-child interaction, which advocates communication, negotiation, and interaction between parents and children, and provides necessary controls to help children. Kuaishou and Bilibili successively released *Report on the Protection of Minors*. While fully implementing their social responsibilities of online protection, they attach importance to the growth needs and learning needs of minors and give them a broader space of protection. Second, because of an aging population and social digitization, Tencent Research Institute released *Invisible Guardianship: Silver Technology Blue Book 2022*, which focuses on technological innovation, empowerment, and the future, and actively promotes the combination of digitization and an aging population, based on joint efforts of society, industry, and the elderly. Didi establishes a team responsible for elderly people who use online ride-hailing, and helps elderly people to see more clearly and understand better, with large-font, no-advertisement and simple interfaces, full-process voice instructions, and payments by sons and daughters.

In preventing cyber violence, Douyin, Weibo, Xiaohongshu, Kuaishou, Douban, Bilibili, Baidu, and other website platforms publish guidance on preventing cyber violence, which help Internet users to prevent cyber violence quickly and effectively by risk warning, one-button protection, private-message protection, and reporting and complaints. Internet platforms enhance their awareness of responsibilities and proactively perform their functions.

2. Social organizations utilize their advantages and promote the healthy development of the Internet ecosystem

Presently, social organizations have become an important part of Internet governance mechanism in China and participate in the construction of Internet infrastructure and the creation of healthy Internet ecosystem in China by integrating social resources and mobilizing social forces. In May 2023, the Internet Society of China released *Self-discipline Convention on Strengthening the Transparency of Rules on Internet Platforms*, which aims to maintain a fair and orderly market environment, protect the legitimate rights and interests of relevant parties on Internet platforms, and promote the healthy and sustainable development of the Internet industry in China. The China Federation of Internet Societies, the China Netcasting Services Association, and the China Association of Performing Arts jointly launched the initiative on the development of the live streaming industry at the Douyin Live Streaming Industry Ecology Conference in 2003, hoping to strengthen the formulation of industrial standards, provide support for the standardized development of the industry, and promote the healthy and orderly development of the live streaming industry.

On Internet Commonweal Day, the Internet Society of China released *Implementation Plan of Public Action for Elderly-Friendly Barrier-free Transformation of Internet Applications*, to further promote the information-based construction that fully takes into account the needs of the elderly and the disabled, fosters the sustainable development of an inclusive digital society, demonstrates elder-friendly digital technology at the public and social levels, and bridges the digital divide generated in the development of ICT. The China Internet Development Foundation hosted the “2022 National Cloud Competition on Knowledge of Internet Laws and Regulations,” upgraded and revised the National Internet Laws and Regulations Publicity Platform, produced and disseminated the video “Micro Class for Law Popularization,” and focused on improving the legal literacy of Internet users. “Bridging the Digital Divide: Community Digital Literacy Demonstration Project” continuously provides special training and courses for elderly people on the use of social software, online shopping, online ride-hailing, registration with doctors and other life scenarios, helping them to improve digital literacy and better adapt to modern life, thus promoting the construction of a digital community. In March 2023, the China Federation of Internet Societies, UN Women China, and other departments hosted the High-Level Side Event of the 67th Session of the United Nations Commission on the Status of Women, “Narrowing the Gender Gap in the Digital Era: Utilizing Technology and Innovation to Promote Economic Empowerment of Women in the Asia Pacific and African Regions.” The report, with the theme of “Together Digital: Empowering Women Entrepreneurs in a Digital World,” was first released in multiple countries and analyzes the challenges to and opportunities for small and medium-sized enterprises led by women in the digital era. The report shares China’s policies and practices in protecting women’s legitimate rights and promoting women’s development in the digital era.

3. Internet users actively report and refute rumors, offer suggestions, and jointly build a good atmosphere for public participation

In order to combat online rumors, the Reporting Center of Office of the Central Cyberspace Affairs Commission launches the Rumor-Refutation Today Program through the China Internet Joint Rumor-Refutation Platform, innovatively conducts online rumor-refutation labeling work, organizes Tencent, Weibo, and ten other large online platforms to label verified rumors and attach "identification codes" to online rumors, and responds to and exposes online rumors involving public policies, emergencies, medical services, people's livelihood, and other topics or fields in a timely manner. Simultaneously, the Reporting Center guides Internet users to actively provide rumor clues, squeeze the space out of online rumors, block the chain of rumor dissemination, and give online rumors nowhere to hide. Since 2022, the Reporting Center has fully played the role of a reporting "window," opened a series of reporting sections, unclogged reporting channels such as the official website, 12377 hotlines, and email, directly accepted 7.644 million reports, and guided local reporting centers of departments of cyberspace affairs to accept 11.606 million reports and major websites to accept 197 million reports. In response to the hot issues reported by Internet users, the Report Center further publicizes knowledge about Internet laws and regulations by reprinting typical illegal cases on the Internet and effectively creates a good atmosphere for the public to participate in reporting.

Simultaneously, the Reporting Center of Office of the Central Cyberspace Affairs Commission urges Internet enterprises to accept public supervision. In September 2022, the Reporting Center organized a total of 617 website platforms in the nine groups to announce methods of reporting to the public. So far, there are more than 4,100 website platforms that have announced methods of reporting to society, covering such fields as news and information, social interaction, live streaming, audio and video, search engines, browsers, and e-commerce shopping.

In addition, various regions launch campaigns to report and refute rumors, improve social awareness and public participation in online reporting, and promote the integration and coordination of the supervision of online reporting and governance at the grassroots level. In Jiangsu, Taizhou organizes the "Online Reporting Caravan," which introduces the procedures of online reporting to the public on the spot, and encourages the public to actively participate in online reporting. The Guangdong Internet Illegal and Harmful Information Reporting Center establishes a section on its official website to report website platforms involved in false information and fraud and accept public reporting. In Xinjiang, Urumqi initiates a campaign under the theme of "actively participating in online reporting and jointly resisting online rumors," improves the ability of Internet users to identify rumors, encourages Internet users to report online rumor clues through various channels in a timely way, and creates a clean and healthy online environment with the participation of the public.

3.2.3 Strengthening the online protection of minors and empowering their healthy growth

As Internet technology quickly penetrates various fields, the digital environment has an unprecedented impact on the lifestyle of young people, making them "digital natives." According to official data, the number of underage Internet users in China has reached 191 million, with a rate of Internet access of 96.8 percent. It is a prominent trend that children use Internet early.[5] Nowadays, as mobile Internet devices such as smartphones become more popular, Internet has been deeply integrated into the daily life of young people, becoming an indispensable tool for leisure and entertainment, social interaction and online learning, and affecting the values of young people. It is a hot topic in the entire society to positively guide young people to access Internet in the right way.

As an important technological means of the online protection of minors, the "Youth Model" has been improved and upgraded since its pilot launch in March 2019. In the beginning of March 2023, on WeChat, the Youth Model can be started by one touch. Then, teenagers can choose the content suitable for them in prescribed channels. Parents or guardians can set the limits of WeChat Pay, including "limits to daily consumption" and "limits to one-time consumption." The Green Seedling Plan continues to provide high-quality content for teenagers by holding open summer classes, building "cloud theaters," and organizing the live streaming of "exploring museums." In May, Internet enterprises such as Douyin, Kuaishou, WeChat, Bilibili, and TT Voice jointly formulated and released *Self-discipline Standards for the Youth Model of Online Performance (Live Stream and Short Video) Industry*, which clarifies the responsibilities of enterprises, optimizes the Youth Model through multiple-process review, content grading and intelligent identification and detection, and implements the online protection of minors.

In January 2023, "Clean up·Nationwide Campaign to Optimize the Internet Environment in Spring Festival" focused on cleaning up video content that bullies and mocks minors or induces them to engage in dangerous actions, strictly controlling the dissemination of pornographic, vulgar, bloody, and violent information to minors, combating illegal account renting and buying, and preventing minors, especially left-behind children in rural areas, from becoming addicted to the Internet. In 2023, "Clean up·Nationwide Campaign to Purify the Internet Environment for Minors in Summer Vacation" focused on prominent problems such as harmful content in new forms, cyberbullying, cyber obscenity, online fraud, harmful content, addiction to the Internet, and risks of new technologies and applications. The campaign resolutely curbed illegal activities that infringe on the rights and interests of minors, improved the security standards of information content for exclusive products and services such

---

5 Youth Rights and Interests Protection Department of the Central Committee of the Communist Youth League of China and China Internet Network Information Center. *Research Report on Minors Use of Internet in China in 2021*, November 2022.

as learning apps and children's smart devices, and created an online environment conducive to the healthy and safe growth of minors.

Children's growth and education is an important issue that arouses global attention. With the rapid development of AI technology, it is important to know how to use AI to ensure the physical and mental health of minors, guide them to learn, and safeguard their rights and interests. At the 2022 United Nations Internet Governance Forum, the China Federation of Internet Societies introduced the implementation of *Guide to the Construction of Internet Applications for Minors Based on Artificial Intelligence Technology* and effectively explored the models an results of Internet services for minors based on AI technology in combination with enterprise cases. In addition, the China Federation of Internet Societies and the United Nations International Children's Emergency Fund jointly launched a research and case collection promotion project on AI for children. They published *Artificial Intelligence for Children: Research Report on Applications of Artificial Intelligence for Children* and presented cases through a special webpage on Guangming Net. By strengthening publicity and promotion, they set a typical model and presented a model Chinese solution for AI for children to the world.

In addition to restrictive and mandatory measures on online protection, long-term and soft measures represented by online literacy education are committed to cultivating the immunity of minors to online temptations, enhancing their ability to identify online information, and improving their self-control in rational use of the Internet. The practical results are confirmed by academic research and recognized by governmental departments. The Central Committee of the Communist Youth League of China launches a series of online courses "CYLC Micro Courses: Open Courses on Internet Literacy for the Youth," which aims to guide minors to cope with risks such as online addiction, cyberbullying and online fraud through hard and soft means, cultivate and improve the Internet literacy of minors, enhance their awareness and ability to use the Internet in a scientific, civilized, safe, and reasonable manner, and protect the legitimate rights and interests of minors in cyberspace.

3.3 Taking Orientation as the Soul and Giving Priority to Innovation, Media Integration Comes into a New Stage of Making Comprehensive Efforts and Improving Quality and Efficiency

In the early stages, media integration covered changing ideas, developing products, and building platforms. Now, media integration is in full swing and has come into a new stage of making comprehensive efforts and improving quality and efficiency.

Presently, county-level integrated media centers have basically achieved full coverage. In governmental new media, a new pattern of standardized, innovative, and integrated development has taken shape. The media industry takes the construction of new mainstream media as an approach to self-improvement. As media integration deepens, the goal of an intelligent all-media ecosystem will be realized.

3.3.1 Deep media integration is solidly promoted, and the creation of an all-media communication system is accelerated

Deep media integration aims to build an all-media communication system. Promoting the creation of an all-media communication system requires an understanding of the profound impact of technological application on the models of news production and dissemination, following new trends and directions in the development of media integration, comprehensively considering the goals and tasks of the integrated development of mainstream media, and drawing an inclusive circle of online-offline and internal-external public opinion. In 2014, media integration was elevated to a national strategy in China. Since then, media integration has been deepened and integrated into major tasks of the Party and governments. In 2023, "solidly promoting deep media integration" was first included in *Report on the Work of the Government* in the Two Sessions. The report of the 20th CPC National Congress proposes strengthening the creation of an all-media communication system and shaping a new pattern of mainstream public opinion. Over the past year, the integrated development of central, provincial, municipal, and county media has reached a new level.

On New Year's Eve of 2023, "Watching Spring Festival Gala with Vertical Screen" of China Media Group was successfully presented on Tencent Channels, China Media Group Mobile, CCTV News, and other platforms. The China Media Group developed a new communication model that integrated TV, mobile phones, and interactive screens, which optimized and innovated various links such as collection, production, dissemination, and presentation. For example, cutting-edge technologies such as XR and AR were fully utilized to create a vivid and realistic virtual stage, giving the audience an amazing audiovisual feast in a 3D way, through the integration and innovation of technology. In the Two Sessions, *Xia Ke Dao*, new media of the *People's Daily Overseas Edition* launched a series of integrated media products, *Xia Ke Dao's Observation of the Two Sessions*, which interpreted the hot topics and policies of the Two Sessions through integrated communication. Columns on the Two Sessions were established on the *People's Daily Overseas Edition*, new media products like short videos on WeChat and Weibo were launched simultaneously, which evoked a warm response among the public. The Xinhua News Agency released a large-scale H5 interactive report *Working Hard, Chinese People*, which allowed the general public to participate in the annual national event in the form of "likes." The report was disseminated on various platforms and on mobile phones and TVs online and offline, attracting widespread attention. Additionally, local integrated media plays an active role in participating in political dissemination and national governance. In the Two Sessions, Litchi News Client-end of Jiangsu Broadcasting Corporation launched the interactive creative product *Historical Questions: Answers in the New Era*, which centered on several requirements of the "Chinese path to modernization" and answered historical questions in the form of interactive poster groups, with more than ten million visits on the Internet. Mango TV produced a creative H5 picture group *Creating a New Scenery of a Better Life*, which showcased nine measures on people's livelihood, such as rural revitalization, education and culture, and effectively enhanced users' immersive experience.

Noticeably, AI technology deeply participates in content production. In the whole process of intelligent collection, intelligent production, intelligent distribution, and intelligent feedback, AI technology empowers news production and promotes the construction of an intelligent all-media communication system. The "multimodal search" function of the AI Editorial Department of *People's Daily* provides business scenarios such as texts, pictures, videos, multiple languages, and semantic search, and quickly improves the efficiency of information collection of editors and journalists. The app for intelligent interview terminal of the Xinhua News Agency adapts to various scenarios of mobile reporting. One mobile phone can complete the processing of integrated-media articles. "Smart Media Data Chain" and "Smart News" products developed by the AI Editorial Department of CCTV.com can quickly capture real-time hot topics, track the source and development of hot topics, help journalists to accurately collect valuable materials and information, and better complete news production by digging for big data on the Internet.

3.3.2 County-level integrated media stands committed to local news, participate in grassroots governance, and serve rural revitalization

Strengthening the construction of county-level integrated media centers is a fundamental link for promoting the in-depth development of media integration and serves as important leverage for accelerating the construction of the "last mile" of social governance. Driven by a series of national strategic plans, county-level integrated media centers continuously strengthen their functions of guidance and service in integration and innovation, and play a positive role in optimizing social governance at the grassroots level, building the capability in guiding public opinion, and revitalizing rural culture.

Over the past year, county-level integrated media centers have utilized the advantages of approaching the grassroots and the masses with a down-to-earth style, changed the sermonizing method, produced high-quality content, stood committed to local news, explored unique local materials, and created content products suitable for the masses. Programs such as "Beautiful Rural Areas," "Typical Figures," and "Characteristic Agricultural Products" were widely broadcast, watched, and "liked" on more media platforms. Feature films *Great Entrepreneurs* and *Cadres of Our Village* produced by the Zhejiang Changxing Media Group focused on ordinary people and families and showcased tremendous changes of people's life thanks to national policies, with real and touching stories. The Integrated Media Center of Youxi County planed a series of documentaries *Welcoming the 20th CPC National Congress & Talks of Hundred Secretaries of the CPC Village Branches*, which organized 100 secretaries of the CPC village branches throughout the county to tell the stories of the transformation of beautiful rural areas from the first-person point of view, introduce the characteristics of rural industries, and draw a blueprint for the development of rural areas. The Haining Media Center launched *Chaomei's Travel along Hangzhou-Haining Intercity Railway*, in which Chaomei travels to typical villages along the Hangzhou-Haining Intercity Railway and unveils the secret of common prosperity.

While participating in grassroots governance and serving rural revitalization, county-level integrated media centers take great efforts to explore the "news + N" model and have made remarkable progress. County-level integrated media centers fully utilize the advantages of "all-media coordination, full-network dissemination and full coverage," improve the efficiency of social governance at the grassroots level, serve people's life and rural revitalization, and strive to build mainstream public opinion platforms, community information hubs, and comprehensive service platforms. The Dongcheng District Integrated Media Center in Beijing fully utilizes the "1 + 18 + N" communication platform, integrates positive publicity with online services, and creates a multifunctional integrated platform of "news + government affairs + services + supervision + business." The Banan District Integrated Media Center in Chongqing expands "news + ," deepens the integration of "integrated media + shopping mall," provides cultural and economic services to the public, promotes the sales of local agricultural and sideline products, and increases farmer's income through platforms such as the Banan news client-end. The Qiubei County Integrated Media Center in Yunnan and the Xiuwen County Integrated Media Center in Guizhou fully tap into the rural culture of local ethnic minorities, combine their lifestyles, daily customs, handicraft production, and local tourism resources, and publicize these elements through new media platforms. In this way, the two integrated media centers present unique symbols of rural culture, popularize local tourist attractions, and build influential brands in rural tourism.

In the construction of communication channels and systems, county-level integrated media actively joins national mainstream media platforms such as *Ren Min Hao* of *People's Daily*, China Media Group Mobile and *Xian Chang Yun* of the Xinhua News Agency, opens accounts on social platforms such as Douyin, Kuaishou, Channels, and Toutiao, and continuously produces excellent works. The Xinhua News Agency and the China Media Group launch "County-level Integrated Media Section" and "National County-level Integrated Media Smart Platform," respectively, in order to help county-level integrated media centers form a mobile communication matrix with diverse channels, wide coverage, effective communication, and controllable functions, expand media coverage, and augment communication effect.

3.3.3 Government new media strengthens the construction of functions and the interaction between governments and citizens, and invents new models of Internet governance

Over the past year, various regions and departments have vigorously promoted the standardized construction and intensive integration and development of governmental websites and new media; fully leveraged the advantages of fast dissemination speed, wide coverage, and strong interactivity of governmental new media; continuously strengthened the functions of publishing news, disseminating information, interacting with the public, guiding public opinion, and handling affairs of governmental new media; provided more convenient and practical mobile services for people; and guided the public to participate in public management and services in an orderly manner according to the law to jointly build a new model of social governance.

Fourteen thousand governmental websites and more than 103,000 governmental new media in China construct information-publishing matrices, strengthen authoritative information publishing and interpretation, build an overall coordination mechanism, promptly release major decisions and arrangements of the CPC Central Committee and the State Council, and expand the coverage of information. Governmental new media at various levels fully utilizes the advantage of mobile-end communication, and interprets policies and responds to concerns through various means such as posters, short videos, animations, and illustrations. The number of articles published in a year totals more than 20 million. Governments at various levels actively engage in online inquiry about governmental affairs on interactive communication platforms on governmental websites, and listen to public opinion and pool wisdom through various means. 91 percent of provincial, municipal, and county governments can effectively respond to simple and common questions within five working days. Governmental websites at various levels efficiently handle comments from Internet users on "I Find Mistakes for Governmental Websites" platform, and solve problems raised by Internet users regarding inaccurate information and unavailability of website services within three working days. In 2022, a total of 45,000 comments were handled, with a completion rate of up to 99 percent.

Additionally, governmental new media innovates the service models of policies and information and make governmental decision-making more scientific and democratic. Based on Internet technology, the General Office of the State Council interprets policies more accurately and extends the chain of policy interpretation. So far, on the Policy Questions and Answers Platform of the State Council, more than 6,000 policy-related questions and answers have been collected, and two million questions from Internet users have been answered. Before the Two Sessions are held, the General Office of the State Council relies on governmental portals and canvasses opinions of Internet users alongside online media platforms. In total, about one million suggestions are collected, and more than 1,000 representative opinions and suggestions are conveyed to the drafting team of *Report on the Work of the Government*, providing public opinions of Internet users for the drafting of the report.

The National Anti-fraud Center focuses on WeChat channels, opens official accounts on seven platforms such as Weibo and Douyin, and constructs a new media matrix for anti-fraud publicity. A large number of products, including anti-fraud songs, anti-fraud police records, anti-fraud microfilms and anti-fraud costume dramas, are easy to understand and deeply touch people. In addition, to combat new forms of fraud, the National Anti-fraud Center gives early warning and prevention tips in a timely fashion and conducts targeted anti-fraud publicity. The WeChat official account and applet of *Yue Sheng Shi* focus on the needs of people in daily life and provide the service of "handling affairs on mobile apps." Through accurate, people-centered and visual operations, *Yue Sheng Shi* makes the affairs closely related to people's life, such as elder care, social security and housing provident fund, more interesting, and continuously provides information and service guides. On important events, such as the National College Entrance Examination, the Spring Festival Travel Season, and the flood season, the China Meteorological Administration connects meteorological experts and Internet users via live streaming in simple expressions and languages, provides weather information in a timely manner, serves the production and life of people, and brings governmental departments closer to Internet users.

3.3.4 Cutting-edge technologies breed new media models, and two-wheel drive facilitates media integration and upgrading

Technological innovation and application play a leading role in driving media transformation and upgrading and the integration and development of media. Currently, cutting-edge technologies, such as big data, metaverse, and AI develop rapidly and penetrate the field of media. The major mass media explores the models of intelligent production and communication, empowers digital transformation of news media, and achieves mutual promotion and deep integration of technology and content. *Opinions on Accelerating the Deep Integration and Development of Media* proposes to lead and drive the integration and development of media with advanced technology, fully utilize revolutionary achievements of information technology such as 5G, big data, cloud computing, IoT, blockchain, and AI, and strengthen the forward-looking research and application of new technologies in the field of news communication.[6] Giving full play to the key role of new-generation cutting-edge technologies in leading and supporting the integration and development of media has a deep impact on transforming the models of media communication, guiding the construction of the online public opinion ecosystem, and gaining an edge in information communication.

Cutting-edge technologies, such as big data, metaverse, AI virtual uploaders, and MR video immersive interaction, accelerate media innovation, empower deep media integration via multidimensional applications, and help mainstream media to continuously evolve towards "full-process media, all-information media, all-staff media, and all-effect media." *Learning Hall in Metaverse* produced by Rednet uses technologies such as 3D modeling and panoramic rendering to build an online real-time dynamic display system, creates an immersive 3D metaverse space, and presents important speeches of General Secretary Xi Jinping attending the discussions of delegations in the form of posters with famous remarks. The *China Police Daily* and cpd.com launch the program *Dialogues on Cloud with Police Delegates: My Keywords of the Two Sessions*, which first attempts to create the scene in metaverse. Through dialogues between virtual anchors and police delegates in the cloud, police delegates voice their feelings of participating in the Two Sessions as well as stories about performing their duties. CCTV News releases a series of microvideos *Drawing a Blueprint in the First Year*, which utilizes mature AI models to intelligently create artistic images. The presence and full-process voice commentary of *Yang Xiao Xin*, a virtual anchor, lead viewers to quickly transition between reality and virtuality, the present and the future. This not only improves the efficiency of media production, but also greatly enriches the visual experience of users. cqnews.net launches the MR video *A Better New Life from This Spring*, which takes the first-person point of view, uses cutting-edge communication and interaction technology, focuses on hot topics such as healthcare, education, and transportation, and shows various aspects of people's livelihood that benefit from high-quality development. New Media of the Henan Broadcasting System adopts various technologies, such as "parallel space + metaverse + AI character integration," "character shooting + digital virtual + naked-eye 3D," and "3D animation + real-scene interaction," and creates a series of short videos such as *Creating a Better Future* and *The Train to Spring*. In addition, cutting-edge media technologies can be used to report the Two Sessions in a more innovative way.

Simultaneously, cutting-edge technologies continuously expand the fields of application, diversify the forms of presentation and expression, provide vivid examples for promoting the integration and innovation of technology and media, and inject the vitality of technological innovation into news reporting and online

---

6 *Opinions on Accelerating the Deep Integration and Development of Media*. Accessed June 2023. https:/www.gov.cn/xinwen/2020-09/26/content_5547310.htm.

communication. *Journey of Chinese Art on the Scroll* organically fuses artistic elements of poetry, painting, music, dance, drama, and music with high-end technologies of XR, CG, naked-eye 3D, and holographic images, and provides a cultural feast that combines the Chinese spirit and aesthetic taste in filmmaking and production. The Hunan Broadcasting System launches the digital virtual anchor *Xiao Yang*, creates next-generation pan-entertainment content social platform "Mango World" based on VR, and promotes the innovation and integration of new technology and high-quality content. The Guangdong Radio and Television Station accurately captures the content preferences of Generation Z, launches the first Cantonese virtual idol *Yue Xiao Man* as well as the "Intangible Cultural Heritage & New Youth" series of digital collections, and accelerates the exploration of all-media content in a digital world.

10.2478/9788367405867-005

Chapter 4
Construction of Cybersecurity

Without cybersecurity we cannot ensure national security. Cybersecurity concerns national security and social stability, as well as the immediate interests of people, and becomes a major issue that affects overall development. Over the past year, the competition among major powers in cyberspace has continued to deepen, and factors of instability, uncertainty, and insecurity became increasingly prominent in the international landscape. In China, key industries and fields frequently suffer from overseas cyberattacks. With the development of new technologies and applications such as cloud computing, AI, and big data, risks to cybersecurity such as data breaches, security vulnerability, and online fraud often occur. The situation of cybersecurity remains complex and severe. Simultaneously, *The 14th Five-Year Plan* has been implemented in an orderly manner, and the construction of a unified national market has been accelerated. The development of digital economy enters a transitional period, which puts forward higher requirements for cybersecurity.

China fully implements a holistic approach to national security, ensures development with security, promotes security with development, vigorously enhances cybersecurity capabilities, and establishes a solid foundation for cybersecurity. In the past year, China steadily advanced the work of cybersecurity, successively released laws and regulations, supporting systems and standards, and continuously improved the system and mechanism of cybersecurity. China made positive progress in guaranteeing cybersecurity and continuously strengthened the protection of the critical information infrastructure, the management of data security and the protection of personal information. Campaigns against cyber gang crimes were carried out following the law. All of society attached greater attention and increased more investment in cybersecurity. The structure of the cybersecurity industry was continuously adjusted and optimized. The cultivation of cybersecurity talents and the publicity of cybersecurity were promoted in an orderly way. These further strengthened the foundation of cybersecurity work and improved the level of cybersecurity protection.

4.1 Overall Situation of Cybersecurity Remains Severe

Over the past year, China faced prominent problems in cybersecurity. Specifically, ransomware attacks targeted enterprises, with the function of data theft. DDoS

(Distributed Denial of Service) attacks continued to expand, with a significant increase in high-traffic attacks (more than 100 G). The attacks from APT (Advanced Persistent Threat) organizations on key industries in China remained active. Data breaches occurred frequently. New technologies and applications like cloud computing developed rapidly, which caused risks to cybersecurity that cannot be ignored.

4.1.1 Typical cyberattacks cause serious harm

1. Enterprises become the main target of ransomware attacks

In 2022, ransomware became less active than in 2021. Yet, a large number of enterprises were attacked by ransomware. According to the *China Cybersecurity Report 2022* released by RISING, in 2022, a total of 579,200 ransomware samples were intercepted, with 194,900 infections, with a decrease of 68.77 percent from 2021.[1] After enterprises are attacked, they must pay ransoms as soon as possible to recover businesses under economic pressure. This significantly increases the success rate and return rate of ransomware. A Chinese enterprise was once attacked by ransomware. As evinced, ransomware uses data theft as an auxiliary means to protect its own interests. Once the ransomware fails, it profits from selling data. Ransomware that primarily attacks enterprises and possesses the capabilities of data encryption and data theft will become a trend of ransomware attacks.

2. High-traffic DDoS attacks increase significantly

In 2022, DDoS attacks continued to grow, with a significant increase in high-traffic attacks (more than 100 G). According to statistics, in 2022, the number of DDoS attacks increased by 8 percent compared to 2021 (also the largest number from 2018 to 2022), and the threats or risks reached the highest level in recent years. 2022 saw a year-on-year increase of more than 50 percent in over 100-G high-traffic DDoS attacks. On average, an over-100-G high-traffic DDoS attack occurred every hour.[2]

The targets of DDoS attacks become clear, and the persistence of DDoS attacks increases year by year. In the frequency of attacks on affected targets, in 2022, the number of IP addresses that were repeatedly attacked significantly increased compared to 2021. The cycle of DDoS attacks on a single target became persistent.

1 RISING. China Cybersecurity Report 2022, February 2023.
2 Tencent Security. *2022 DDoS Attack Threats Report*, February 2023.

In 2021, 56.91 percent of victims only suffered from one DDoS attack. In 2022, victims identified as attack targets were more susceptible to multiple DDoS attacks, posing bigger challenges to DDoS protection.

3. APT attack remains severe

In 2022, the growth trend of cyberattacks from APT organizations slowed down, yet remained at a high level. APT organizations focused on critical information infrastructure and important information systems such as governments, research institutes, finance, energy, healthcare, electricity, and communications, with various attack intentions such as information theft, economic profit, intelligence espionage, and physical destruction. Economically developed regions were the main target regions for overseas APT organizations to attack.

4.1.2 Threats to cybersecurity in key fields become prominent

1. The risk of data breaches remains prominent

According to statistics from the National Computer Virus Emergency Response Center in Tianjin, in the first quarter of 2023, data breach incidents in China happened frequently, as a blow to industries such as education, healthcare, and finance. In particular, the highest proportion of single data breaches occurred in the range of 100,000 to 1,000,000, accounting for nearly half of the total. Data breaches mainly involved personal information about citizens.

2. Incidents where viruses are implanted into open-source software ecosystem occur frequently

In 2022, official package repositories of Github and Python, the world's largest open-source communities, were implanted with viruses. Similar incidents frequently occurred in recent years, causing a large number of malicious source codes in open-source software. The reliability and security of the open-source software ecosystem attract widespread attention. Currently, open-source software and its ecosystem become the most important basic components and facilities in software development in various industries; therefore, software developers must ensure the reliability of the source of open-source software and continuously monitor the software when introducing open-source projects into their own software. Relevant industries should actively promote the application of security approaches and measures such as open-source ecology monitoring systems, software composition analysis (SCA), and software bills of materials (SBOM), in order to help enterprises and developers better avoid and solve the risks to software security that arise from open-source software more quickly.

3. The situation of the threats to cloud security remains serious

According to *2022 State of Public Cloud Security Report* released by Orca Security, many security problems are exposed in the field of cloud computing applications, such as the interruption of cloud services, the breach of sensitive data, and the vulnerabilities of cloud infrastructure. Specifically, there are:

Cloud-based violent attacks. In 2022, the number of cyber violent attacks targeting enterprises and organizations increased by 31 percent over 2021, and the peak number of attacks related to major geopolitical and socioeconomic events.

API threat. With the popularity of cloud-based microservice architecture, the use of API has become common. Currently, more than 83 percent of traffic in the entire Web application system is accessed through API. More than 44 percent of surveyed enterprises report that they are creating and maintaining more than 100 API applications. A survey shows that 50 percent of surveyed enterprises admit to having experienced API-related security incidents in the past twelve months.[3]

Errors in cloud configuration. In 2022, many serious cloud-based data security incidents were caused by errors in cloud configurations. Seventy-two percent of enterprises and organizations had at least one storage bucket with public "read" permissions, and 36 percent of enterprises and organizations stored unencrypted personal privacy data in these cloud services.

4. The risks to ICV cybersecurity increase

IoV signifies a complex network system formed by the deep integration of the Internet, mobile communications technology, automobile, electronics, transportation, and other fields. At present, the number of IoV users in China exceeds 140 million, and the application scenarios continuously expand, with an upward trend in the scale. The risks to IoV cybersecurity are mainly distributed in terminal, communications, application services, and data. In the risks to terminal security, vehicles enter the era of software definition, with a surge in code volume. Vehicle network protocols such as CAN and FlexRay lack security design, and networked devices lack capabilities in high-level security verification and protection, making them vulnerable to attacks

3 "Google: Cloud Computing Triggers API Security Crisis." Accessed July 2023. https://www.secrss.com/articles/50429.

such as resetting and tampering. In the risks to communications security, the current IoV communications security authentication mechanism remains weak, with security risks such as DoS attack, data theft, data tampering and identity forgery. In the risks to the security of application and service, IoV encompasses typical service scenarios such as OTA upgrading, remote diagnosis, assisted driving, and vehicle-road collaboration. Once service platforms and applications lack security management, proper protection, and timely evaluation and detection, they become an access for large-scale attacks on IoV devices and networks, affecting the network ecosystem. In the risks to data security, IoV collects and processes important data that involves national security, such as information on surrounding environments and roads, critical infrastructure, traffic flow, and pedestrian distribution, as well as personal information and data such as vehicle audio-video recordings, location trajectories, and biological features, within a wide range and with high accuracy. Currently, the security guarantee of the entire life cycle of IoV data is weak, and the processing of data is not standardized. There are security risks such as plaintext transmission of sensitive data and illegal cross-border transmission of data, which are susceptible to malicious theft, breach, or analysis for bad purposes.

4.2 New Progress is made in Cybersecurity Protection and Data Security Protection

Over the past year, China has solidly promoted cybersecurity protection and guarantees, continuously improved cybersecurity policies and standard systems, strengthened the protection of critical information infrastructure, enhanced the management of data security and the protection of personal information, accelerated the construction of cybersecurity service and product certification systems, and continually raised the level of the management of cybersecurity vulnerabilities.

4.2.1 Security protection of critical information infrastructure is actively promoted

Critical information infrastructure is the top priority in cybersecurity protection. Over the past year, the security protection of critical information infrastructure was continuously promoted, and the security protection system and capability of critical information infrastructure were continuously enhanced. In November 2022, national standards for the security protection of critical information infrastructure, *Requirements for the Security Protection of Information Security Technology and Critical Information Infrastructure (GB/T39204-2022)*, was released, which was officially implemented on May 1, 2023, providing a strong standard guarantee for operators to carry out the protection of critical information infrastructure.

4.2.2 Protection of data security and personal information is implemented

1. The system and standard for the protection of data security and personal information improve

Basic management systems for the protection of data security and personal information are advancing steadily. In December 2022, the CPC Central Committee and the State Council officially released *Twenty Articles on Data*, which comprehensively arranges and deploys the construction of a basic data system in China from four aspects, i.e., data property rights, data circulation and transactions, data revenue distribution, and data security governance. Security is integrated in the entire process of data supply, circulation and use, and regulatory bottom lines and red lines are established.

Positive progress is made in the protection and certification of data security and personal information. In November 2022, to comprehensively improve the capabilities of protecting data security and detecting risks, and ensure the controllability of the risks to data security, the State Administration for Market Regulation and the Cyberspace Administration of China jointly released *Announcement on the Implementation of the Protection and Certification of Personal Information* and the implementation rules, which encourages personal information processors to improve their capabilities in personal information protection through certification. After the management and certification of data security were carried out in June 2022, this further improved the protection and certification of personal information and provided a basis for standardizing personal information processing, promoting the rational use of personal information, and implementing the protection and certification of personal information.

The standardization of data security progresses in an orderly manner. By February 2023, national standard systems on data security covered more than fifty standards in five categories,[4] including basic or general standards, security technology, security management, security evaluations, and typical applications. Specific fields included gait recognition, gene recognition, voiceprint recognition, facial recognition, intelligent vehicles, instant communication, express and logistics, online shopping, online payments, online audio and video, online ride-hailing, personal information security engineering, etc.

4 "The Status Quo and Development of Domestic Data Security in 2022." https://mp.weixin.qq.com/s?src=11&timestamp=1724051806&ver=5453&signature=V2N1YVj2UTYHTnjdeyaGLgvHvZsvq9bbpuZ1HWrzyMSxTq2nx8V1X8AzreYu022GyGtiFbJfsBSrsFazyLpgBYrxHer*GpTqBNVG3ScyWWdACj0lrYCENOagzpHEQzsd&new=1. Accessed July 2023.

2. The management of data export security accelerates

The management system for data export security quickens, which further guarantees the orderly and free flow of data following the law. *Twenty Articles on Data* and *Measures on Security Evaluation of Data Outbound Transfer* propose to promote cross-border data flow in a standard, orderly, and secure way. In August 2022, to guide and assist data processors in applying for data export security evaluation in a standard and orderly way, the Office of the Central Cyberspace Affairs Commission formulated *Guidelines for Application* for *Security Evaluation of Data Outbound Transfer (First Edition)*, which explains the specific requirements for application methods, procedures, and materials regarding security evaluation of data outbound transfer. In February 2023, the Office of the Central Cyberspace Affairs Commission released *Measures on Standard Contract of Personal Information Outbound Transfer*, which clarifies the standard contract and provides specific guidance for personal information outbound transfer with the standard contract. In September, the Office of the Central Cyberspace Affairs Commission published *Regulations on Standardizing and Promoting Cross-border Data Flow (Draft for Comments)*, which aims to further standardize and promote the legal, orderly, and free flow of data, based on ensuring national data security and protecting personal information rights and interests.

Security evaluation of data outbound transfer is carried out in an orderly manner. In 2022, the joint research project of Beijing Friendship Hospital, Capital Medical University and Amsterdam UMC in the Netherlands was the first data-outbound-transfer project in China that passed the security evaluation. This marks the first case of national data-outbound-transfer security evaluation system in Beijing and provides practical guidance for strengthening the management of the security of medical and health data outbound transfer and promoting international medical research and cooperation. Simultaneously, the second case, the Air China Project, submitted by the Office of Cyberspace Affairs Commission of Beijing, was approved, which is of great significance for improving the level of the management of data-outbound-transfer security and optimizing the business environment. The Office of Cyberspace Affairs Commission of Shanghai actively formulates *Practical Q & A on the Security Evaluation and Application of Data Outbound Transfer* and conducts Q & As on the application of data outbound transfer. By January 31, 2023, Shanghai had received sixty-seven formal application materials for security evaluation of data outbound transfer. Specifically, thirty-five were approved in completeness inspection and submitted to the Office of the Central Cyberspace Affairs Commission. Seventeen would be approved in completeness inspection, involving retail, automobile, finance, medicine, and other fields.[5]

5 "Practical Q & A on the Security Evaluation and Application of Data Outbound Transfer (2)." Accessed July 2023. https://mp.weixin.qq.com/s/4lYcOmFNVOOtn_YqS6v3HA.

3. The protection of data security and personal information is strengthened in key industries and fields

In August 2022, the National Health Commission issued *Measures on the Management of Cybersecurity for Medical and Health Institutions*, which further standardizes the management of cybersecurity and data security of medical and health institutions, promotes the development of "Internet + healthcare," and accelerates the high-quality development of the health industry. In October 2022, the State Post Bureau solicited public opinions on *Regulations on the Management of the Security of Personal Information of Postal Users (Draft)*, requiring postal enterprises that handle the personal information of postal users and reach the number specified by national departments of cyberspace affairs to designate persons in charge of personal information protection for postal users, to implement full-process management of postal waybill-number resources, to use effective technological means such as radio-frequency identification, virtual security number, and electronic paper to de-label waybill information, and to prevent the breach of waybill information in the delivery. In December 2022, the Ministry of Industry and Information Technology released *Measures on the Management of Data Security in the Fields of Industry and Information Technology (Trial)*, which focuses on solving the problems of "who will manage, what will be managed, and how to manage" regarding data security in the fields of industry and information technology and establishes a two-level regulatory mechanism of "Ministry of Industry and Information Technology and local industrial regulatory departments."

4.2.3 Review of cybersecurity is continuously strengthened

The review of cybersecurity is an important part of national cybersecurity guarantee system. In May 2023, the Office of Cybersecurity Review conducted a cybersecurity review of Micron's products sold in China legally. As investigated, Micron's products caused serious risks to cybersecurity, posing big security risks to the supply chain of critical information infrastructure in China and affecting the national security of China. Therefore, the Office of Cybersecurity Review concluded that Micron would not legally pass the cybersecurity review . On the basis of laws and regulations like *Cybersecurity Law*, operators of critical information infrastructure in China should stop purchasing Micron's products. In June 2022, the Office of Cybersecurity Review launched cybersecurity review of CNKI. In September 2023, based on laws and regulations such as *Cybersecurity Law*, *Personal Information Protection Law*, and *Administrative Penalty Law*, the Office of the Central Cyberspace Affairs Commission comprehensively considered the nature, consequences, and duration of CNKI's illegal processing of personal information (especially cybersecurity review), imposed an administrative penalty related to cybersecurity review on CNKI, ordered CNKI to stop illegal processing of personal information, and fined CNKI 50 million *yuan*.

4.2.4 Certification system of cybersecurity services and products is continually improved

Promoting the construction of the certification system of cybersecurity services and improving the level and service quality of cybersecurity service organizations play an important role in strengthening the work of cybersecurity. In March 2023, to carry out national unified certification of cybersecurity services, the State Administration for Market Regulation, the Office of the Central Cyberspace Affairs Commission, the Ministry of Industry and Information Technology and Ministry of Public Security jointly issued *Implementation Opinions on Carrying out the Certification of Cybersecurity Services*, which requires the strengthening of the organization, implementation, and supervision of the certification of cybersecurity services, encourages Internet operators and others to widely accept the results of the certification of cybersecurity services, and promotes the healthy and orderly development of the cybersecurity service industry.

In order to strengthen the security management of products dedicated to cybersecurity, promote mutual recognition of the results of security certification and testing, and avoid repeated certification and testing, in April 2023, the Office of the Central Cyberspace Affairs Commission, the Ministry of Industry and Information Technology, the Ministry of Public Security, the Ministry of Finance and National Certification and Accreditation Administration jointly issued *Notice on Adjusting the Security Management of Products Dedicated to Cybersecurity*. As required, from July 1, 2023, products dedicated to cybersecurity listed in the *Catalogue of Key Network Devices and Products Dedicated to Cybersecurity* shall comply with the mandatory requirements of relevant national standards such as *Technological Requirements for Information Security Technologies and Products Dedicated to Cybersecurity* and can only be sold or provided after passing the security certification or security testing by qualified institutions. In July 2023, the Office of the Central Cyberspace Affairs Commission, the Ministry of Industry and Information Technology, the Ministry of Public Security and National Certification and Accreditation Administration jointly issued *Notice on Adjusting Catalogue of Key Network Devices and Products Dedicated to Cybersecurity*, updating *Catalogue of Key Network Devices and Products Dedicated to Cybersecurity*.

4.2.5 f Password evaluation system is actively promoted

The State Cryptography Administration accelerates the construction of security evaluation system for the application of commercial passwords ("password evaluation"), actively cultivates seventy-three commercial password-evaluation pilot institutions, comprehensively strengthens the filing and review of evaluation results and standardized management of evaluation business, organizes assessments of password-evaluation personnel, and implements assessments on 685 password-evaluation personnel from seventy-three password-evaluation pilot institutions. The State Cryptography Administration has conducted password evaluation of nearly 8,000 important systems. The Administration continuously improves the password evaluation system, released the second edition of *FAQ of Password Evaluation*, revised *Implementation Guidelines for the Applications of Information System Passwords*, compiled *The White Paper on the Password Evaluation Industry 2022* and *Password Evaluation Report Template 2022*, and organized the compilation of twenty-nine guiding documents for national password applications in typical scenarios.

4.2.6 Formulation of standards on cybersecurity is solidly carried out

Standards on cybersecurity play a fundamental, normative, and leading role in safeguarding national security and ensuring the healthy development of digital economy. In 2022, under the guidance of the Standardization Administration and industrial regulatory authorities, China achieved fruitful results in the standardization of cybersecurity, which effectively promoted the high-quality development of the cybersecurity industry. By August 2023, the National Technical Committee on Information Security Standardization had released 370 national standards on cybersecurity; 65 have been released since 2022. Simultaneously, China strengthens the research and formulation of standards on commercial passwords. The State Cryptography Administration releases two national standards on commercial passwords, including *Standards on the Functions and Interfaces of Information Security Technology Trusted Computing Password Supporting Platforms*, and nine industrial standards on commercial passwords, including *Technical Requirements for the Application of Network Identity Service Passwords* and *Implementation Guidelines for Cloud-based Electronic Signature Service Technology*. The standard system for commercial passwords continuously improves.

China actively promotes the formulation of international standards on cybersecurity. In November 2022, the Secretariat of National Technical Committee on Information Security Standardization organized the collection of proposals for the SC27 international standard, including data security, personal information protection, critical information infrastructure, consumer IoT, industrial Internet, IoV, quantum information, IPv6, and other fields. In the first half of 2023, a total of twenty-four international standard documents, including *Information Security, Cybersecurity and Privacy Protection Password Protocol Verification, Part 2: Evaluation Methods and Activities for Password Protocol*, were voted on and reviewed.

Positive progress has been made in the implementation and promotion of standards on cybersecurity. In April 2023, the themed event of “National Standards on Cybersecurity Entering Campus” was successfully held at Shandong University, which aimed to further strengthen the promotion of national standards on cybersecurity, promote the training of talents in this field, and enhance the knowledge and skills of cybersecurity standardization for the general public. In October 2022, the "2022 World Standards Day: National Standards on Data Security Promotion Conference" was held in Beijing, focusing on the promotion and interpretation of six online platform services, such as online shopping, instant messaging, online payment, online audio-video, online ride-hailing, and express and logistics, as well as four national standards on the data security of biometric recognition, including facial features, genes, gait, and voiceprints. The event helps to promote the understanding and use of national standards on data security by all relevant parties and enhances the capabilities and levels of organizations in data security protection.

4.3 Governance of Cybersecurity and the Punishment of Cybercrimes are Deepened

Over the past year, the settlement and governance of various cybersecurity incidents were intensively launched, the illegal collection and use of personal information by apps were continuously regulated, the governance of prominent problems on cybersecurity was solidly promoted, and illegal activities in cyberspace were punished in accordance with the law.

4.3.1 Campaign of personal information protection continues to be launched

1. The illegal collection and use of personal information by apps are continuously regulated

Since 2021, the Office of the Central Cyberspace Affairs Commission has continued to regulate the illegal collection and use of personal information by apps, and organized special inspections on more than 2,000 common types of apps, such as input method, map navigation, and security management that are widely used by the public. Apps with serious problems have been published and removed, which effectively deters illegal behavior. App operators have significantly enhanced their awareness of personal information protection. In 2023, the Office of the Central Cyberspace Affairs Commission organized a comparative test on the collection of personal information by common or high-download apps. By July 2023, a test report on the collection of personal information by fifty-six apps in eight categories, including online shopping, map navigation, browsers, news and information, online audiovisual, e-books, photo beautification, and cloud storage, had been released, which guides operators to improve their apps. In order to establish and improve the channel for complaints and reports on the illegal collection and use of personal information by apps, the Office of the Central Cyberspace Affairs Commission timely accepts, handles, and replies to complaints and reports on the illegal collection and use of personal information by apps through the minister's mailbox, website, mailbox, WeChat official account, and other channels. So far, more than 40,000 complaints and reports have been received, giving full play to the role of social supervision.

Local departments steadily carry out the governance of app infringement on users' rights. In 2022, the Office of Cyberspace Affairs Commission of Zhejiang, the Zhejiang Provincial Department of Public Security, the Zhejiang Administration for Market Regulation, and the Zhejiang Communications Administration strengthened the closed-loop management of app security. In total, more than 159,100 apps were tested, focusing on 1,039 apps with a great impact on society and a large number of downloads. Five hundred copies of *Notice of the Verification for Apps with Problems* were issued, 135 apps that were not rectified in a timely manner were announced to the public, and twenty-two apps were removed. In Zhejiang, apps and data security management platforms in the telecom and Internet industries were put into use, and 159,100 apps were monitored and detected in an all-round and timely manner, in terms of privacy compliance and security vulnerability. In September 2022, the Shanghai Communications Administration conducted an inspection of the infringement on users' rights by apps, announced 127 apps with problems such as "illegal collection of personal information," "illegal use of personal information," and "requests for permission by apps in a compulsory, frequent and excessive way," and urged operators to rectify these apps.

2. Relevant departments strictly crack down on the illegal online sale of personal information of citizens

Criminals maliciously steal personal information of citizens for the purpose of committing crimes. In response to this prominent problem, the Ministry of Public Security and relevant departments maintained a tough stance and focused on investigating and handling malicious theft of personal information of groups such as primary and secondary school students and the elderly, illegal intrusion into computer systems to obtain personal information, illegal theft of express delivery information, and illegal online sale of personal information of citizens. More than 16,000 cases of infringing on personal information of citizens have been investigated and handled, which effectively safeguards the security of personal information of citizens. In response to serious infringement of citizens' privacy and other criminal activities such as illegal production and sale of equipment for eavesdropping and taking photos, as well as stealing personal privacy and spreading them online for sale, the Ministry of Public Security and relevant departments carriedout a campaign to crack down on eavesdropping, secretly taking photos, and voyeurism. A total of more than 340 cases were investigated and handled, more than 90 production dens for equipment for illegal eavesdropping and taking photos were destroyed, and 141,000 pieces of equipment for eavesdropping and taking photos were confiscated, which effectively crack down on such criminal activities.[6]

4.3.2 Cybercrimes like black industry are punished according to the law

The Ministry of Public Security promotes the "Clean up 2022" campaign, handles prominent online crimes and illegal activities that seriously endanger order in cyberspace and the rights of the public in accordance with the law, and achieves significant results. By the end of December 2022, public security organs had investigated and handled a total of 83,000 cases and taken practical actions to maintain security and order in cyberspace.[7]

1. Remarkable achievements are made in closing online accounts in the black industrial chain

In order to root out illegal and criminal activities in cyberspace and effectively safeguard the legitimate rights and interests of people, in September 2022, the Ministry of Public Security deployed the campaign of closing online accounts in the black industrial chain. By February 2023, more than 11,000 cases had been investigated and handled, more than 130 code-receiving platforms had been shut down, more than 800 modem pool dens had been destroyed, more than 10,000 black industrial devices such as modem pools and GOIP had been seized, more than 2.4 million mobile phone black cards had been confiscated, and more than 42 million online accounts in the black industrial chain had been closed. Additionally, the top ten typical cases of the campaign, such as "Public security organs in Jiangsu concluded the case of a man surnamed Zhang and others who illegally used information network," were announced.

---

6 "Public Security Organs Achieve Significant Results in the 'Clean up Campaign 2022'". Accessed July 2023. https://www.mps.gov.cn/n2255079/n8819345/n8819484/n8819511/c8826464/content.html.

7 "Public Security Organs Achieve Significant Results in the 'Clean up Campaign 2022.'" Accessed July 2023. https://www.mps.gov.cn/n2255079/n8819345/n8819484/n8819511/c8826464/content.html.

2. Campaign against cyber gang crimes is solidly carried out

Stepping up efforts to combat cyber gang crimes plays an important role in building a higher-level peaceful China and the rule of law in China. In September 2022, nine departments, including the Ministry of Public Security, the Department of Publicity of the CPC Central Committee, the Office of the Central Cyberspace Affairs Commission, the Supreme People's Court, the Supreme People's Procuratorate, the Ministry of Industry and Information Technology, the Ministry of Justice, the People's Bank of China, and the China Banking and Insurance Regulatory Commission, jointly issued a notice to deploy an eighteen-month campaign to crack down on cyber gang crimes nationwide, and promote rooting out criminal gangs on an ongoing basis in cyberspace. By February 2023, a total of more than 400 criminal gangs in cyberspace had been dismantled, including more than 20 organized crime groups, more than 320 criminal gangs, and more than 50 gangs, and more than 8,800 various cases had been solved. The campaign achieved significant phased results.[8]

3. Telecom and online fraud is combated in accordance with the law

Telecom and online fraud occurs frequently. Departments of cyberspace affairs, public security, industry and information technology, and financial regulation jointly combat telecom and online fraud and achieve positive results. The Office of the Central Cyberspace Affairs Commission and the Ministry of Public Security co-developed a National Fraud-related Black Sample Database, which covers and handles 7.83 million fraud- related websites, 585,000 fraud-related apps, and 520,000 fraud-related phone calls. The Internet Early Warning and Dissuasion Platform has warned and dissuaded users more than ten billion times, with remarkable early-warning effect. The Office of the Central Cyberspace Affairs Commission focuses on key fraud-related fields, such as Internet access, domain-name registration, server hosting, online live streaming, and promotional service, which evokes strong response in society, effectively combating the industrial chain of telecom and online fraud and accelerating the formation of a healthy Internet ecosystem. The Ministry of Industry and Information Technology continuously promotes "Closing Online Illegal Accounts Campaign 2.0," launches "security governance of harmful apps," strictly implements the real-name system, steps up efforts to combat virtual operator cards, strengthens the governance of key businesses such as SMS ports, voice-dedicated lines, and cloud services, and continuously enhances the ability to respond

8 "Ministry of Public Security Deploys a Campaign to Combat and Punish Cyber Gang Crimes." Accessed July 2023. http://www.gov.cn/xinwen/2023-02/17/content_5741893.htm.

in a timely manner throughout the entire process. A total of 110 million high-risk fraud-related phone cards are handled, and 1.82 billion fraud-related calls and 2.15 billion SMS messages are intercepted. The People's Bank of China deepens the governance of the capital chain, continuously improves the normalized governance pattern of the payment industry, organizes commercial banks, payment institutions, and settlement institutions to assist public security organs in blocking the transfer of a large amount of fraud-involved funds and recovers a large number of losses for the people.

The publicity of anti-fraud knowledge is an important approach to fighting telecom and online fraud. In 2022, the Office of the Central Cyberspace Affairs Commission released promotional materials such as *Office of the Central Cyberspace Affairs Commission Extensively Cracking down on a Group of Fake Investment and Fraud Platforms* and *Office of the Central Cyberspace Affairs Commission Exposing a Group of Typical Cases of Telecom and Online Fraud Involving Minors* targeting vulnerable groups and typical fraud cases, which aroused strong response from all sides and jointly created a good atmosphere for anti-fraud in all of society.

4.4 Cybersecurity Industry and Technology Steadily Develop

Over the past year, the cybersecurity product system in China continuously improved. Local governments actively deployed and promoted the development of cybersecurity industry clusters and constructed platforms for technological innovation and ecology. Significant results were achieved in the development of the cybersecurity industry.

4.4.1 Environment for the development of cybersecurity and data security industries is continuously optimized

Policies and documents for the development of the cybersecurity industry are continuously released, and the environment for the development of the cybersecurity industry is continuously improved. The report of the 20th CPC National Congress makes clear arrangements for strengthening the construction of the guarantee system for cybersecurity and data security. In June 2022, the State Council issued *Guiding Opinions on Strengthening the Construction of Digital Government*, proposing to enhance the capability of security guarantees and strengthen the security for the construction of digital government. In January 2023, the Ministry of Industry and Information Technology, the Office of the Central Cyberspace Affairs Commission, and fourteen other departments jointly issued *Guiding Opinions on Promoting the Development of the Data Security Industry*, providing strong policy support for expanding and strengthening the data security industry. In November 2022, the Ministry of Industry and Information Technology and the China Banking and Insurance Regulatory Commission issued *Opinions on Promoting the Standardized and Healthy Development of the Cybersecurity Insurance Industry (Draft for Comments)*, which plays an important role in accelerating the integrated development of the cybersecurity industry and financial services and in promoting the high-quality development of the cybersecurity industry.

As the creation of a digital China accelerates, relevant policies and documents are continuously released in key industries and fields to promote the development of the cybersecurity industry. In the financial industry, the China Banking and Insurance Regulatory Commission issued *Guiding Opinions on the Digital Transformation of the Banking and Insurance Industry*, proposing to strengthen the protection of cybersecurity, data security and privacy. The People's Bank of China issued *Development Plan for Fintech 2022–2025*, which clearly requires protection data security and proposes key tasks such as improving a secure and efficient Fintech innovation system, establishing a secure and ubiquitous financial network. The Civil Aviation Administration of China released *Guiding Opinions on the Development of Civil Aviation Big Data*, proposing tasks such as building a data resource system and a data security system.

Various regions intensively formulate policies and documents on cybersecurity and promote the development of the cybersecurity and data security industries. Shanghai, Hebei, and Jiangsu, respectively, release *Action Plan for Building a Cybersecurity Industry Cluster in Lingang New Area of China (Shanghai) Pilot Free Trade Zone 2022–2025*, *Regulations on Promoting the Development of Digital Economy in Hebei*, and *Regulations on Promoting the Development of Digital Economy in Jiangsu*, raising higher requirements for cultivating and developing the industrial chain of data security service, conducting research and development of key core technologies in the field of cybersecurity, improving the security guarantee system of industrial Internet or industrial information, and promoting the development of the cybersecurity industry.

4.4.2 The cybersecurity market continues to develop and grow

1. The scale of the cybersecurity market steadily increases

In recent years, the cybersecurity industry in China maintained a trend of growth as a whole. However, affected by the macro-economy, the growth rate of the cybersecurity industry fluctuated, as shown in Figure 4-1. In 2022, the scale of the cybersecurity market in China approximated 63.3 billion *yuan*, with a year-on-year growth of 3.1 percent. As digitization accelerates, the application scope of technologies such as cloud computing, AI, big data, and 5G keeps expanding. While using new technologies to improve efficiency, enterprises face more cybersecurity threats and

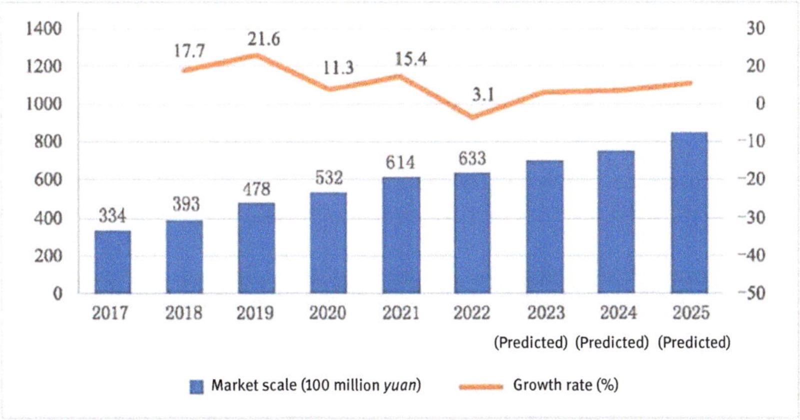

Figure 4-1 Scale and growth rate of the cybersecurity market in China from 2017 to 2025.

Source: China Cybersecurity Industry Alliance.

continuously increase investment to cybersecurity. As predicted, the growth rate of the cybersecurity market in China will exceed 10 percent in the next three years, and the market scale will exceed 80 billion *yuan* by 2025.[9]

2. The cybersecurity product and service system improves

In China, the layout of the cybersecurity industry is relatively complete. Divided by four dimensions, i.e., cybersecurity product, solution, application scenario, and service, the business fields of cybersecurity enterprises cover seven basic security fields (security of network and basic architecture, endpoint security, identity and access management, application security, data security, development security, and security management), six security solutions (zero trust, data security governance, threat management/scalable threat detection and response or XDR, attack surface management, security operation/hosting detection and response service or MDR, security hosting service or MSS, and security access service edge), four application scenarios (cloud security, mobile security, industrial Internet security, and IoT security), and nine security services (security solution and integration, security operation and maintenance, risk assessment, penetration testing and red-blue confrontation, emergency response, attack-defense training/target range, training and certification, education on security awareness, and the all testing of security). In addition, positive progress is made in

9 China Cybersecurity Industry Alliance. *Analysis of the Cybersecurity Market and Corporate Competitiveness in China in 2023*, June 2023.

the evaluation of the security of commercial password, the evaluation of the level of cybersecurity protection, and the evaluation of the security of cloud computing service. As shown in Figure 4-2, by April 2023, there were a total of 4,743 registered enterprises in the cybersecurity industry in China. In recent years, the number of registered enterprises in the cybersecurity industry has continued to increase. In 2022, the number of newly registered enterprises reached a historic peak, reaching 328. This indicates that the cybersecurity industry in China thrives.[10]

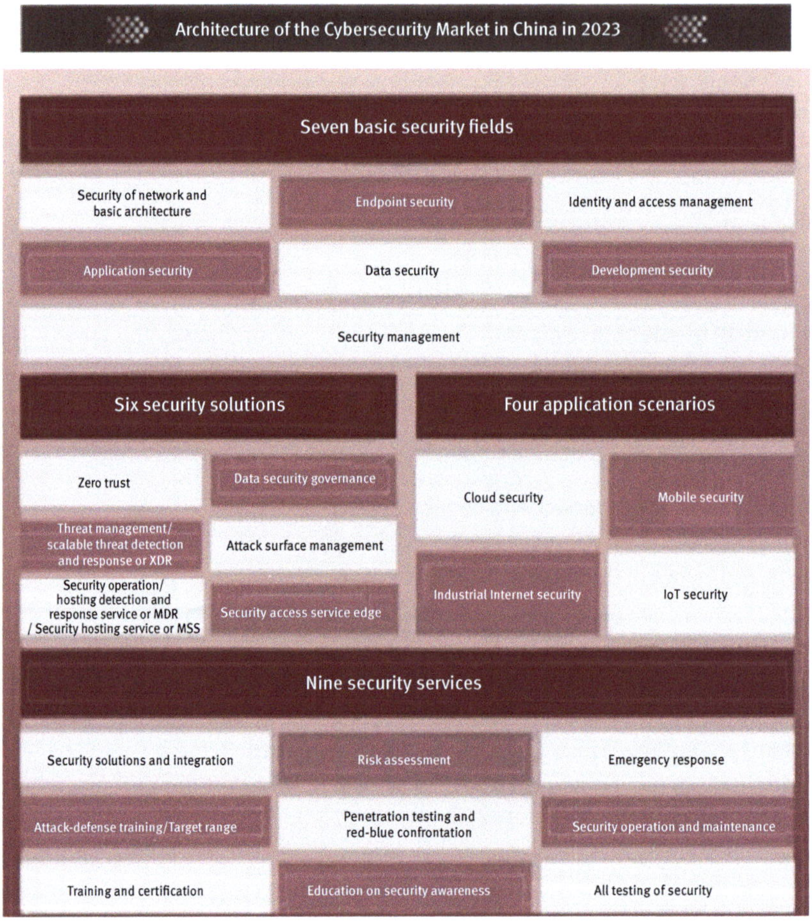

Figure 4-2 Architecture of the cybersecurity market in China in 2023[a].

[a]"Cybersecurity Reviews: A Panorama of the Cybersecurity Market in China in 2023," May 2023.

10 "Analysis of the Current Situation and Development Prospects of the Cybersecurity Industry and Market in China in 2023." Accessed July 2023. https://bg.qianzhan.com/trends/detail/506/230607-3096c0cf.html.

3. The concentration ratio of the cybersecurity market enlarges

Currently, the cybersecurity market in China has reached a stage of steady growth, and the advantages of top enterprises in scale and resources became prominent. In 2022, the CR1[11] and CR8 of the cybersecurity market in China were 9.83 percent and 44.91 percent, respectively, with a year-on-year increase. From 2018 to 2022, the market share of the top four enterprises rose from 21.71 percent to 28.59 percent in 2022. This signals that the concentration ratio of the cybersecurity market in China is further enlarging and that a few leading enterprises dominate the market.[12]

In 2022, the market share of five cybersecurity enterprises, i.e., Qi'anxin, Venustech, Sangfor, TOPSEC, and CETC all exceeded 5 percent. The growth rate of the revenue of most of the top enterprises was higher than the industrial average, as shown in Figure 4-3. In 2022, the market share of top enterprises increased slightly compared to 2021. As estimated, the market share of top enterprises will grow slightly in the next two to three years.

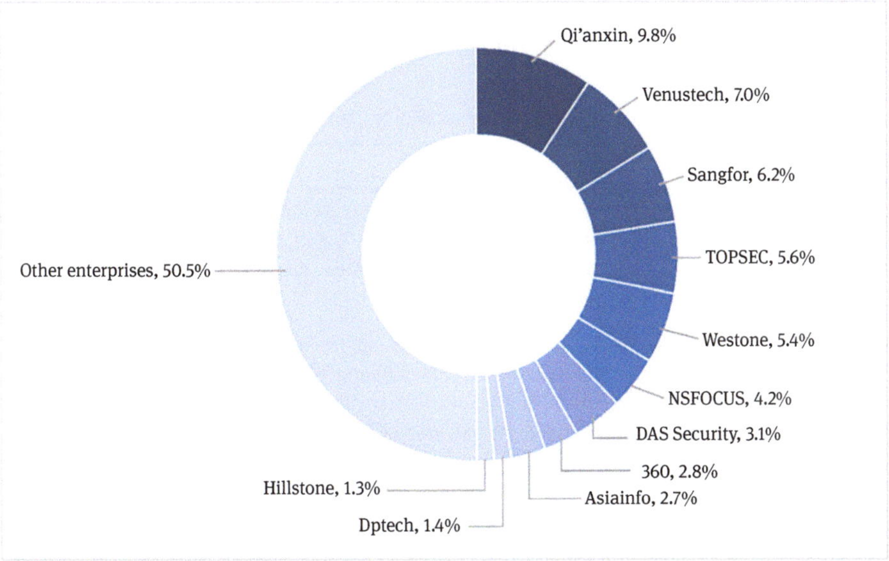

Figure 4-3 Market share of major cybersecurity enterprises in China in 2022.

Source: China Cybersecurity Industry Alliance.

11 CRn Index refers to the total market share of the top N largest enterprises in relevant market of the industry. For example, CR4 stands for the market share of the four largest enterprises in the industry.

12 China Cybersecurity Industry Alliance. *Analysis of the Cybersecurity Market and Corporate Competitiveness in China in 2023*, June 2023.

4. The data security market flourishes

In recent years, the scale of the data security market in China has continued to grow. Research shows that from 2017 to 2021, the scale of the data security market in China jumped from 2.29 billion *yuan* to 7.09 billion *yuan*, with a CAGR of 32.6 percent, projected to reach 10.95 billion *yuan* by 2023.[13] By October 25, 2022, there were thirty-five events of investment in China in the field of data security, with an investment amount of 6.284 billion *yuan*. As expected, the number and amount of investments continue to increase.[14]

Regarding the entities of the data security market, there are comprehensive manufacturers, such as Qi'anxin, Venustech, NSFOCUS, TOPSEC, and DAS Security, as well as manufacturers specializing in data security, such as DBSEC. Data security technology involves specific fields such as privacy computing, data-flow monitoring, data classification and grading, and data sharing and exchanges. As the scenarios of data security become more complex, products and technologies on data security develop continuously. Cybersecurity enterprises focus on solutions such as data security operation platform, zero trust data security platform, and data security monitoring platform in the field of data security, as shown in Table 4-1.

Table 4-1 Distribution of enterprises in the data security market[a]

Field	Major Enterprises
Governance of data security	DBSEC, DataSecOps, Wondersoft, Certificate Authority, Leadsec, Koal Software, VRV, DPTech, Sky Guard, MeiChuangTech, Kuaiye Information, Cloudsky Sec, Surfilter, Westone, DAS Security, Venustech, Sangfor, etc.
Database security	DBSEC, Anxin Tianxing, Strait Information, SPINFO, VRV, Koal Software, WINICSSEC, MeiChuangTech, Gile Technology, Sangfor, Goldencis, Donjin, High Dimensional Data, Cloudsky Sec, Yuanwang Information, Tencent, WebRay, DAS Security, fisec, LeagSoft, Venustech, Certificate Authority, Juming Network, etc.
Prevention of data breaches	ESAFENET, VRV, Wondersoft, LeagSoft, TOPSEC, Sangfor, NSFOCUS, Sky Guard, Venustech, etc.
Protection of personal privacy	Liuliu Security, Cipher Gateway, iTrusChina, Zhiyou Wang'an, Cloudsky Sec, Sky Guard, SPINFO, Qi'anxin, DataSecOps, IDLINK, MeiChuangTech, Donjin, etc.

13 "Prediction and Analysis of the Data Security Market in China in 2023." Accessed July 2023. https://www.askci.com/news/chanye/20230204/142740267549206055842008.shtml.

14 "The Future of the Data Security Industry as a New Trend." Accessed July 2023. http://wap.seccw.com/Index/detail/id/15915.html.

Table 4-1 *(Continued)*

Field	Major Enterprises
Document Encryption	Anxin Tianxing, Certificate Authority, VRV, Westone, Wondersoft, etc.
Disaster recovery backup	Anxin Tianxing, Gile Technology, VRV, Sangfor, Koal Software, etc.

[a]*Guide to Data Security Products*. Accessed July 2023. https://mp.weixin.qq.com/s/aA-vN7DcTiVnfXFtCvAxEw.

4.4.3 A sound ecosystem in the cybersecurity industry quickly takes shape

1. The construction of cybersecurity industrial park is actively carried out

Building cybersecurity industrial parks is an important approach and an effective path to promote resource aggregation, industrial development, and technological breakthroughs. In recent years, the Beijing National Cybersecurity Industrial Park, the Changsha National Cybersecurity Industrial Park, and the Chengdu-Chongqing National Cybersecurity Industrial Park have been successively established, which have attracted more than 500 cybersecurity enterprises.[15] The industrial chain of cybersecurity and data security is continuously improved, and the synergistic effect is continuously strengthened.

Located in Tongzhou District, the Beijing National Cybersecurity Industrial Park (Tongzhou Park) forms an overall layout of "three-park coordination, multi-point linkage and nationwide influence," with the Haidian Cybersecurity Industrial Park and the Economic Development Zone Information and Innovation Park. In November 2022, three major projects, i.e., the Cybersecurity Leading Talents Training Base, the Office and Service Supporting Facilities in Launch Area, and the Northwestern Polytechnical University Beijing Research Institute, were officially started. Currently, Cybersecurity Leading Talents Training Base of Tongzhou Park accelerates. Changsha National Cybersecurity Industrial Park focuses on the cultivation and development of an industrial cluster of new-generation independent security computing systems and establishes an industrial chain that covers the entire field of chip, operating system, host, software, cybersecurity service, etc. Founded in February 2023, the Chengdu-Chongqing National Cybersecurity Industrial Park actively builds the construction of "two cities, seven parks and one region" and forms a new pattern of "multi-point support, nationwide influence, complementary advantage and coordinated development."

15 "Strengthening the Defense Line of Cybersecurity and Ensuring a New Development Pattern with a New Security Framework." Accessed July 2023. http://www.cinic.org.cn/hy/tx/1425995.html?from=singlemessage.

Various regions actively promote the construction of cybersecurity industrial parks. The first cybersecurity industrial demonstration park in Shanghai was founded in 2022. It actively releases construction plans and supporting policies and becomes a new center for industrial clusters. Shanghai government guides social capital to establish the Cybersecurity Industry Fund of at least two billion *yuan* to support the development of the cybersecurity industry.

2. Significant achievements are made in the construction of the industrial Internet security ecosystem

Industrial Internet-related competitions, security drills, talent selection, and other activities at the national, local, and industrial levels become more diverse, and the national technical support capability for industrial Internet takes initial shape. In October 2022, the Standardization Administration approved and released a national standard, *Overall Network Architecture of Industrial Internet (GB/T 42021-2022)*. As the first national standard in the field of the industrial Internet network in China, it marks a solid step in the construction of the industrial Internet system in China. Security technology monitoring service systems at the national, provincial, and corporate levels are basically established, which cover 9.8 million Internet-connected devices, nearly 140,000 industrial enterprises, and 165 key platforms, and effectively enhance the capabilities in monitoring, early warning, and threat handling.[16] Industrial Internet enterprises in twenty provinces, autonomous regions, and municipalities directly under the central government engage in "Security Promotion Activity." Guangdong, Jiangsu, Hunan, and other regions actively promote the construction of resource pools for industrial Internet security products, technical support organizations, and security service institutions. Enterprises commonly enhance their awareness of security protection and increase their investment to security protection. More than 1,000 enterprises actively carry out classification and grading-based management of security, detect and handle security risks, and improve the level of security protection.

3. Associations and alliances build platforms to boost the development of the cybersecurity industry

The Cyber Security Association of China connects industrial organizations, co-hosts "2022 Digital Security and Rule of Law Summit Forum" and "Artificial Intelligence and Personal Information Protection Forum" with industrial organizations, promotes excellent cases in the field of data security protection in China, and serves the

16 "The Functions of Industrial Internet Are Continuously Optimized and Integrated." Accessed July 2023. https://www.cinn.cn/p/266804.html.

development of the cybersecurity industry. The China Cybersecurity Industry Alliance is committed to improving the level of cybersecurity technology industry and service, and strengthening and expanding the cybersecurity industry. In 2022, the alliance formulated and released a series of achievements such as an industrial analysis report, technological report, and alliance technological standard, built an industrial platform for technological innovation, strengthened industrial self-discipline, and promoted the work in key fields such as data security, cybersecurity service, IoV security, and the interconnection of cybersecurity products.

4.5 The Training of Cybersecurity Personnel and the Publicity and Education about Cybersecurity are Solidly Promoted

Improving public awareness of cybersecurity and cultivating cybersecurity talents play an important part in cybersecurity. In 2022, as the publicity for and education about cybersecurity was deepened, the awareness of cybersecurity among the public was significantly enhanced, and positive progress was made in the development of cybersecurity talents.

4.5.1 Demand for cybersecurity personnel continues to rise

1. Beijing, Guangdong, and Zhejiang have the biggest demand for cybersecurity talent

Currently, the supply of cybersecurity talent fails to meet the demand in China. According to the statistics from the Cybersecurity Teaching Guidance Committee of the Ministry of Education, in 2019, there was a gap of 700,000–1,400,000 cybersecurity personnel. There were about 100,000 cybersecurity staff in China, with a gap ratio of 93 percent. According to *The White Paper on Practical Skills of Cybersecurity Talents*, the demand for cybersecurity professionals will reach 3.27 million by 2027 in China.[17]

Regionally, Beijing, Guangdong, and Zhejiang have the biggest demand for cybersecurity talent. Specifically, Beijing accounts for 18 percent, Guangdong accounts for 15.2 percent, and Zhejiang accounts for 10.2 percent. Shanghai ranks fourth. *The White Paper on Practical Skills of Cybersecurity Talents* shows that the demand for cybersecurity talents in the four regions takes up nearly 50 percent of national demand.

---

17 2022 National Cybersecurity Promotion Week. *The White Paper on Practical Skills of Cybersecurity Talents*, September 2022.

2. A large number of cybersecurity personnel are needed in the energy and communications industries

The demand for cybersecurity personnel varies in industries, organizations, and enterprises. A survey shows that the energy industry ranks first in the demand for cybersecurity talent.[18] In the segmented industries, the demand of the energy industry accounts for 21 percent, followed by communications, politics and law, finance and transportation, accounting for 16 percent, 14 percent, 9 percent, and 7 percent, respectively. Noticeably, cybersecurity enterprises and the healthcare industry rank among the top ten, both accounting for 6 percent. The education industry (excluding student groups) accounts for 2 percent, with a low proportion, as shown in Figure 4-4.

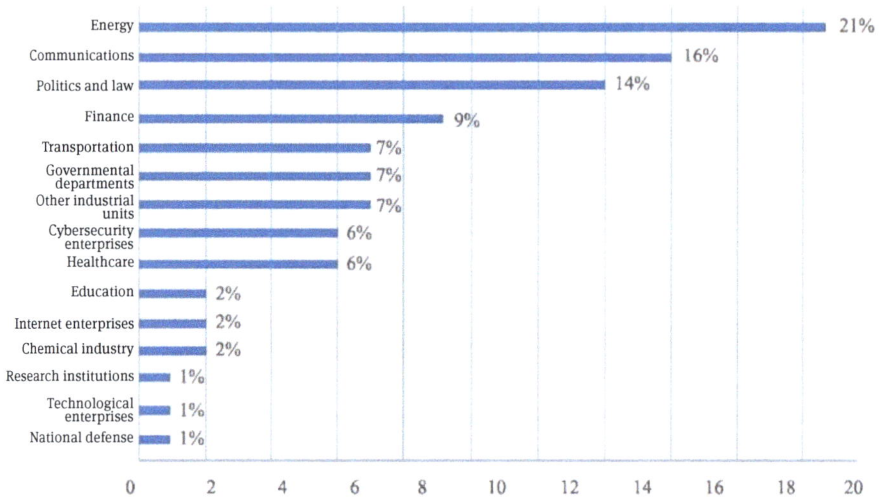

Figure 4-4 Distribution of demand for cybersecurity talents in different industries.

Source: National Cybersecurity Promotion Week.

3. The proportion of cybersecurity personnel from relevant majors increases, a prominent trend of young professionals

A survey shows that most job seekers in the cybersecurity industry come from the majors of computer science and technology, information security, and network

18 2022 National Cybersecurity Promotion Week. *The White Paper on Practical Skills of Cybersecurity Talents*, September 2022.

engineering. In addition to information security, cybersecurity-related majors such as information security and management and cyberspace security rank among the top ten. Compared with 2021, the proportion of cybersecurity personnel from relevant majors significantly increased. This indicates that the training of cybersecurity professionals achieved initial results in China.

There is a prominent trend among young professionals. In terms of age, cybersecurity personnel aged 25–40 account for more than 80 percent, and these aged 30–40 account for more than 50 percent. Comparing the data in 2021 and 2022, young cybersecurity personnel aged below 30 or 25 saw significant growth.[19]

4.5.2 Various regions actively promote the training of cybersecurity personnel

1. First-class Cybersecurity College Construction and Demonstration Project continuously advances

The First-Class Cybersecurity College Construction and Demonstration Project was jointly launched by the Office of the Central Cyberspace Affairs Commission and the Ministry of Education from 2017 to 2027. The project centers on universities, based on the principle of "voluntary application and quality-based selection." National departments strengthen guidance and support, and give full play to the initiative of local governments, enterprises, and society so as to jointly build world-class cybersecurity colleges. In 2017 and 2019, eleven universities in two groups were selected for the project. Since the implementation of the project, under the guidance and with the support of relevant departments and local governments, eleven universities have achieved significant results in policy guarantees, funding investment, basic conditions, teaching staff, student training, and research and innovation. Great progress is made in the construction of cybersecurity colleges.

In July 2022, under the guidance of the Office of the Central Cyberspace Affairs Commission, Internet and IT enterprises, first-class cybersecurity colleges, the Cyber Security Association of China and the China Internet Development Foundation jointly launched the Innovation Funding Plan for Students in Cybersecurity Colleges. Currently, six enterprises, including TOPSEC, Qi'anxin, Ant Group, NIO, Huawei, and Didi, participate in the plan. The plan was implemented in 2022. Since then, the six enterprises have proposed 103 tasks for innovation based on their needs for innovation. Students apply for and complete the tasks. Two hundred forty students have been funded. This establishes a new model of joint technological innovation

19 Talent Exchange Center of Ministry of Industry and Information Technology. *Report on the Development of Talents in the Cybersecurity Industry 2022*, September 2022.

between enterprises and universities and achieves desirable results. In 2023, in the First Wuhan Cybersecurity Innovation Forum, an exchange meeting on the integration and innovation achievements of cybersecurity education and technology industries was organized. Students who received the funds of Innovation Funding Plan for Students in Cybersecurity Colleges (Phase-I), as well as mentors from universities and enterprises, participated in the event.

2. The construction of the National Cybersecurity Talent and Innovation Base accelerates

The National Cybersecurity Talent and Innovation Base is located in the Linkonggang Economic and Technological Development Zone, Wuhan, Hubei. With a mission of national strategy, it was fully launched in September 2016. In May 2023, the Phase-I project of the National Cybersecurity Talent and Innovation Base Sharing Center was completed and put into use, which greatly improved the functional support of the National Cybersecurity Base Park and promoted industrial development.

On May 16–17, 2023, the First Wuhan Cybersecurity Innovation Forum was successfully held in the National Cybersecurity Talent and Innovation Base. The forum was guided by the Office of the Central Cyberspace Affairs Commission and the Hubei Provincial Government and hosted by the Wuhan Municipal Government. Under the theme of "Driven by Innovation, Building a Healthy Ecology of the Integration and Development of Cybersecurity Education, Technology and Industry," the forum focused on technological innovation and talent cultivation for cybersecurity, explored strategic and forward-looking issues of cybersecurity, trends in cutting-edge technologies, trends in industrial development and industrial solutions, and organized exchange events on the achievements of cybersecurity innovation. More than 500 academicians, experts, entrepreneurs, and university teachers and students participated in the forum. The forum released ten outstanding achievements of cybersecurity innovation, as well as two themed reports, *Report on the Construction of Cybersecurity Talents in China 2022* and *Personal Information Protection Index Report on Commonly Used Apps by the Public.*

3. The training of professionals in data security and cryptography continuously improves

To promote the professionalism of data security personnel, the Cyber Security Association of China formulates national professional standards for personnel in data security engineering and technology. In March 2023, the Ministry of Human Resources and Social Security, the Office of the Central Cyberspace Affairs Commission, and the Ministry of Industry and Information Technology issued *National Occupational Standards for Data Security Engineering Technicians*, which provides a standardized and detailed description of professional activities of data security engineering personnel, clarifies the fields, content, knowledge levels, professional abilities, and practical requirements of professional and technical personnel at all levels, and plays an important role in promoting the cultivation and development of data security talents.

The training of cryptographic personnel continues to be strengthened. By April 2023, fifteen universities in China offered undergraduate programs in Cryptographic Science and Technology, and nine local universities established schools or departments of cryptography. The newly revised *Catalogue of Graduate Education Disciplines 2022* officially includes cryptography as an interdisciplinary category. *Occupational Classification Code of the People's Republic of China (2022 Edition)* adds a new occupation of "cryptographic engineering technician." The Ministry of Human Resources and Social Security and the State Cryptography Administration jointly issued *National Vocational Skill Standards for Cryptographic Technology Applicants* and *National Vocational and Technical Skill Standards for Cryptographic Engineering Technicians*, which provide guarantees for further improving the quality of training cryptographic professionals.

4.5.3 Publicity and education about cybersecurity is positively advanced, and awareness about cybersecurity is significantly enhanced

1. National Cybersecurity Promotion Week is held continuously

Organizing National Cybersecurity Promotion Week and enhancing public awareness and skills in cybersecurity play an important part in the work of national cybersecurity. Since 2014, National Cybersecurity Promotion Week has been held for nine consecutive sessions. On September 5–11, 2022, National Cybersecurity Promotion Week was staged nationwide, under the theme of "Cybersecurity serves the people, Cybersecurity depends on the people." Important events, such as the opening ceremony, Cybersecurity Expo, and Cybersecurity Technology Summit Forum, were held in Hefei, Anhui. During the week, various regions carried out online and offline activities such as cybersecurity education cloud classes, cybersecurity competitions, and cybersecurity at the grassroots level, as well as six series of themed days such as campus day, telecom day, and personal information protection day. In National Cybersecurity Promotion Week in 2022, the topics on themed events were read 3.86 billion times, 1.3 billion public short messages were pushed, and short videos were viewed more than 500 million times, creating a strong atmosphere for safeguarding cybersecurity nationwide.

Panel 4-1

The First Group of National Cybersecurity Education, Technology and Industry Integration, and Development Pilot Zones Officially Unveiled

On September 5, 2022, the first group of National Cybersecurity Education, Technology and Industry Integration, and Development Pilot Zones were officially unveiled. They are Hefei High-tech Industrial Development Zone in Anhui, Haidian District in Beijing, Yanta District in Xi'an, Shaanxi, Changsha High-tech Industrial Development Zone in Hunan, and Jinan High-tech Industrial Development Zone in Shandong.

The pilot zones are jointly organized and implemented by the Office of the Central Cyberspace Affairs Commission, the Ministry of Education, the Ministry of Science and Technology, and the Ministry of Industry and Information Technology. By promoting the construction of pilot zones, China aims to explore new mechanisms and models for the integration and development of cybersecurity education, technology, and industry; formulate a series of systems and policies to encourage and support integration and development; cultivate a number of innovative carriers to support integration and development; summarize experiences and practices that can be followed, copied and promoted; and accelerate the formation of a healthy ecosystem for the cultivation of cybersecurity talents and the development of technological and industrial innovation nationwide.

2. Public awareness of cybersecurity is enhanced by organizing themed publicity and education, as well as annual meetings on cybersecurity

Through innovative content supply, a multi-angle communication matrix, and an accurate push to the public, relevant departments launch cybersecurity publicity and education on important occasions. By June 1, 2022, *Cybersecurity Law* was implemented for five years. The Office of the Central Cyberspace Affairs Commission initiated a themed publicity and education campaign. A series of short videos on law popularization were released, with more than ten million views. More than twenty platforms pushed themed screens on mobile media, covering 300 million people. More than twenty columns were established, with more than 20 million clicks. Relevant topics on Weibo, Douyin, Kuaishou, and other platforms were read more than 400 million times.[20]

20 Office of the Central Cyberspace Affairs Commission. "Enhancing the Cybersecurity Awareness and Skills among the Public on a Regular Basis." Accessed July 2023. http://news.china.com.cn/2022-09/02/content_78402341.htm.

Organizing a cybersecurity conference is an important approach to strengthening cybersecurity publicity and education. In August 2022, CNCERT/CC organized the China Cybersecurity Annual Meeting, under the theme of "Jointly Guaranteeing Security for Digital Information Infrastructure," providing a bridge and link for technological and business exchanges among various sectors of industry, academia, research, and applications in domestic cybersecurity. In July, the Cyber Security Association of China and other organizations jointly hosted the "2022 Beijing Cybersecurity Conference," inviting more than 500 experts and leaders in the cybersecurity industry from more than ten countries and regions, and organizing more than fifty themed activities.

3. The evaluation of Internet users on the satisfaction with cybersecurity remains stable

In August 2022, 135 cybersecurity industry associations and related social organizations nationwide launched a survey of the satisfaction of Internet users with cybersecurity. A total of 3,031,775 survey samples were collected, and the *2022 General Report on the Survey of the Satisfaction of Internet Users with Cybersecurity* was released in December, which comprehensively reflected the attitudes of Internet users and industrial personnel towards cybersecurity in China. As shown, the satisfaction index of cybersecurity in 2022 was 73.399 (according to the original statistical standard, the satisfaction index was 73.469), with a year-on-year increase of 0.047 percent over 2021. Close to sixty percent, or 58.48 percent of Internet users rated the overall state of cybersecurity governance in China as satisfactory or very satisfactory.[21] As the data shows, in 2022, the evaluation of Internet users on the satisfaction with cybersecurity remained stable, better than 2021, reflecting remarkable results achieved in cybersecurity governance in 2022.

21 "2022 General Report on the Survey of the Satisfaction of Internet Users with Cybersecurity Week Was Officially Staged." Accessed July 2023. https://baijiahao.baidu.com/s?id=1752011596450048639&wfr=spider&for=pc.

10.2478/9788367405867-006

Chapter 5
Law-based Governance of Cyberspace

The report of the 20th CPC National Congress stresses that "The comprehensive advancement of law-based governance has been a profound revolution in China's governance. Law-based governance is important for the Party's success in governing and rejuvenating the country, for the wellbeing of the people, and for the long-term stability of the Party and the country." In March 2023, the State Council Information Office released the white paper *Law-based Governance of Cyberspace in China in the New Era*. As the first white paper on law-based governance of cyberspace in China, it plays a great role in learning and implementing the spirit of the 20th CPC National Congress and accelerating building China into a country with cyber strength as well as a digital nation. Over the past year, China took the rule of law as an important approach to Internet governance and made phased results in law-based governance of cyberspace. The legislative system in cyberspace was continuously improved, and the law enforcement in cyberspace was carried out in a fair, civilized and orderly way. Smart justice enhanced the effectiveness of cyberspace governance, and the popularization of the laws relating to cyberspace deepened the public understanding of the law.

5.1 Legislation in Cyberspace is Continuously Promoted

The legal system for the governance of cybersecurity basically takes shape. *Combating Telecom and Online Fraud Law* is issued, the management system for cross-border data flow is continuously improved, and the legislative protection and support for critical information infrastructure are continually strengthened. In medical care, electric power companies, and other industries, the cybersecurity responsibilities are clarified. The law on the digital economy is optimized, the framework of basic data system is determined, and the protection of data intellectual property is enhanced. Local legislation on the digital economy is accelerated. Multiple measures are taken to promote the governance of online content, combat cyber violence, strengthen the protection of special groups, and standardize the governance of Internet information and content. Relevant departments standardize the healthy development of new technologies and applications, quicken the formulation of the systems for the development of the AI industry, clarify the requirements for the operation and management of ICV, strengthen the regulation of the information security of deep synthesis technology, and focus on precise management of online ride-hailing services.

5.1.1 Legislation in cybersecurity is vigorously promoted

With the change in the cybersecurity landscape and the emergence of new problems, the legislation on cybersecurity has been adjusted accordingly. Over the past year, China improved institutional design in such fields as the protection of critical information infrastructure and the regulation of data outbound transfer and data cross-border flow and deepened law-based governance of cyberspace. *Combating Telecom and Online Fraud Law* is issued. In recent years, China has deepened its efforts to crack down on illegal and criminal activities related to telecom and online fraud. In order to effectively prevent, curb, and punish telecom and online fraud, strengthen the combat against telecom and online fraud, protect the legitimate rights and interests of citizens and organizations, and maintain social stability and national security, in September 2022, the 36th meeting of the Standing Committee of the 13th National People's Congress voted to pass *Combating Telecom and Online Fraud Law of the People's Republic of China*, which would come into effect on December 1, 2022. The law covers seven chapters and fifty articles, including General Provisions, Telecom Governance, Finance Governance, Internet Governance, Comprehensive Measures, Legal Responsibilities, and Supplementary Provisions. In terms of rules, the law clarifies the concept and scope of application of telecom and online fraud, stipulates the working mechanism and functional division, establishes the publicity for, education about, and prevention of telecom and online fraud, improves basic management systems, coordinates the construction of various technological countermeasures, determines punitive measures and appeal and relief channels, and provides comprehensive legal support for combating telecom and online fraud.

The management system for cross-border data flow continuously improves. In order to implement the requirements of relevant regulations on data outbound transfer in *Cybersecurity Law*, *Data Security Law* and *Personal Information Protection Law*, supporting departmental rules and normative documents, such as *Measures on Security Evaluation of Data Outbound Transfer*, *Measures on Standard Contract of Personal Information Outbound Transfer*, and *Announcement on Implementing the Protection and Certification of Personal Information* have been successively issued since 2022, which further clarify the requirements for data outbound transfer, and protect personal information and rights, social public interests, and national security. So far, the framework for the management system of the security of data outbound transfer has been basically established, and the paths for legal data outbound transfer have been clarified in rules (including security evaluation, standard contracts, and the protection and certification of personal information), which provide practical guidance for the implementation of the three paths. *Measures on Security Evaluation of Data Outbound Transfer* officially clarifies the procedures and requirements of the security evaluation of data outbound transfer, especially the requirements for the security evaluation of important cross-border data, reflects the unique role of important data in cross-border data protection, and highlights national security-oriented requirements for cross-border data. According to the *Measures*, the scope of the security evaluation of data outbound transfer covers important data and personal information, and spotlights the system design for the self-evaluation of risks to data outbound transfer. *Measures on Standard Contract of Personal Information Outbound Transfer* specifies the applicable scenarios of providing personal information to overseas organizations via signing standard contracts, determining the main content of standard contracts, and providing examples of standard contracts. *Implementation Rules for the Protection and Certification of Personal Information* in *Announcement on Implementing the Protection and Certification of Personal Information* is the first special system on the protection and certification of personal information in China. It officially establishes the status of the protection and certification of personal information in the Chinese legal system for personal information protection, further improves the certification and accreditation system for data security in China, and promotes building a more scientific and efficient governance system for data security.

In June 2023, the Office of the Central Cyberspace Affairs Commission and Innovation, the Technology and Industry Bureau of the Government of the Hong Kong Special Administrative Region signed *Memorandum of Cooperation on Promoting Cross-border Data Flow in Guangdong-Hong Kong-Macao Greater Bay Area*. Under the framework of the national data cross-border security management system, the two sides established security rules for cross-border data flow in the Guangdong-Hong Kong-Macao Greater Bay Area, promoted cross-border data flow in a secure and orderly way, and fostered high-quality development of the Guangdong-Hong Kong-Macao Greater Bay Area. Grounded in the basic idea of balancing security and development, the regulatory system for cross-border data flow provides a practical legal basis for outbound data transfer.

In September 2023, the Office of the Central Cyberspace Affairs Commission solicited opinions on *Regulations on Standardizing and Promoting Cross-border Data Flow (Draft for Comments)*, aiming to ensure national data security, protect personal information and rights, and further regulate and promote the legal, orderly, and free flow of data.

Legislative protection and support for critical information infrastructure are consolidated. Critical information infrastructure plays a pivotal role in the operation of the digital society. In recent years, China has strengthened and improved legislative protection and support for critical information infrastructure. In April 2023, the 2nd meeting of the Standing Committee of the 14th National People's Congress voted to pass the newly-revised *Anti-Espionage Law of the People's Republic of China*, which would come into effect on July 1, 2023. The newly revised law clearly defines "acts such as cyberattacks on state organs, confidential units or critical information infrastructure as espionage." Additionally, key industries and fields continuously release and improve normative documents for the protection of critical information infrastructure. In April 2023, the Ministry of Transport issued *Management Measures on the Protection of the Security of Critical Information Infrastructure of Highways and Waterways*, which clarifies the identification standards for critical information infrastructure of highways and waterways and determines the protection responsibilities of corresponding operating entities, in order to build a collaborative governance system for critical information infrastructure of highways and waterways among transport-management departments at various levels. In August 2022, the National Health Commission, the National Administration of Traditional Chinese Medicine, and the National Disease Control and Prevention Administration issued *Management Measures on Cybersecurity of Medical and Health Institutions*, which specifies protection requirements for critical information infrastructure of medical and health institutions, in order to ensure the secure and stable operation of critical information infrastructure and protect the integrity, confidentiality, and availability of data. In December 2022, the National Energy Administration issued *Management Measures on Cybersecurity in the Power Industry* and *Management Measures on the Grading-Based Protection of Cybersecurity in the Power Industry*, which require operators of critical information infrastructure in the power industry to prioritize the procurement of secure and trustworthy cybersecurity products and services and conduct risk assessments by relevant requirements. The legislative protection of critical information infrastructure extends to specific fields, providing accurate and professional protection systems for key industries under a unified legislative protection framework.

The responsibilities for cybersecurity in key fields are clarified. Medical care, the electric power industry, and other industries relate to the national economy and people's livelihood. The secure and stable operation of their business systems is closely bound up with national security, public security, and the daily life of citizens. Cybersecurity is a prerequisite for the operation of their business systems. Therefore, under the general legislative framework of cybersecurity, industrial standards for cybersecurity are formulated in key industries based on industrial characteristics. In August 2022, *Management Measures on Cybersecurity of Medical and Health Institutions* was released, which clarifies basic principles, division of labor of management, execution standards, and requirements for supervision and punishment for the management of cybersecurity and data security of various medical and health institutions, reflects an overall balance between security and development, and signals general direction for the management of cybersecurity for various medical and health institutions. In December 2022, the newly revised *Management Measures on Cybersecurity in the Power Industry* clarified the responsibilities and work of the National Energy Administration and its dispatched agencies, as well as local energy regulatory departments and power-dispatching agencies responsible for the supervision and management of cybersecurity in the power industry. The Administration stipulated requirements for protection of security of critical information infrastructure, procurement of cybersecurity products and services, risk assessments, monitoring and early warning and information notification, building emergency capability, ensuring security during important periods, emergency response, disaster recovery backup, data security, financial support, talent cultivation, management of security-dedicated products, and summary reporting among power enterprises. In various industries, industrial standards on cybersecurity tally with industrial characteristics, clarify specific responsibilities for cybersecurity of institutions, enhance the awareness of cybersecurity, and effectively ensure cybersecurity in key industries.

5.1.2 Law on the digital economy is gradually improved

The digital economy possesses great significance for optimizing resource allocation, promoting industrial upgrading, and fostering economic circulation. In central and local legislation, supporting polices are formulated to boost the innovation and development of the digital economy in a standardized and healthy way.

The framework of basic data system is clarified. The contributions of data elements are rated by the market, which determines the returns of entities. This mechanism enables all people to better share in the development achievements of the digital economy and promotes common prosperity. In December 2022, the CPC Central Committee and the State Council issued *Twenty Articles on Data, which centers on accelerating* the compliant and efficient circulation and use of data and empowering real economy, proposes twenty policies and measures from four aspects, i.e., data property rights, data circulation and transaction, distribution of data profits, and governance of data security, and builds basic data systems in China, aiming to fully unleash the value of data elements and promote the sharing of the dividends of the development of the digital economy for all people. *Twenty Articles on Data* proposes to establish a three-right framework for data property rights system (the right to hold data resources, the right to process and use data, and the right to manage data products), which provides guidance for the legislative construction of the allocation of data rights in the market-oriented allocation of data elements. The classification and grading-based framework of "general data, important data, and core data" is established in line with the *Data Security Law*. The formulation of relevant measures and regulations clarifies the data classification and grading-based protection system. *Regulations on the Management of Data Security in Cyberspace (Draft for Comments)* have been published, covering personal information protection and obligations of Internet platform operators. Special industrial standards have also been established based on data classification and grading in key industries. For example, in December 2022, the Ministry of Industry and Information Technology issued *Measures on the*

Management of Data Security in the Industry and Information Technology Fields (Trial), which takes data grading-based protection as an overall principle, and strengthens the full lifecycle security management of general data, the protection of important data, and the strict protection of core data. The *Measures* clarifies the classification and grading standards for the data on industry and information technology, which can be divided into industrial data, telecom data and radio data (classification) and general data, important data and core data (grading). Notably, the classification and grading standards for the data can be applied flexibly. Data processors in the industry and information technology fields may further divide data on this basis. Additionally, national standards outline detailed and specific regulations on the classification and identification of important data. For example, in September 2022, the National Information Security Standards Committee issued *Requirements for the Classification and Grading of Data on Information Security Technology and Network (Draft for Comments)*, which further clarifies and implements the requirements for data classification and grading in *Data Security Law*, and elaborates on basic principles, frameworks, methods, and procedures for data classification and grading.

The protection of intellectual property is continuously strengthened. The high-quality development of the digital economy hinges on comprehensive support of the modernization of the governance system of intellectual property. Some provinces and cities first explored the management system of intellectual property registration. In June 2023, the Zhejiang Administration for Market Regulation, the Office of Cyberspace Affairs Commission of Zhejiang, and other nine departments jointly issued *Measures on Data Intellectual Property Registration in Zhejiang (Trial)*, which would come into effect on July 1, 2023. The *Measures* puts forward requirements for intellectual property registration in terms of scope of application, registration application and supervision and management, and establishes a protection system for intellectual property registration with clear ownership, traceable sources, compliant operation, and a governance system. Efforts are taken to address issues such as unclear data ownership, insufficient data innovation and utilization, and difficulty in providing evidence for protection of data rights. In June 2023, the Beijing Municipal Intellectual Property Office and three other departments issued *Management Measures on Data Intellectual Property Registration in Beijing (Trial)*, which includes five parts, i.e., General Provisions, Registration Content, Registration Procedures, Management and Supervision, and Supplementary Provisions; clarifies the main matters of intellectual property registration such as objects, subjects, and procedures; actively promotes the application of registration certificates in administrative law enforcement, judicial trial and legal supervision; fully leverages the role of registration certificates; and effectively protects the legitimate rights and interests of data processors. Relevant management departments of intellectual property encourage the advancement of registration certificates and promote the innovation, development, dissemination, and utilization of data as well as the realization of data value. This further strengthens the application of registration certificates in administrative law enforcement, judicial trial and legal supervision, fully leverages the role of registration certificates, enhances the protection of data intellectual property, and effectively protects the legitimate rights and interests of data processors.

Local legislation on the digital economy is accelerating. Currently, various regions successively release regulations on data and take legislative means to revitalize data resources, unleash data value, and empower real economy. In 2022, with the rapid development of the digital economy in China, various provinces and cities actively research and introduce local regulations to promote the development of the digital economy, and stimulate and utilize the economic value of data elements. For example, local regulations, such as *Regulations on Promoting Digital Economy in Beijing*, *Regulations on Promoting Digital Economy in Henan*, *Regulations on Promoting Digital Economy in Jiangsu*, and *Regulations on Promoting Digital Economy in Hebei* have been successively issued. Simultaneously, various provinces and cities energetically introduce regulations on the opening and sharing of public data. In recent years, Zhejiang, Jiangsu, Guangdong, Shandong, and other regions have actively explored the system for the opening and utilization of public data, and successively released special normative documents on the opening of public data, such as *Regulations on Public Data in Zhejiang*, *Measures on the Opening of Public Data in Shandong*, and *Interim Measures on the Opening of Public Data in Guangdong*. In addition to provincial-level normative documents, many cities have issued special documents on the opening of public data, such as *Management Measures on the Opening of Public Data in Guangzhou* and *Implementation Plan for the Authorization and Operation of Public Data in Hangzhou (Trial)*. Several provinces and cities, including Beijing, Shanghai, Guangdong, and Zhejiang, actively explore and practice the procedures and models of the authorization and operation of public data, launch innovative mechanisms such as chief data officer, data asset voucher, data customs, and a regulatory sandbox, and promote and implement the authorization and operation of public data.

5.1.3 Measures on the governance of the online environment are effectively implemented

The report of the 20th CPC National Congress stresses that in the new era, "the online environment has seen continuous improvement," and "All this has brought overarching and fundamental changes in China's ideological landscape." In 2022, regulatory authorities continued to build and improve a comprehensive system of cyberspace governance, issue special regulations for common scenarios in Internet information services such as pop-up information push and post comments, and optimize specific rules of the governance of online content.

The governance of cyber violence is strengthened. The Internet is not a place beyond the rule of law. To counter cyber violence, regulatory authorities step up efforts to strengthen the management responsibilities of Internet platforms, and guide Internet users to strictly observe laws and regulations, respect social ethics, jointly resist cyber violence, and resolutely prevent Internet users from being subjected to cyber violence. In November 2022, the Office of the Central Cyberspace Affairs Commission issued *Notice on Strengthening the Governance of Cyber Violence*, which focuses on four aspects, i.e., establishing and improving early warning and prevention mechanisms against cyber violence, strengthening the protection of parties involved in cyber violence, curbing the spread of misinformation on cyber violence, and strictly punishing illegal platforms and accounts in accordance with the law. It aims to improve the mechanisms and measures on the entire chain of governance of cyber violence, guide websites and platforms to provide the function of one-click protection, optimize the rules on private messages, establish immediate reporting channels, and protect parties involved from being subjected to cyber violence. In April 2023, the Supreme People's Procuratorate issued *Opinions on Strengthening the Law in Cyberspace by Procuratorial Organs in the New Era*. The *Opinions* propose to strictly punish crimes infringing on citizens' personal rights such as cyber violence, explore the industrial chain and interest chain behind cybercrimes, severely crack down on crimes such as spreading rumors and attracting traffic, extorting public opinion, click farming and controlling comments and paid post deletions by paid posters, jointly address prominent issues such as making and spreading rumors, false information, and illegal profit-making of We Media, strengthen the announcement and exposure of typical cases, and purify the online environment for public opinion. In July 2023, the Office of the Central Cyberspace Affairs Commission released *Regulations on the Governance of Information on Cyber Violence (Draft for Comments)*, and solicited opinions, aiming to effectively strengthen the governance of information on cyber violence and create a good online ecosystem. In September 2023, the Supreme People's Court, the Supreme People's Procuratorate, and the Ministry of Public Security issued *Guiding Opinions on Punishing Illegal Crimes of Cyber Violence in Accordance with the Law*, which clarifies legal provisions applicable to behaviors such as online defamation, online insults, cyber hunt, offline harassment, and malicious marketing or hype through cyber violence incidents, and stipulates the aggravating circumstances of cyber-violence-related crimes by utilizing deep synthesis, organizing paid posters, and other behaviors, aiming to continuously improve the long-term mechanism of the governance of cyber violence.

The governance of Internet information and content is standardized. The governance of Internet content plays an important part in the modernization of the capabilities in national governance and social governance. In September 2022, the Cyberspace Administration of China, the Ministry of Industry and Information Technology, and the State Administration for Market Regulation jointly released *Regulations on Internet Pop-up Information Push Service*, which would be implemented on September 30, 2022. The *Regulations* puts forward governance requirements for pop ups, such as pop-up ads, message bombardment, and pop ups from internal software. For example, there are specific requirements such as prohibiting the push of illegal and harmful information, and the setting of algorithmic models inducing user addiction and excessive consumption. The *Regulations* fills the gap in the structural deficiency of the legislative system of pop-up regulations, improves the applicability, connectivity, and operability of relevant laws and regulations, and provides a clear basis and practical guidance for enterprises to standardize the operation of the push of Internet pop-up information. In November 2022, the Cyberspace Administration of China issued the newly revised *Regulations on the Management of Internet Post Comment Services*, which strengthens the standardization and management of Internet post comment services, and promotes the healthy development of Internet post comment services. The *Regulations* mainly clarifies the management responsibilities of post comment service providers for post comments, as well as the behavioral norms of post comment service users and public account production operators. In addition, legal obligations have been established for the users of post comment services, and "harmful information" has been included within the regulatory scope of post comment services.

The protection of special groups in cyberspace is enhanced. The white paper *Law-based Governance of Cyberspace in China in the New Era* emphasizes that "while establishing a legal system for protecting the rights in cyberspace, we should protect the digital rights of special groups." The legislation on online protection for special groups such as minors, the elderly, and women enables them to integrate into digital society more equally and widely, and enjoy the dividends of the digital era. On January 1, 2023, the fully revised *Law on the Protection of the Rights and Interests of Women of the People's Republic of China* officially came into effect. Regarding acts or phenomena that infringe on women's rights and interests through the use of information networks, Article 27 and Article 82 stipulate that it is prohibited to organize, force, lure, shelter, and introduce women to engage in obscene performances in any place or on the Internet, and that anyone who belittles and harms women's personalities through mass media or other means must bear administrative responsibilities in accordance with the law. This further establishes a special protection mechanism for women in cyberspace. In May 2023, the General Office of the CPC Central Committee and the General Office of the State Council issued *Opinions on Promoting the Construction of Basic Elderly Care Service System*, emphasizing that based on the National Integrated Government Service Platform, China will promote cross-departmental data sharing, establish a precise identification and dynamic management mechanism for elderly people with difficulties, optimize institutional arrangements related to the permanent population and radius of service range, and transition from "finding services for people" to "finding people for services." China will deepen the integration of resources in the identification, treatment, and service delivery of disabled elderly people as well as the construction of barrier-free environments, and strengthen the guarantee of elder care services for disabled elderly people. In June 2023, the 3rd meeting of the Standing Committee of the 14th National People's Congress passed *Law on the Construction of*

Barrier-Free Environments of the People's Republic of China, which would come into effect on September 1, 2023. The law stresses the need to strengthen the construction of barrier-free environments and eliminate tangible or intangible obstacles in various fields such as public facilities, transportation, information exchanges, and social services so as to ensure that disabled people and elderly people can participate equally and fully in social production and life. The law reflects the intrinsic requirement of safeguarding the human rights and interests of disabled people and elderly people, and promoting the development of China's human rights cause.

The management of mobile app distribution platforms is strengthened. In order to strengthen the legal supervision and comprehensive governance of mobile Internet apps and promote the healthy and orderly development of app information services, in June 2022, the Office of the Central Cyberspace Affairs Commission issued the newly revised *Regulations on the Management of Mobile Internet App Information Services*, which would be implemented on August 1, 2022. New business forms of apps such as applets, fast apps, and browser plug-ins will be regulated, with clear requirements for standardizing the filing management of mobile app distribution platforms. As required, app providers and app distribution platforms must fulfill the responsibilities of information content management and establish and improve management systems of the management of information content security, the governance of information content ecology, the protection of data security and personal information and minors protection, in order to ensure cybersecurity and maintain a good Internet ecology.

5.1.4 Development of new technologies and new business models is standardized

The innovation and application of digital technologies not only promote social development and facilitate social life but also bring new risks and challenges to cyberspace governance. Over the past year, in response to new technologies and applications such as AI, algorithms, and deep synthesis, relevant departments have successively introduced special regulations, prioritized urgent needs, and enriched the laws in specific fields in a fast and flexible way.

Special legislation promotes the development of the AI industry. AI is a strategic technology that will drive a new round of technological revolution and industrial transformation. China has successively issued a series of policies to support the development of AI as it enters a new stage of development in China. At the national level, in July 2023, the Office of the Central Cyberspace Affairs Commission, in collaboration with the National Development and Reform Commission, the Ministry of Education, the Ministry of Science and Technology, the Ministry of Industry and Information Technology, the Ministry of Public Security, and th eNational Radio and Television Administration released *Interim Measures on the Management of Generative Artificial Intelligence Services*. As stated, China adheres to the principle of balancing development and security and promoting innovation and legal governance and takes effective measures to encourage the innovation and development of generative AI. Specific measures are proposed to promote the development of generative AI technology. At the local level, Shenzhen and Shanghai have successively passed special legislation to promote the healthy development of the AI industry. In September 2022, Shenzhen released the first special law on the AI industry in China, *Regulations on Promoting the Development of the Artificial Intelligence Industry in Shenzhen Special Economic Zone*. In order to solve the problem of applying AI products, Shenzhen proposes an access system of innovative products and first establishes an AI statistical and monitoring system. Low-risk AI products and services are allowed to conduct tests, experiments, and pilots. In the same month, Shanghai published *Regulations on Promoting the Development of the Artificial Intelligence Industry in Shanghai*. As the first provincial-level local regulation in the field of AI, it constructs a basic institutional framework for the standardized development of the AI industry and clarifies the key areas and directions of AI development as well as relevant supporting policies and management mechanisms. In addition, it specifies industrial norms, prohibitive behaviors, and punitive rules, breaks the bottlenecks in the development of the AI industry, and accelerates the standardized development of AI-related industries, technologies, and applications.

The regulation of information security of deep synthesis technology is improved. In order to regulate the behaviors of deep synthesis service providers in technological development and application, regulatory authorities actively explore feasible regulatory paths for deep synthesis technology. In November 2022, the Cyberspace Administration of China, the Ministry of Industry and Information Technology, and the Ministry of Public Security issued *Regulations on the Management of Deep Synthesis in Internet Information Services*. It imposses specific requirements for the responsibilities of providers, technological supporters, and users of deep synthesis services, further clarifies and optimizes the application scenarios of deep synthesis technology, and determines the obligations of providers and users of deep synthesis services in information security. As stipulated, national departments of cyberspace affairs are responsible for coordinating the governance, regulation, and management of deep synthesis services nationwide. Simultaneously, various industries formulate industrial standards on deep synthesis technology and service. For example, in April 2023, the China Mobile Communications Association Metaverse Consensus Circle and the China Communications Industry Association Professional Committee of Blockchain jointly released *Industrial Tips on the Application of Generative Artificial Intelligence (Like ChatGPT) in Metaverse*, which proposes to strictly comply with relevant national and industrial laws and regulations, enhance the awareness of compliance and prudent operation, and comprehensively improve the level of risk control.

The requirements for the operation and management of ICV are clarified. In terms of the institutional support of ICV, China actively explores the formulation of regulations on ICV road testing and demonstration applications, access and registration, cybersecurity and data protection, and handling of traffic violations and accidents. In August 2022, in order to adapt to the development trend of autonomous driving technology, encourage and standardize the application of autonomous vehicle in the field of transport service and ensure transport safety, the Ministry of Transport organized the drafting of *Guides on the Safety and Services of Autonomous Vehicles Transport (Trial)*, on the basis of systematically investigating the pilot, demonstration, and operation of autonomous vehicles, which specifies that transport operators, vehicles, and personnel should meet requirements when autonomous vehicles engage in transport operations. In the same month, the Ministry of Natural Resources issued *Notice on Promoting the Development and Maintenance of Surveying and Mapping Geographic Information Security in Intelligent Connected Vehicles*, which clarifies the application and implementation of relevant laws, regulations, and policies on surveying and mapping geographic information and data collection and management in ICV applications. In October 2022, the Ministry of Industry and Information Technology issued *Regulations on Production Access Permits for Road Motor Vehicles (Draft for Comments)*, which proposes special requirements for the management of ICV in terms of the management of production access permits and the obligations of production enterprises. In November 2022, the Ministry of Industry and Information Technology issued *Notice on the Pilot Work of Intelligent Connected Vehicles Access and Road Traffic (Draft for Comments)*, which elaborates on the pilot work of ICV access and road traffic. Since 2022, multiple ministries and commissions have released documents to clarify the requirements for the management of ICV and actively promote the pilot work of ICV. In the legislation on autonomous driving, China has progressed from standards for the testing of ICV to standards for the commercial application of ICV. Simultaneously, local legislation actively explores the standards for ICV. For example, in June 2022, Shenzhen issued *Regulations on the Management of Intelligent Connected Vehicles in Shenzhen Special Economic Zone*, which standardizes the entire industrial chain of ICV. In November 2022, the Shanghai Municipal Transportation Commission released *Implementation Rules for the Demonstration and Operation of Intelligent Connected Vehicles in Shanghai*, providing practical guidance for enterprises to carry out the demonstration and operation of ICV. The legislation at the national and local levels explores the standards on ICV and establishes a solid foundation for the high-quality development of the ICV industry.

Relevant departments focus on the precise management of online ride-hailing services. While formulating rules to maintain market order, relevant departments encourage the innovation in operation models and cultivate or develop new business models. In 2016, *Interim Measures on the Management of the Operation and Service of Online Taxi Booking* and *Notice on Strengthening During-After-the-Event Joint Regulation of the Online Taxi Booking Industry* were successively released. In November 2022, the Ministry of Transport, the Ministry of Industry and Information Technology, the Ministry of Public Security, the Ministry of Commerce, the State

Administration for Market Regulation, and the Office of the Central Cyberspace Affairs Commission jointly issued *Decision on Amending Interim Measures on the Management of the Operation and Service of Online Taxi Booking*, which took effect from the date of publication. In the amendments, the regulation on the fine for not carrying transportation certificates and driver's licenses of online taxi booking as required is deleted, and the amount of fines for engaging in online ride-hailing without obtaining the two certificates is lowered. The *Decision* implements specific requirements in *Decision of the State Council on Cancelling and Adjusting Several Penalty Matters*, promotes "streamlining of administration, delegating powers, and improving regulation and services" reform, and optimizes the business environment, which effectively balance regulation and market demand, and alleviate practical problems of taxi booking and ride-hailing in cities.

5.2 Law Enforcement in Cyberspace is Standardized

In order to give full play to law enforcement and regulation, relevant national departments focus on prominent problems in data security, personal information protection and other fields, continuously strengthen law enforcement and regulation, and effectively safeguard a fair, equitable, civilized, and orderly cyberspace. In addition, relevant national departments crack down on malpractice in information content such as online rumors and cyber violence in accordance with the law, strengthen the law enforcement in the field of personal information protection, carry out law enforcement in the anti-monopoly work on platforms, actively launch campaigns against telecom and online fraud, issue *Regulations on Administrative Law-Enforcement Procedures of Departments of Cyberspace Affairs* and *Regulations on Administrative Penalty Procedures in the Fields of Industry and Information Technology*, and promote standardized and orderly law enforcement in cyberspace.

5.2.1 Combating malpractice in information content according to the law

Over the past year, in order to further purify online ecology and environment, various departments have severely cracked down on illegal activities such as spreading online rumors and false information, as well as cyber violence. According to statistics, from January 2022 to the end of June 2023, departments of cyberspace affairs nationwide totally summoned 14,126 websites and platforms for talks, warned 9,626 websites and platforms, fined and punished 645 websites and platforms, suspended or updated 809 websites and platforms, removed 540 mobile apps, canceled the licenses or records of illegal websites with administrative departments in charge of telecom, closed 32,937 illegal websites, and transferred 17,631 related case leads, according to the law.

Departments of cyberspace affairs at various levels participate in a serious of "clean up" campaigns, further strengthen law enforcement, and work with administrative departments in charge of telecom to cancel a number of unlicensed websites that provide Internet news information services in violation of regulations and seriously disrupt Internet communication order, close websites and platforms that provide downloading services for pornographic mobile apps, and remove a group of mobile apps that spread pornographic information. According to laws and regulations, relevant websites and platforms punish a group of accounts that illegally publish information on virtual currency, as well as accounts that publish or hype false information and violate public order and good customs.

The standardization and management of mobile Internet apps are strengthened. Since 2022, widely used apps that affect public opinion, such as *Kongkong Yuyin*, have violated laws and regulations, failing to conduct security evaluation as required. These apps are removed according to the law. Widely used new technologies and apps that affect public opinion, such as *Hai Ou* and *Shi Mi Da*, have been launched without security evaluation as required. These apps are also removed according to the law.

5.2.2 Enhancing law enforcement in the field of personal information protection

The Office of the Central Cyberspace Affairs Commission continuously enhances law enforcement in the field of personal information protection, and severely cracks down on violations of laws and regulations. The Office exposes typical law enforcement cases of personal information protection, educates and guides Internet enterprises to operate in accordance with laws and regulations, and promotes the healthy, standardized, and orderly development of enterprises. For Internet enterprises negligent in performing their obligations of the protection of cybersecurity and data security, the Office takes measures such as fines, rectification, warnings, and punishment of leaders. In 2022, 135 apps, such as *Chaofan Qingli Guanjia*, were investigated and handled in accordance with the law, which engaged in illegal processing of personal information through malicious means such as coercion, inducement, and fraud, which prompted strong public reaction. After investigation, 55 apps such as *Chaofan Qingli Guanjia* excessively asked for unnecessary permissions, shared precise location information with third parties without separate consent, lacked privacy policies, and unduly collected and uploaded contact lists. These apps violated laws and regulations such as the *Personal Information Protection Law*, resulted in a negative impact, and were removed. Eighty apps such as *Dongfang Toutiao* frequently asked for unnecessary permissions, failed to prompt privacy policies upon initial launch, failed to inform relevant rules on processing personal information, defaulted on the selection of privacy policies, and failed to cancel accounts, which violates laws and regulations such as the *Personal*

Information Protection Law. They were ordered to rectify the situation within a limited time in accordance with the law. If not, they would be removed.

5.2.3 Normalizing and standardizing actions against monopolies and unfair competition in the digital market

Over the past year, regulatory departments strictly enforced the law against monopolies and unfair competition in the digital market, anti-monopoly law enforcement became a normalized mechanism, and the normalized regulation of monopolies deepened. In July 2022, the State Administration for Market Regulation made administrative penalties on twenty-eight cases of failing to declare as required or illegally participating in the concentration of business operators. The exposed cases were transactions that should have been declared, most of which involved digital platforms and enterprises with the VIE architecture. The State Administration for Market Regulation published the seventh group of Internet enterprises since December 14, 2020, when it first punished a group of Internet enterprises for failing to declare according to the law.

Simultaneously, regulatory departments strengthen guidance on the compliance of competition. Based on investigating and handling monopoly cases in accordance with the law, the State Administration for Market Regulation urges enterprises to stop monopolistic behaviors such as "picking one out of two" in an all-round way, earnestly implement measures on rectification, and enhance the awareness about compliance, so as to continuously optimize competition in the market. The State Administration for Market Regulation consolidates the evaluation, monitoring and early warning of market competition, improves preventive regulatory measures, effectively prevents and resolves monopoly risks of Internet platforms, maintains fair competition in the market, and creates a good environment for the standardized, healthy, and sustainable development of platform enterprises.

5.2.4 Standardizing law enforcement procedures for cyberspace administration

Administrative law enforcement procedures for departments of cyberspace affairs improve. To further standardize and ensure the performance of duties by departments of cyberspace affairs according to the law, protect the legitimate rights and interests of citizens, legal persons, and organizations, and safeguard national security and the public interest, in March 2023, the Office of the Central Cyberspace Affairs Commission issued *Regulations on Administrative Law-Enforcement Procedures for Departments of Cyberspace Affairs*, which comprehensively revised *Regulations on Administrative Law-Enforcement Procedures for the Management of Internet Information and Content*, and would take effect on June 1, 2023. The newly revised *Regulations* standardizes administrative law enforcement procedures for departments of cyberspace affairs. The first procedure is to clarify procedural requirements for multiple stages such as filing, investigation, and evidence collection, review, decision-making, delivery, and execution, stipulating that departments of cyberspace affairs should record the entire process in written, audiovisual, and other forms in accordance with the law, and archive and preserve the records. The second one is to improve the avoidance system, hearing system, and the system of statements and defenses of the parties, so as to effectively protect the rights of all parties. The third one is to clarify the procedures for legal review, and specify the scope of cases, review institutions and review personnel that should undergo legal review, stipulating that the decision of administrative penalty cannot be made for cases that have not undergone legal review or have not passed the review. The fourth procedure is to clarify the system of collective discussion and decision-making for the punishment of major cases. When imposing administrative penalties on complex or major illegal acts, heads of departments of cyberspace affairs shall make collective discussions and decisions. The fifth procedure is to stipulate the deadlines for the handling of cases in administrative penalty by departments of cyberspace affairs and the specific circumstances of case closure.

In May 2023, the Ministry of Industry and Information Technology released *Regulations on Administrative Penalty Procedures in the Fields of Industry and Information Technology*, which officially came into effect on September 1 and revised the current *Regulations on Administrative Penalty Procedures in the Communications Industry*. The revisions cover four areas. First, on the basis of the needs of administrative law enforcement in the fields of industry and information technology, the scope of application expands from communications to industry and information technology. Second, in line with the requirements of *Administrative Penalty Law* as well as the "Three Systems" in administrative law enforcement, the principles of administrative penalties, the disclosure of administrative penalty information, the qualification requirements for law enforcement personnel, the recording of the entire law enforcement process, and the disclosure of administrative penalty decisions are added, and provisions related to avoidance are adjusted and optimized. Third, in some illegal activities through telecom networks, it is hard to determine locations. Residence, networks, and other places are stipulated as locations, so that departments of industry and information technology can determine the jurisdictions. When two or more departments have jurisdiction, the principle of "filing first" works. The resolution procedures for disputes over jurisdiction are optimized, and relevant regulations on transfer of jurisdiction are adjusted. Fourth, common procedures are adjusted and optimized. In filing, regulations such as filing conditions and time limits are improved. In investigations, the procedures for investigation and evidence collection are optimized, basic requirements for law enforcement are clarified, and provisions for suspending investigations are added. In hearings, adjustments are made to the regulations on the application of hearings and hearing personnel.

In decision-making, the provision that major illegal acts should be collectively discussed is added, and the deadline for handling cases is adjusted. In delivery, the requirements for delivery methods and addresses are clarified.

5.3 A Smart Judiciary Improves the Effectiveness of Cyberspace Governance

The People's Court and the People's Procuratorate comprehensively improve the level of a smart judiciary, continuously optimize the models of the Internet judiciary, strengthen the judicial guarantee for digital economy, promote the deep integration of modern technology and judicial practice, and make positive efforts to foster the construction of law in cyberspace and serve the development of the digital economy.

5.3.1 A smart court information system is popularized and applied

The intelligence-assisted case-handling system of a smart court ushers in a new era of a smart judiciary, including the information-based construction and application of related systems, such as "smart service," "smart trial," "smart execution," and "smart management." Presently, Chinese courts have established information systems of a smart court that supports "full-business online handling, full-process legal disclosure and comprehensive intelligent service" for the fourth-level courts nationwide, significantly improving the efficiency and quality of judicial work. According to the data, all the courts in China have now used "People's Court Online Service" applet and "filing on mobile phones," allowing parties to fully experience the convenience of "litigation and case handling on mobile phones." In 2022, the information-based court was required to focus on the pilot of full-chain-element-based trial technology, fully promote the intelligent application of trials, strengthen the collaborative ability between the Supreme People's Court and various higher people's courts in case-handling systems, meet the requirements of the reform of the trial levels and functions of the four-level courts, enhance the intelligence level of the governance of ecological environment, build a Chinese Environmental Resources Trial Information Platform, upgrade the website of the China Maritime Trial, and raise the intelligence level of maritime trial. In 2022, the brain service capability of smart courts continued to improve. The first one was to optimize the intelligent recommendation function of personalized data. The unified working platform can push real-time and dynamic data to police. The second one was to improve the judicial knowledge base, and complete the application and deployment of internal and external network resources required for generation of cause of action, element extraction and document generation.

The third one was to expand universal intelligence for application scenarios, complete the design and planning of basic AI modules for AI platforms, and provide intelligent services such as the intelligent publicity about legal information, the portraits of parties, and the recognition of images and texts to courts nationwide. Some regions explore a more advanced smart judiciary. For example, the courts in Zhejiang vigorously built all-area digital courts featuring deep integration of online and offline models, sharing and collaboration of internal and external networks, and wired and wireless interconnection" based on the top-level design of "platform + intelligence." In the future, Chinese courts will continue to deepen the construction of smart courts, improve the model of the Internet judiciary, have people enjoy more digital dividends, and build higher-level digital justice.

5.3.2 New breakthroughs are made in the digital procuratorial model

As the National Conference on Digital Procuratorial Work of Procuratorial Organs was held, accelerating the construction of procuratorial organs and driving the high-quality development of procuratorial work in the new era of the "digital revolution" became a highlight of procuratorial work in 2022. Various regions established digital procuratorial organs, determined personnel responsible for digital procuratorial work, published *Guidelines for Case Handling in Digital Procuratorial Work*, introduced management methods for big data-based legal supervision models, drafted rules on digital procuratorial work, and guided the standardized and long-term development of digital procuratorial work. According to data from the Supreme People's Procuratorate, in 2022, lawyers examined more than 70,000 case files on the Internet, with a year-on-year increase of 159 percent, covering 34,000 lawyers, with a year-on-year increase of 162 percent. Nearly 2,000 occurrences of live streaming of procuratorial hearing were conducted, and the number of viewers grew by 2.2 times year on year, promoting fairness through openness. Currently, national procuratorial organs have entered the stage of "Smart Procuratorial Work 4.0" which is data-based, scientific, and intelligent, shifting from the stage of electronic procuratorial work ("all data-based business") to the stage of smart procuratorial work ("all business-based data"). The model "AI + procuratorial work" has been applied. For example, Guizhou and Shanghai adopt an intelligence-assisted case-handling system. Zhejiang uses intelligent public prosecution based on intelligent voice technology. The Jiangsu Provincial People's Procuratorate uses case management robots. Additionally, local procuratorial organs actively explore and continuously deepen intelligent procuratorial work. According to the data of the Supreme People's Procuratorate, by March 2023, procuratorial organs in various regions had developed more than 800 digital supervision models, discovered more than 200,000 clues, and supervised more than 61,000 judicial precedents, involving various fields of procuratorial work.

In February 2023, the Shenzhen Municipal People's Procuratorate adhered to the overall principle of "focusing on new fields, enhancing new capabilities and achieving new breakthroughs," invested in the construction of a "procuratorial cloud" and "data integration platform," issued *Action Plan for Digital Procuratorial Work of Procuratorial Organs in Shenzhen 2023–2025*, advanced and deepened the construction of digital procuratorial models in the new era, and played a leading role in exploring new paths of legal supervision and closed-loop management in procuratorial organs nationwide.

5.3.3 Big data empowers the judicial assistance mechanism

Judicial departments reinvent the "big data + " model, expand the scope of judicial assistance, improve the accuracy, science, and effectiveness of assistance through digital procuratorial work in multiple dimensions, break bottlenecks in legal supervision, promote the modernization of social governance, and empower the new pattern of judicial assistance. In 2022, the Supreme People's Procuratorate and the All-China Women's Federation jointly deepened the themed events of "Caring about Women in Difficulties, Strengthening Special Judicial Assistance" and "Judicial Assistance to Promote Comprehensive Rural Revitalization." Local procuratorial organs analyze cases of judicial assistance, utilize national procuratorial work application system and local big data resources, empower discovering clues of judicial assistance and improving the efficiency of judicial assistance with big data, discover clues of judicial assistance in a timely manner, and coordinate judicial assistance and social assistance. In May 2023, the Supreme People's Procuratorate published the first group of typical cases of judicial assistance empowered by big data, summarized the experiences and practices of grassroots procuratorates in establishing big data-based models for judicial assistance, promoted the sharing and two-way connection of information on judicial assistance and social assistance, and accelerated the high-quality and efficient development of procuratorial work through the "digital revolution." The wide application of digital procuratorial work, which shifts from "artificial detection" to "intelligent screening," from "one-department work" to "multi-department collaboration," and from "case handling" to "supervision of judicial precedents," empowers new models of judicial assistance and promotes the modernization of social governance.

5.3.4 Judicial rights and interests in cyberspace are protected

The system of public interest litigation promotes the law-based governance of cyberspace. The 20th CPC National Congress stresses the need to improve the system of public interest litigation. The law-based governance of cyberspace is a key field for expanding the coverage of public interest litigation. According to data from the Supreme People's Procuratorate, from January 2022 to March 2023, more than 8,200 cases of public interest litigation on personal information protection were filed and handled by procuratorial organs nationwide, including more than 3,300 cases of civil public interest litigation and more than 4,900 cases of administrative public interest litigation. One hundred twenty-eight cases of public interest litigation on governance of cyberspace (excluding personal information protection) were filed, including sixty cases of civil public interest litigation and sixty-eight cases of administrative public interest litigation. In March 2023, the Supreme People's Procuratorate released a group of typical cases of public interest litigation on personal information protection handled by procuratorial organs. Governance of cyberspace has become an important field in which public interest litigation serves national governance. Procuratorial organs focus on damage to the public interest, such as infringing on the personal information security of citizens, infringing on the rights and interests of e-commerce consumers, and endangering cybersecurity and data security. In addition, procuratorial organs comprehensively use various methods of supervision, urge administrative organs to fully perform their duties in accordance with the law via administrative public interest litigation, and investigate the responsibilities of the civil subject for damage to public interest through civil public interest litigation, civil suits collateral to criminal proceedings, and supporting litigation. Simultaneously, for network operators and e-commerce platform operators who undertake the function of public management and social responsibilities, procuratorates in various regions urge them to rectify through civil public interest litigation and procuratorial proposals in order to supervise and support the standardized, orderly and stable development of enterprises. Additionally, the system of public interest litigation strengthens the protection of minors in cyberspace. The model "procuratorial work + public interest litigation" for minors effectively protects minors from the adverse impact of cyberspace.

Judicial work serves and ensures the development of the digital economy. The Supreme People's Procuratorate issues *Opinions on Strengthening Rule-by-Law in Cyberspace of Procuratorial Organs in the New Era*, which proposes to equally protect the rights and interests of various market entities in the digital economy. Therefore, procuratorial organs step up efforts to punish crimes such as using the Internet to publish false information, defame the commercial reputation of enterprises, or engage in extortion. By utilizing various methods, procuratorial organs strengthen judicial protection of the rights and interests of e-commerce consumers, people having new forms of employment and other entities, and conduct in-depth research on the data ownership involved in new types of cases such as data transactions and data services. In trial work, courts actively explore scientific investigation and judgment for cases in the digital economy, clarify rules for the development of the digital economy and technological innovation, and guide the healthy and orderly development of digital industry in accordance with the law. For example, in November 2022, the People's

Court of Jiading District, Shanghai released the first group of typical cases of the Shanghai High People's Court Digital Economy Judicial Research and Practice (Jiading) Base. In April 2023, the Guangdong Provincial High People's Court published the first group of typical cases in intellectual property protection in the digital economy. In the same month, the Jiangxi Provincial High People's Court released ten typical cases of serving and guaranteeing the development of the digital economy. People's courts in various regions create a favorable legal environment for the development of the digital economy by fully leveraging the exemplary, leading, and promotional role of typical cases.

Procuratorial organs actively combat telecom and online fraud. According to data from the Supreme People's Procuratorate, from January 2022 to March 2023, procuratorial organs nationwide cracked down on telecom and online fraud in accordance with the law, and prosecuted more than 37,000 people for telecom and online fraud. Procuratorial organs take greater efforts to combat overseas gangs engaged in telecom and online fraud, deepen the "Root out" campaign, work with theMinistry of Public Security to supervise two groups of eight major cross-border fraud cases twice, disclose supervision matters and progress to society in a timely manner, and achieve good social results. Procuratorial organs summarize the experience in anti-fraud work, identify various chains of telecom and online fraud, and build an entire-chain mechanism for preventing telecom and online fraud. Meanwhile, procuratorial organs strengthen the coordination among multiple departments, and establish an entire-chain, all-industry, and whole-society pattern that combats, prevents, and controls telecom and online fraud.

5.4 Education about the Law in Cyberspace is Widely Accepted among the Public

Education about the law in cyberspace plays a fundamental role in law-based governance of cyberspace and meets the intrinsic requirement for the healthy development of Internet and information technology. Over the past year, education about the law in cyberspace became more targeted and effective, which significantly enhanced the legal literacy and awareness of Internet users.

5.4.1 Innovating the form of legal education in cyberspace

In order to enhance public awareness of the law and create a strong social atmosphere for people to learn, understand, observe, and use the law, various departments organize online law-and-regulation knowledge contests, publish annual typical cases about education about the law, produce documentaries or animations aboutthe law through the Internet, use new technologies to carry out legal education more accurately, continually reinvent the forms of legal education in cyberspace, and make great progress in legal education.

Organizing Online Law-and-Regulation Knowledge Cloud Contest. In September 2022, the 2022 National Online Law-and-Regulation Knowledge Cloud Contest (Cloud Contest) was held. Guided by Xi Jinping's Thought on the Rule of Law and the important idea of General Secretary Xi Jinping on building China into a country with cyber strength, the Cloud Contest deepens the understanding of the law among cadres of departments of cyberspace affairs, Internet professionals, and Internet users, promotes the governance, operation, and access to the Internet according to the law, and creates a good legal environment for building China into a country with cyber strength. The Cloud Contest covers laws and regulations such as Xi Jinping's Thought on the Rule of Law, *Constitution of the People's Republic of China*, *Civil Code of the People's Republic of China*, *Law on the Protection of Minors*, *Cybersecurity Law*, *Data Security Law*, *Personal Information Protection Law*, and *Regulations on the Management of Internet News Information and Service*, realizing full coverage of key legal content and highlighting the authority of the content of legal education. As a major approach to supporting the Cloud Contest, the promotion platform includes multiple in-depth columns, including legal education information, typical cases, policy interpretation, insightful reviews, industrial observation, and theoretical research, with rich and detailed content.

Publishing excellent cases about legal education in cyberspace of departments of cyberspace affairs in 2022. Since the issuance of The 8th Five-Year Plan for Law Popularization and Education in Departments of Cyberspace Affairs 2021-2025, various regions have conscientiously implemented the plan, taken the initiative to perform their duties, comprehensively deepened the plan, achieved remarkable progress, and formed a number of experiences and practices that can be replicated and promoted. The Office of the Central Cyberspace Affairs Commission organizes a review of relevant experiences and practices, strengthens the promotion and application of achievements, gives full play to the exemplary and leading role of cases, and continuously creates new sopportunities for legal education in cyberspace.

Carrying out a series of activities of "National Law Popularization in Cyberspace Campaign." In February 2023, Office of the Central Cyberspace Affairs Commission launched "National Law Popularization in Cyberspace Campaign," an important brand activity for legal education in cyberspace. The event is an important measure for departments of cyberspace affairs to learn and implement the spirit of the 20th CPC National Congress, fully implement *The 8th Five-Year Plan for Law Popularization and Education in Departments of Cyberspace Affairs 2021–2025*, and strengthen legal education in cyberspace. A series of legal education activities have been carried out in Zhejiang, Jiangxi, Sichuan, Heilongjiang, and Guangxi.

Using new technologies to carry out legal education more accurately. In 2022, the Supreme People's Court showcased its work and typical cases in "Xirang Metaverse

Virtual Interaction Space," bringing a more innovative and immersive experience to the public through an interactive path, with a total exposure of nearly 100 million. In 2023, the Supreme People's Court achieved human–computer interaction for the first time, and launched the first AI virtual judicial assistant "Justice" and the first AI digital human for report interpretation "Lin Kaikai." The Supreme People's Court first achieves metaverse-based real-time interaction and application in the domestic judicial system and explores legal education with generative AI.

Enriching the form of legal education in cyberspace. In 2023, the Supreme People's Procuratorate centered on its work report and released a series of interpretive works, including *The Statements in the Work Report of the Supreme People's Procuratorate Are Hardcore*, as well as the first themed song for procuratorial work, *The Positive Spirit of the Youth*, which innovatively used the form of "AI anchor + 3D data display + animation" to vividly visualize the main content of the report. The Supreme People's Procuratorate planned and launched the first short documentary on legal education, *Returning to the Crime Scene: Prosecutors of People*, which presented procuratorial work in multiple forms and produced a significant effect.

5.4.2 Increasing publicity and legal education in cyberspace

Various departments actively carry out education about laws and regulations in cyberspace that closely relate to people's lives. For example, the Supreme People's Court strengthens the publicity and education about the *Constitution of the People's Republic of China* on cloud platforms and in micro-classes about the *Civil Code of the People's Republic of China*. The Supreme People's Procuratorate releases online anti-fraud short dramas to publicize *Law on Combating Telecom and Online Fraud*. The National Anti-Fraud Center actively publishes *Manual for Preventing Telecom and Online Fraud 2023*, which deepens the publicity and education about major laws among the public.

Various departments increase publicity and education about the *Constitution of the People's Republic of China*. In December 2022, the Supreme People's Court planned and launched special activities of "Approaching Courts on Cloud Plarforms," "My Stories of Law," and "Constitution Publicity Week in 2022." Through live streaming on cloud platforms, the public was guided to learn and understand the development and implementation of the Constitution at the China Court Museum, to enter the Smart Court Laboratory of the Supreme People's Court, to visit ten courts, including Beijing Financial Court online, and to experience the judicial atmosphere in an immersive way. In this way, the Supreme People's Court promotes the spirit of the Constitution to the public, disseminates the concept of rule of law, and guides all the people to respect, observe, and safeguard socialist law.

Various departments widely publicize the work about combating telecom and online fraud. The Supreme People's Procuratorate releases online short drama

Anti-fraud Elites: Prosecutors of People on Kuaishou, and co-creates *Prosecutors Talking about Tool Men of Criminals, or Hardcore Rap* with UPs on Bilibili, so as to warn the public of the crime of helping information network crime and not to become accomplices in telecom and online fraud. In June 2023, in order to further expand the coverage of anti-fraud publicity and enhance the anti-fraud awareness of the public, the National Anti-Fraud Center published *Manual for Preventing Telecom and Online Fraud 2023*, which introduced important facts, such as "Top Ten High-Incidence Cases in Telecom and Online Fraud," "Seven Anti-Fraud Tools for Preventing Telecom and Online Fraud," and *Law on Combating Telecom and Online Fraud* to the public. In addition, the National Anti-Fraud Center exposed and criticized the methods of fraud, analyzed typical cases, and provided anti-fraud tips.

5.4.3 Strengthening legal education in cyberspace for key groups

The Supreme People's Procuratorate focuses on legal education for key groups in an accurate way and continuously carries out online publicity of the protection of minors. The China Disabled Persons' Federation, the Ministry of Justice, and other organizations give online warnings on the protection of the rights and interests of disabled people, and continually enhance the awareness of key groups to protect their own rights and interests in accordance with the law.

The Supreme People's Procuratorate continues to promote the themed publicity of the protection of minors. For three consecutive years, the Supreme People's Procuratorate has organized a themed online publicity activity of "Protecting the Youth," reported the legal supervision of the campaign of "Caring for the Youth with Procuratorial Organs," and released typical cases. It also launched the first documentary on the protection of minors produced by procuratorial organs, *Protecting the Youth*, to safeguard the legitimate rights and interests of minors and enhance their awareness of protection.

Relevant departments enhance the awareness of protecting the rights and interests of disabled people in accordance with the law. In April 2023, the Online Knowledge Contest on Legal Protection of the Rights and Interests of Disabled People was officially started, which aimed to promote public attention and support for the development of social undertakings on behalf of disabled people in accordance with the law and enhance the awareness and ability of disabled people to protect their own rights and interests. The contest focuses on laws and regulations closely related to the protection of the rights and interests of disabled people, such as the *Constitution of the People's Republic of China*, the *Civil Code of the People's Republic of China*, and the *Law on the Protection of Disabled Persons of the People's Republic of China*; the contest is open to the public, as well as disabled people, their relatives, friends, and related personnel.

10.2478/9788367405867-007

Chapter 6
The Construction of a Digital Government

Globally, the digital transformation of economy and society accelerates, and digital productivity plays a key role in driving economic growth and social development. Digital transformation becomes leverage for the Chinese government to actively follow the trends of the times, seize the opportunities for development, and proactively address challenges. Under the strong leadership of the CPC Central Committee with Comrade Xi Jinping at its core, China actively adapts to the trend of a new round of technological revolution and industrial transformation, takes the construction of a digital China as overall strategy for information-based development in the new era, regards the construction of digital government as the fundamental and pioneering project for implementing the strategies of building China into a digital country with cyber strength, views strengthening digital capabilities and improving the level of digital governance and service as a new stage and a new task in the construction and development of digital government, systematically deploys the construction of digital government, and urges various regions and departments to continuously enhance the capabilities of digital services. In China, governments at all levels utilize new-generation information technology to continuously improve the construction of digital government so as to actively follow current trends, seize opportunities for development, and proactively address challenges.

Over the past year, China saw fast construction and development of digital government. The system of policies continuously improved, and the construction of platforms continually advanced. Significant progress was made in the construction of a data governance system, and digital services and regulatory capabilities were further optimized. Remarkable achievements were made in the modernization of the national governance system and governance capabilities.

6.1 The System of Policies Continuously Improves

The Fourth Plenary Session of the 19th CPC Central Committee and the Fifth Plenary Session of the 19th CPC Central Committee propose to promote the construction of a digital government, strengthen orderly sharing of data, and improve the digital and intellectual level of public service, social governance, and other fields. In *The 14th Five-Year Plan for Economic and Social Development*, there is a special chapter on "Improving the Level of the Construction of Digital Government." The State Council has successively issued *Guiding Opinions on Strengthening the Construction of Digital Government* and other documents, which continuously improve the system of policies on the construction and management of digital government.

6.1.1 China introduces many policies and documents

Under the overall strategic deployment of a digital China, since 2022, China has issued a series of policies and documents based on the construction and development of digital government, covering overall strategy, government data, and government services.

In terms of overall strategy, in February 2023, China issued *Overall Layout and Planning for the Construction of Digital China*, which regards digital government as a key direction in the deep integration of digital technology and the "Five-sphere Integrated Plan," proposes the development of efficient and collaborative digital government, and further clarifies the orientation, direction, and requirements for the construction and development of a digital government. Specifically, it requires the acceleration of innovation on systems and rules; the optimization of rules and regulations in tune with the construction of digital government; strengthening the construction of digital capabilities; promoting the interconnection of information system networks, on-demand data sharing, and efficient business collaboration; improving the level of digital services; quickening the model of "handling one affair one time;" deepening online and offline integration; and enhancing and standardizing the management of government mobile Internet apps.

Concerning government data, in September 2022, the General Office of the State Council issued *Guidelines for the Construction of National Integrated Government Big Data System*, which gives full play to the role of government data in enhancing governmental performance, boosting the construction of digital government, and promoting the modernization of the national governance system and governance capability. The *Guidelines* provide requirements and principles for the construction and development of government big data in China, in line with the data resources system in *Guiding Opinions on Strengthening the Construction of Digital Government* issued by the State Council. Currently, to address the most fundamental and urgent issues in the construction of digital government, China clarifies the rights and responsibilities of national, local. and industrial departments in government data with integrated management, investigates national government data resources with an integrated data catalog, strengthens data collection and improves data quality with integrated data resources, achieves on-demand flow of government data nationwide with integrated data sharing and exchanges, promotes the analysis and application of government big data with integrated data services, improves the efficiency and capability of digital government with integrated computing facilities, consolidates the foundation of the construction and management of government big data with integrated standards, and enhances the bottom line of government big data system with integrated security guarantee.

With respect to government services, at the national level, China raises higher requirements for handling one affair one time and "cross-provincial government services," while significantly improving the level of government services. In October 2022, the General Office of the State Council issued *Guiding Opinions on Accelerating the Promotion of "Handling One Affair One Time" to Build Upgraded Government Services*, which clearly stresses the need to promote handling one affair one time of the entire lifecycle of government services for enterprises and individuals, optimize service models, and strengthen capability building. Simultaneously, the General Office of the State Council released *Opinions on Expanding the Scope of "Cross-Provincial Government Services" in Government Services to Further Improve Service Efficiency*. As clarified, China will expand the scope of cross-provincial government services, improve the efficiency of cross-provincial government services, strengthen the support for cross-provincial government services, propose twenty-two new tasks for cross-provincial government services in government services nationwide, and continuously deepen the reform of cross-provincial government services in government services.

6.1.2 Local governments continually strengthen planning and layout

In recent years, local governments at all levels in China have actively promoted the construction and development of digital government, and launched large-scale planning, construction, and implementation. From July 2022 to the end of June 2023, Guangdong, Ningxia, Henan, Tibet, Yunnan, Shandong, Fujian, Guangxi, Heilongjiang, Zhejiang, and other regions introduced or updated plans or implementation opinions on the construction of digital government, as shown in Table 6-1. Since 2020, provincial-level governments in China have formulated more than thirty plans or guiding opinions on digital government, which continuously improve the systems and rules and the construction and management of digital government in China.

The plans or policies on the construction of digital government introduced by various regions generally involve enhancing digital governance capabilities, constructing digital governance systems, building government data systems, forging government infrastructure, and promoting key tasks and projects related to digital government. Compared to traditional e-government construction, under the guidance of *Guiding Opinions on Strengthening the Construction of Digital Government* issued by the State Council, the policies on digital government introduced by various regions in recent years are characterized by three shifts in direction.

In management systems, departmental leadership shifts to unified construction and management. In overall strategy, various regions emphasize people-centered and demand-oriented construction of digital government. By implementing the concept of holistic governance, various regions break traditional models of construction and management for departmental business, solve the lack of coordination and

Table 6-1 Policies and documents on digital government issued by provincial governments from July 2022 to the end of June 2023

Provincial Government	Documents	No.	Date
Guangdong	Implementation Opinions of Guangdong Provincial People's Government on Further Deepening the Reform and Construction of Digital Government	Yue Fu (2023) No. 47	June 8, 2023
Ningxia	Implementation Opinions of Ningxia Autonomous Region People's Government on Strengthening the Construction of Digital Government	Ning Zheng Fa (2023) No. 17	May 16, 2023
Henan	Implementation Plan of Henan Province for Strengthening the Construction of Digital Government 2023–2025	Yu Zheng (2023) No. 17	April 26, 2023
Tibet	Plan of Tibet Autonomous Region for Strengthening the Construction of Digital Government 2023–2025	Zang Zheng Fa (2023) No. 12	April 16, 2023
Yunnan	Overall Plan of Yunnan Province for the Construction of Digital Government	Yun Zheng Fa (2023) No. 8	March 2, 2023
Shandong	Implementation Plan of Shandong Province for the Construction of Digital Government	Lu Zheng Zi (2023) No. 15	January 29, 2023
Fujian	Overall Plan of Fujian Province for the Reform and Construction of Digital Government	Min Zheng (2022) No. 32	December 26, 2022
Guangxi	Implementation Opinions of Guangxi Zhuang Autonomous Region People's Government on Strengthening the Construction of Digital Government	Gui Zheng Fa (2022) No. 31	November 30, 2022
Heilongjiang	Implementation Opinions of Heilongjiang Provincial People's Government on Strengthening the Construction of Digital Government	Hei Zheng Fa (2022) No. 23	September 28, 2022
Zhejiang	Implementation Opinions of Zhejiang Provincial People's Government on Deepening the Construction of Digital Government	Zhe Zheng Fa (2022) No. 20	July 30, 2022

isolated information islands caused by fragmentation in the construction of digital government, and meet the needs of comprehensive business across departments, levels, and regions. In this way, various regions abandon department-led models of construction and management and adopt the system of unified construction and management with clear rights and responsibilities.

In the construction model, decentralized construction shifts to holistic construction. In recent years, the development of digital government has featured the deployment and construction of new infrastructure such as government clouds and data platforms. By continuously building large platforms and systems, various regions achieve the integration of government business models and significantly enhance interdepartmental collaboration, which improves governmental ability to solve complex problems and provide better service experience and more suitable production and living environments for the public and for industrial enterprises.

In the technological model, traditional information-based construction of digital government shifts to digital and intelligent construction of digital government. As data becomes a key factor of production, various regions have focused on defining and reconstructing business with data, promoted the integration of technology, business, and data with unified data sharing, unclogged the channels for information exchange, and achieved integrated collaboration and governance of governmental affairs. The full development of new-generation information technology such as big data and AI provides more intelligent and efficient technological tools for governmental affairs. In recent years, in the deployment and construction of digital government, various regions not only met basic needs of providing convenient and efficient services, but also explored the use of big data for comprehensive analysis to complete economic regulation, market supervision, social governance, emergency response, and other work.

6.2 Construction of Platform System is Continuously Promoted

In the construction of digital government, governments at various levels and in various regions continually invest funds, vigorously promote the construction of infrastructure, accelerate the construction of integrated government service platforms and government data platforms, deepen the integration of government information systems, support the application of digital government in different fields and industries, and achieve significant results, providing efficient governmental services.

6.2.1 Functions of relevant national platforms continually improve

The issuance and use list of electronic certificates are included in the dynamic management of the National Integrated Government Service Platform. Electronic certificates are preliminarily applied in such fields as transportation and travel and culture and tourism, and the digitization of ID cards and the "one card" service for social security of residents are piloted and promoted. By the end of March 2023, the National Integrated Government Service Platform had gathered more than 900 types of electronic certificates from 32 regions and 26 departments of the State Council, and provided a total of 8.35 billion electronic certificate sharing and application services, which effectively reduced certificates and materials and saved time.

By the end of November 2022, a national regulations database was completed and launched; the database collected more than 10,000 effective regulations of departments and local governments. In the national regulations database, current regulations are sorted out, published, and updated in a timely manner. As an important approach to solving the long-standing problem of ignorance of regulations and inconvenient access to regulations, the national regulations database helps to further clarify the rules on market regulation, create a market- and law-oriented international business environment, and improve the quality of the construction of law-based government.

Breakthroughs are made in the construction of a platform for the National People's Congress to perform its duties. Since the opening of the information platform for the work of deputies to the National People's Congress, it has gathered more than 2,700 deputies, more than 3,000 staff members, and more than 20,000 groups for handling proposals and suggestions, which significantly facilitates the work and connection of deputies. A cloud listening system, online video conferencing, voice transcription technology, and other technologies are widely applied, which provide strong support for broadcasting, interviewing, recording, and other work done during the National People's Congress.

The smart court is further transformed and upgraded. On judicial data middle platform and judicial knowledge service platform of smart court brain, thirty-three high-quality services are integrated. More than 800 million incidents of services are provided to 3,470 courts nationwide, covering 80 percent of core business scenarios of trial execution as well as 100 percent of high courts and middle courts and 97 percent of grassroots courts. The proportion of electronic litigation in courts nationwide increased from 24 percent in 2021 to 28 percent in 2022. A national unified judicial blockchain platform completes a total of 2.85 billion pieces of data on the chain for the preservation of evidence.

6.2.2 Local governments maintain large-scale investment in the construction of platforms

By analyzing the bidding information released by governmental procurement websites at various levels and in various regions across the country from January to December 2022, a total of 66,588 projects on digital government and service were selected from 31 provinces, autonomous regions, and municipalities directly under the central government. Specifically, in the number of construction projects, the top five provinces were Zhejiang (5,785), Guangdong (5,551), Jiangsu (5,324), Sichuan (4,149), and Shandong (3,862), as shown in Figure 6-1.

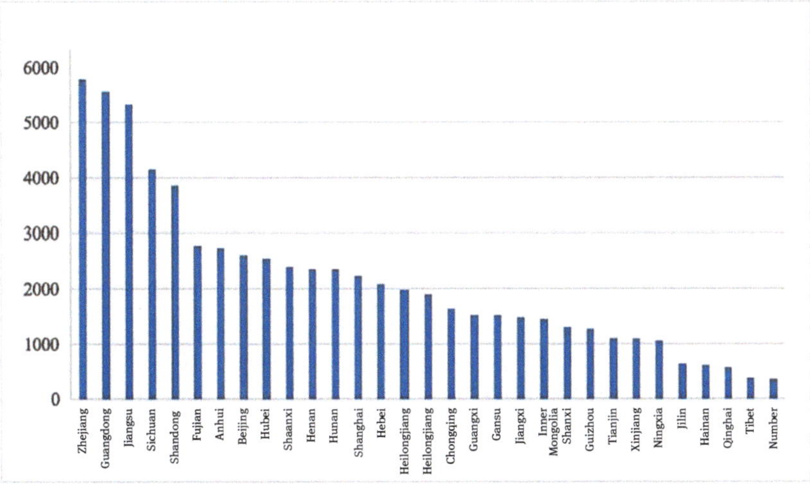

Figure 6-1 Number of projects on digital government and service in thirty-one provinces, autonomous regions, and municipalities directly under the central government in China in 2022.

In investment scale, in 2022, a total of 100.866 billion *yuan* was invested to the projects on digital government and service in 31 provinces, autonomous regions, and municipalities directly under the central government. Specifically, in total amounts, the top five provinces were Guangdong (10.562 billion *yuan*), Zhejiang (8.12 billion *yuan*), Sichuan (7.656 billion *yuan*), Jiangsu (6.758 billion *yuan*), and Shandong (5.925 billion *yuan*), as shown in Figure 6-2.

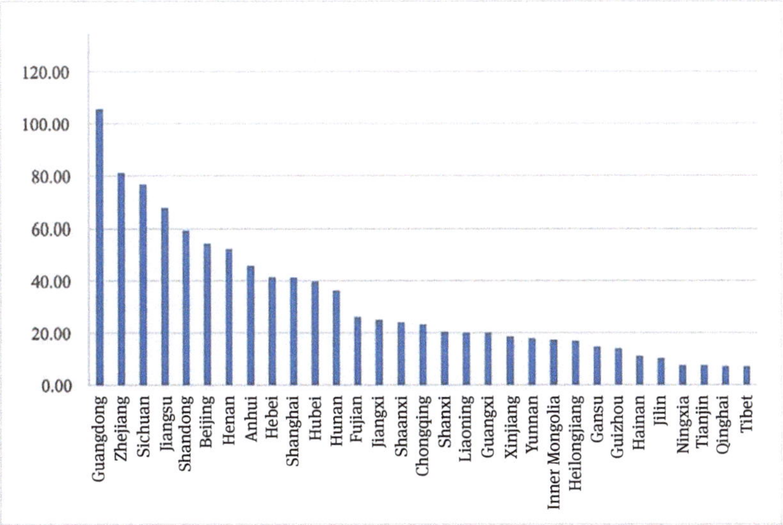

Figure 6-2 Investment scale of projects on digital government and service in thirty-one provinces, autonomous regions, and municipalities directly under the central government in China in 2022.

In regional investment, in 2022, the number of projects on digital government and service in the eastern, central, and western regions was 33,492, 15,211, and 17,885, respectively, with cumulative investment reaching 51.488 billion *yuan*, 24.636 billion *yuan*, and 24.741 billion *yuan*, respectively. Both in the number of projects and the scale of investment, the eastern region was higher than the central and western regions, with capital investment accounting for more than 50 percent, as shown in Figure 6-3.

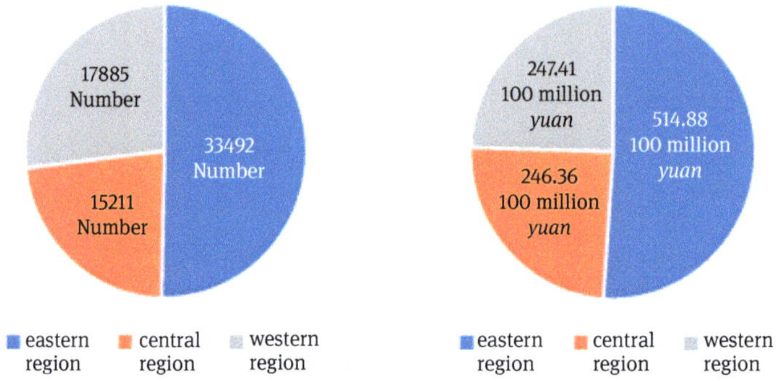

Figure 6-3 Number and investment of projects on digital government in eastern, central, and wstern regions in 2022.

6.2.3 Investment and construction cover multiple key fields

In specific fields, in 2022, the investment in the construction of digital government in thirty-one provinces, autonomous regions, and municipalities directly under the central government covers comprehensive fields such as transportation, finance and taxation, education, health, civil affairs, judiciary, agriculture, and forestry, especially the fields of education, transportation, and health.

In the field of education, in 2022, there were a total of 2,115 projects in 31 provinces, autonomous regions, and municipalities directly under the central government, with a total investment scale of 3.876 billion *yuan*, accounting for 3.84 percent of the total investment to the construction of digital government in 2022. In the number of projects, the top five regions were Sichuan (180), Zhejiang (177), Jiangsu (146), Guangdong (134), and Shanghai (115), as shown in Figure 6-4. In the amount of investment, the top five regions were Shaanxi (374 million *yuan*), Henan (343 million *yuan*), Sichuan (337 million *yuan*), Zhejiang (272 million *yuan*), and Shanghai (252 million *yuan*), as shown in Figure 6-5.

In the field of transportation, in 2022, there were a total of 1,812 projects in 31 provinces, autonomous regions, and municipalities directly under the central

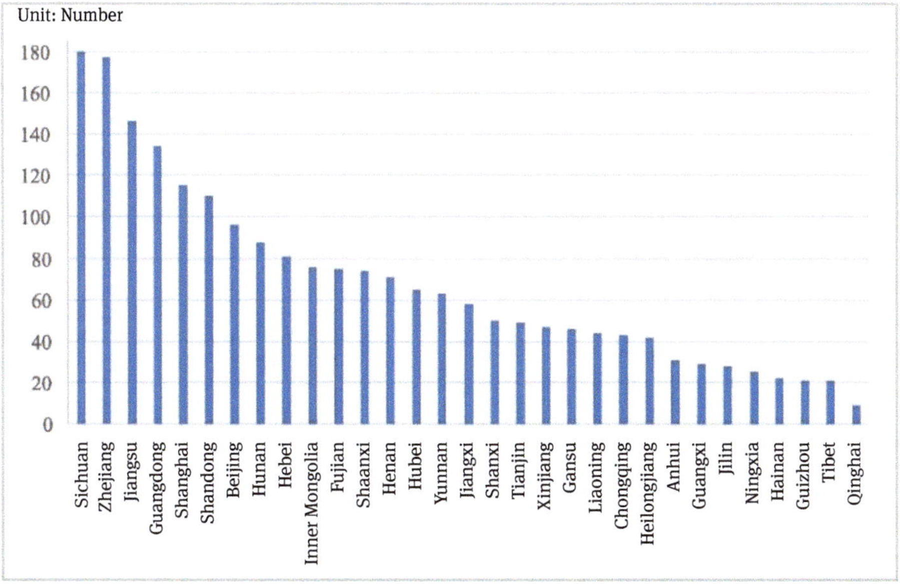

Figure 6-4 Number of projects in the field of education in thirty-one provinces, autonomous regions, and municipalities directly under the central government in China in 2022.

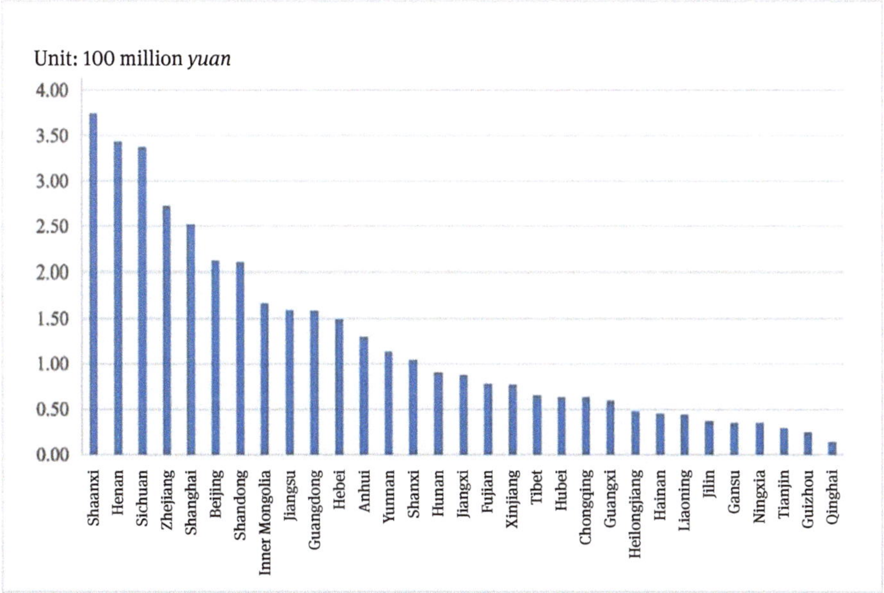

Figure 6-5 Amount of investment in the field of education in thirty-one provinces, autonomous regions, and municipalities directly under the central government in China in 2022.

government, with a total investment scale of 4.029 billion *yuan*, accounting for 4.0 percent of the total investment in the construction of digital government in 2022. In the number of projects, the top five provinces were Guangdong (159), Zhejiang (158), Jiangsu (125), Sichuan (118), and Shandong (110), as shown in Figure 6-6. In the amount of investment, the top five regions were Guangdong (513 million *yuan*), Henan (356 million *yuan*), Sichuan (338 million *yuan*), Beijing (316 million *yuan*), and Hunan (265 million *yuan*), as shown in Figure 6-7.

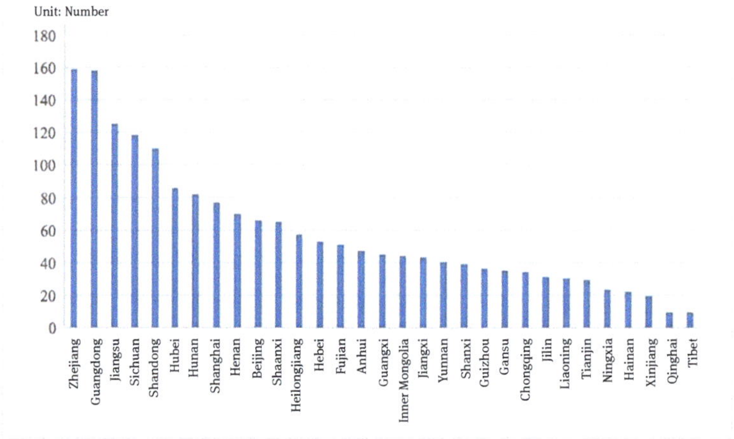

Figure 6-6 Number of projects in the field of transportation in thirty-one provinces, autonomous regions, and municipalities directly under the central government in China in 2022.

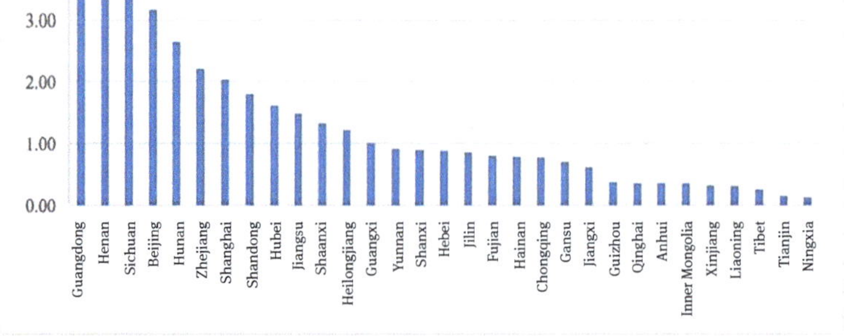

Figure 6-7 Amount of investment in the field of transportation in thirty-one provinces, autonomous regions, and municipalities directly under the central government in China in 2022.

In the field of health, in 2022, there were a total of 1,262 projects in 31 provinces, autonomous regions, and municipalities directly under the central government, with a total investment of 1.4 billion *yuan*, accounting for 1.4 percent of the total investment in the construction of digital government in 2022. In the number of projects, the top five regions were Zhejiang (142), Jiangsu (125), Guangdong (120), Shanghai (88), and Sichuan (87), as shown in Figure 6-8. In the amount of investment, the top five provinces were Guangdong (167 million *yuan*), Sichuan (132 million *yuan*), Shandong (112 million *yuan*), Zhejiang (88 million *yuan*), and Hunan (87 million *yuan*), as shown in Figure 6-9.

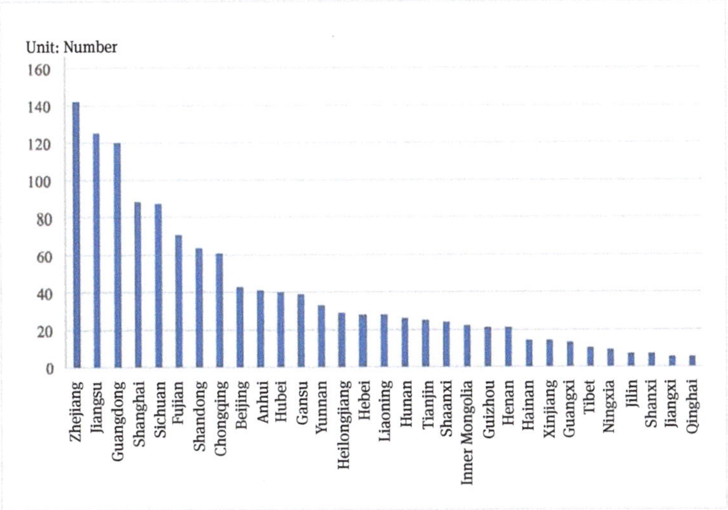

Figure 6-8 Number of projects in the field of health in thirty-one provinces, autonomous regions, and municipalities directly under the central government in China in 2022.

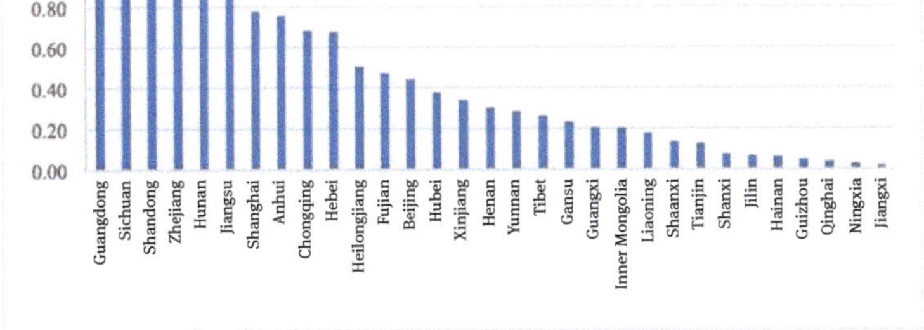

Figure 6-9 Amount of investment in the field of health in thirty-one provinces, autonomous regions, and municipalities directly under the central government in China in 2022.

6.3 Significant Progress is Made in the Opening and Sharing of Government Data

The effective governance and efficient utilization of government data play a key role in the construction of digital government. In recent years, with the rapid development of new-generation information technology such as big data and AI, governments at various levels have attached great importance to the value of data. Under the coordinated deployment of policies such as *Guidelines for the Construction of National Integrated Government Big Data System*, significant progress has been made in the construction of government data resources systems.

6.3.1 Establishment of institutions and policies is gradually optimized

According to a survey conducted by the School of Public Policy & Management, Tsinghua University, in thirty-one provinces, autonomous regions, and municipalities directly under the central government, at the end of 2022, thirty provinces, autonomous regions, and municipalities directly under the central government had established governmental departments in charge of data management or clarified their responsibilities. Specifically, some regions established special departments responsible for the management of government data, such as Guangdong and Shanghai. Some regions incorporated the management of government data into the responsibilities of departments of big data, such as Guizhou, Zhejiang, Shandong, and Guangxi. Some provinces included the management of government data in the responsibilities of departments of government services, such as Jiangsu, Henan, Hebei, and Hunan. In some regions, departments of cyberspace affairs, general offices of provincial governments, and relevant leading groups were in charge of the management of government data. In various regions, there are significant differences in the division of responsibilities, institutional categories, and administrative level of departments for the management of government data, as shown in Table 6-2.

In the formulation of local laws and regulations, the management of government data attracts wide attention. In line with local conditions, multiple provinces, autonomous regions, and municipalities directly under the central government have issued laws and regulations on government data to promote effective governance of government data, as shown in Table 6-3.

Table 6-2 Names of provincial departments for the management of government data

Region	Name
Beijing	Beijing Municipal Bureau of Economy and Information Technology (Beijing Big Data Management Bureau)
Tianjin	Tianjin Internet Information Office
Hebei	Hebei Provincial Government Service Management Office
Shanxi	Shanxi Provincial Administrative Approval and Service Management Bureau
Inner Mongolia	Inner Mongolia Autonomous Region Big Data Center
Liaoning	Liaoning Provincial Business Environment Development Bureau (Liaoning Provincial Big Data Management Bureau)
Jilin	Jilin Provincial Government Services and Digital Construction Management Bureau
Heilongjiang	Heilongjiang Business Environment Construction Supervision Bureau
Shanghai	Shanghai Municipal Data Development Management Office (E-government Office)
Jiangsu	Jiangsu Provincial Government Service Management Office
Zhejiang	Zhejiang Provincial Big Data Development Management Bureau
Anhui	Anhui Provincial Data Resources Management Bureau
Fujian	Office of the Leading Group for the Construction of Digital Fujian in Fujian Province
Jiangxi	Jiangxi Provincial Government Services Office
Shandong	Shandong Provincial Big Data Bureau
Henan	Henan Provincial Administrative Approval and Government Information Management Bureau
Hubei	Hubei Provincial Government Services Office
Hunan	Hunan Provincial Government Services Bureau
Guangdong	Guangdong Provincial Government Service and Data Management Bureau
Guangxi	Guangxi Zhuang Autonomous Region Big Data Development Bureau
Hainan	Hainan Provincial Big Data Management Bureau
Chongqing	Chongqing Municipal Big Data Application, Development and Management Bureau
Sichuan	General Office of Sichuan Provincial People's Government
Guizhou	Guizhou Province Big Data Development and Management Bureau
Yunnan	None
Tibet	Tibet Autonomous Region Big Data Development and Management Bureau
Shaanxi	Shaanxi Provincial Government Services and Big Data Bureau
Gansu	Gansu Provincial Big Data Center
Qinghai	Qinghai Provincial Government Information and Government Servies Office
Ningxia	Office of the Leading Group for Promoting the Construction of Digital Government in Ningxia Hui Autonomous Region
Xinjiang	Xinjiang Uygur Autonomous Region Government Services and Public Resources Trading Center

Table 6-3 Special laws and regulations on the management of government data issued by some provincial-level departments

Region	Law and Regulation	No.	Date
Fujian	Measures on the Management of Government Data in Fujian Province	Fujian Provincial Government Order No. 178	October 15, 2016
Ningxia	Measures on the Sharing and Management of Government Data Resources in Ningxia Hui Autonomous Region	Ningxia Hui Autonomous Region People's Government Order No. 100	September 4, 2018
Shanghai	Measures on the Management of Public Data and One-stop Government Services in Shanghai	Shanghai Municipal People's Government Order No. 9	September 30, 2018
Jilin	Measures on the Management of Public Data and One-stop Government Services in Jilin Province (Trial)	*Ji Zheng Fa* (2019) No. 4	January 4, 2019
Chongqing	Interim Measures on the Management of Government Data Resources in Chongqing	Chongqing Municipal People's Government Order No. 328	July 31, 2019
Liaoning	Measures on the Sharing and Management of Government Data Resources in Liaoning Province	Liaoning Provincial People's Government Order No. 330	November 26, 2019
Shanxi	Measures on the Management of Government Data Assets in Shanxi Province (Trial)	Shanxi Provincial People's Government Order No. 266	November 28, 2019
	Measures on the Management and Application of Government Data in Shanxi Province	No. 65 Announcement of the Standing Committee of Shanxi Provincial People's Congress	November 27, 2020
Shandong	Measures on the Management of E-government and Government Data in Shandong Province	Shandong Provincial People's Government Order No. 329	December 25, 2019
	Measures on the Management of Health Big Data in Shandong Province	Shandong Provincial People's Government Order No. 335	August 20, 2020
	Measures on the Opening of Public Data in Shandong Province	Shandong Provincial People's Government Order No. 344	January 31, 2022
Zhejiang	Interim Measures on the Management of the Opening and Security of Public Data in Zhejiang Province	Zhejiang Provincial People's Government Order No. 381	June 12, 2020
	Regulations on Public Data in Zhejiang Province	No. 3 Announcement of the 6th Meeting of the 13th Zhejiang Provincial People's Congress	January 21, 2022

Table 6-3 *(Continued)*

Region	Law and Regulation	No.	Date
Hunan	Measures on the Management of the Sharing of Government Information Resources in Hunan Province	Hunan Provincial People's Government Order No. 301	November 28, 2020
Anhui	Measures on the Management of Government Data Resources in Anhui Province	Anhui Provincial People's Government Order No. 299	December 30, 2020
Hubei	Measures on the Application and Management of Government Data Resources in Hubei Province	Hubei Provincial People's Government Order No. 419	January 25, 2021
Jiangsu	Measures on the Management of Public Data in Jiangsu Province	Jiangsu Provincial People's Government Order No. 148	December 18, 2021
Hebei	Measures on the Management of the Sharing and Application of Government Data in Hebei Province	Hebei Provincial People's Government Order (2022) No. 7	November 3, 2022
Jiangxi	Measures on the Management of Public Data in Jiangxi Province	Jiangxi Provincial People's Government Order No. 254	January 12, 2022
	Measures on the Management of the Sharing and Opening of Government Information Resources in Jiangxi Province	Jiangxi Data Sharing Office (2020) No. 1	January 9, 2020
Tianjin	Interim Measures on the Management of the Sharing of Government Information Resources in Tianjin		2018
	Interim Measures on the Management of the Opening of Public Data Resources in Tianjin	Jin Wang Xin Ban Tong (2020) No. 8	July 21, 2020
Guizhou	Measures on the Management of Government Data Source Resources in Guizhou Province	*Qian Fu Ban Fa* (2023) No. 13	June 8, 2023

6.3.2 Construction of a data catalog system is continuously strengthened

According to a survey conducted by the School of Public Policy & Management, Tsinghua University, all thierty-one provinces, autonomous regions, and municipalities directly under the central government, as well as Xinjiang Production and Construction Corps, have compiled catalogs of government data. Among them, twenty-four regions have compiled catalogs of government data at the provincial, municipal, and county levels, five regions have compiled catalogs of government data at the provincial and municipal levels, and two regions have compiled catalogs of government data at the provincial level. Nineteen regions have basically achieved full coverage of government data, accounting for 59.4 percent. Twenty-four regions have basically achieved a correlation between data catalogs and departmental rights and responsibilities, accounting for 75 percent. Simultaneously, the compilation of data catalogs by national ministries and commissions continuously advances. Among thirty-nine surveyed national ministries and commissions, thirty-one have compiled catalogs of government data, accounting for 79.5 percent. In particular, seven departments have compiled data catalogs of relevant departments in various regions, accounting for 17.9 percent. Twelve departments have basically achieved a correlation between data catalogs and departmental rights and responsibilities, accounting for 30.8 percent. Fourteen departments have basically achieved full coverage of government data, accounting for 35.9 percent.

In establishing and improving the working mechanisms and standards for the compilation of the catalogs of government data, twenty-five regions have released relevant policies, documents, and standards, accounting for 78.1 percent. Twenty-two national ministries and commissions have issued relevant policies and documents, and seventeen ministries and commissions have released relevant standards, accounting for 56.4 percent and 43.6 percent, respectively. Various regions and departments have taken multiple measures such as assessment, supervision, and notification, and solidly promoted the compilation of the catalogs of government data. More than ten regions and more than twenty departments have initially established identification mechanisms, self-examination mechanisms for compliance, security, and availability, as well as return and correction mechanisms for data sources.

In constructing, maintaining, and updating catalog systems of government data, all provincial-level regions have established catalog systems, and sixteen regions have adopted the model of provincial integrated construction, accounting for 50 percent. Twenty-two national ministries and commissions have established catalog systems of government data, accounting for 56.4 percent at the ministerial level. Presently, twenty-three regions have updated catalog systems of government data, accounting for 71.9 percent. Sixteen regions have updated the correlation between data and systems, accounting for 50 percent. Nine regions have simultaneously updated catalog systems of government data on relevant national platforms, accounting for 28.1 percent. Seventeen ministries and commissions have updated catalog systems of government data, Fifteen ministries and commissions have updated the correlation between data and systems, and nine ministries and commissions have simultaneously updated catalog systems of government data on relevant national platforms (less than provincial-level regions).

As a whole, progress on the compilation of catalog systems of government data provides strong support for promoting and improving the construction of government data systems and lays a solid foundation for comprehensive compilation of catalog systems of government data in line with the requirements of "three-formulation" in *Guidelines for the Construction of National Integrated Government Big Data System.*

6.3.3 Significant results are produced in the sharing of government data

In recent years, various regions and departments have accelerated the sharing of government data, continuously optimized data-sharing systems and platforms, accumulated massive government data resources, continually released interfaces for data sharing, updated data entries, promoted data connectivity and sharing among governments at various levels, and achieved significant results in the sharing of government data. By June 2023, eighty-two central departments (after reform of Party and State institutions) had access to national data sharing and exchange platforms, and thirty-one provinces, autonomous regions, and municipalities directly under the central government, as well as Xinjiang Production and Construction Corps, had access to national data sharing and exchange platforms through provincial-level prefix areas. National data sharing and exchange platforms gathered and published more than 16,000 shared catalogs of departmental data with more than 21,000 types of online resources, and more than 67,000 shared catalogs of local data with more than 4,900 types of online resources. Through service interfaces, a total of 12.412 billion queries/verifications were provided to fifty-three departments, thirty-one provinces, autonomous regions, and municipalities directly under the central government, as well as Xinjiang Production and Construction Corps. Through the exchanges of database tables and quantity files in prefix areas, a total of 162.194 billion database tables and 405.90 TB files were exchanged. Compared to the corresponding period in 2022, shared catalogs and online resources steadily multiplied, the cumulative number of data sharing and exchanges significantly increased, and the sharing of government data continuously deepened.

According to the data from the national data sharing and exchange platform, from July 2022 to June 2023, the highest level of monthly query/verification services was 465 million, with the cumulative number of services reaching more than 4.483 billion. Compared to the corresponding period (from July 2021 to June 2022), the average monthly number of query/verification interface calls increased from 340 million to more than 374 million. Figure 6-10 shows query/verification interface calls on national data sharing and exchange platforms from July 2022 to June 2023.

The concentration ratio of the demand for the sharing of government data nationwide remains high. From July 2022 to June 2023, the Ministry of Public Security, the State Administration for Market Regulation, the Ministry of Education, the Ministry of Civil Affairs, the National Development and Reform Commission, the National

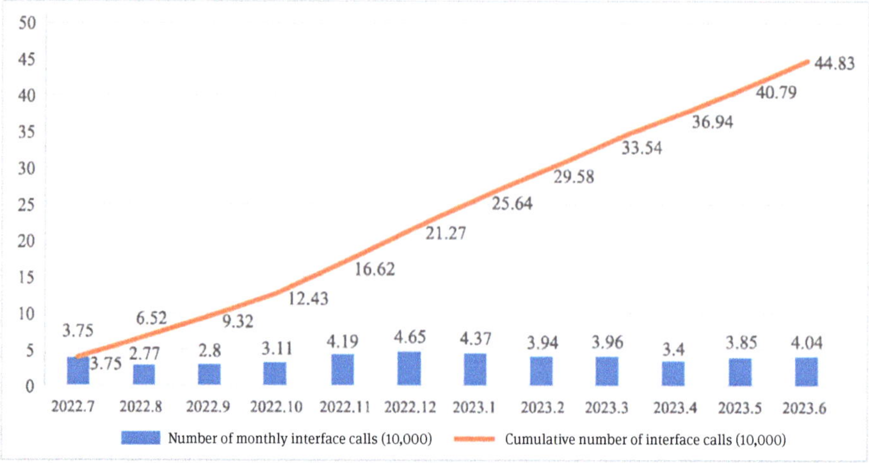

Figure 6-10 Query/verification interface calls on the National Data Sharing and Exchange Platform from July 2022 to June 2023.

Source: National Data Sharing and Exchange Platform.

Health Commission, and the Ministry of Housing and Urban-Rural Development provided a total of more than 4.319 billion data query/verification services, accounting for more than 96 percent of all query/verification services on national data sharing and exchange platforms. Figure 6-11 shows the proportion of data query/verification services provided by various departments from July 2022 to June 2023.

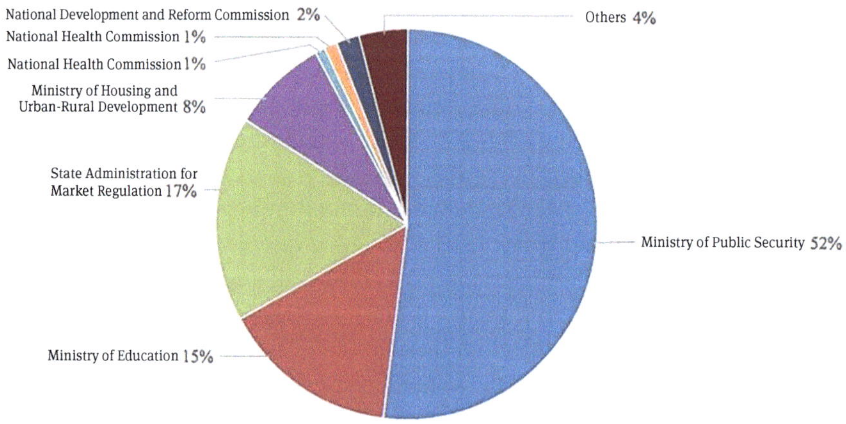

Figure 6-11 Proportion of dta query/verification services provided by various departments from July 2022 to June 2023.

Source: National Data Sharing and Exchange Platform.

Various provinces, autonomous regions, and municipalities directly under the central government have large and widespread demands for the use of the data from ministries and commissions. Via national data sharing and exchange platforms, various regions connect with more than 140 vertical management systems of relevant departments of the State Council, with a total of more than 256 million queries/verifications of data. This further breaks apart the information islands caused by vertical-horizontal segmentation and tackles the vexing problems of multiple records of transaction data and repeated login of transaction entities. From July 2022 to June 2023, in the number of data queries/verifications on national data sharing and exchange platforms, the top ten regions were Guangxi, Jiangsu, Shandong, Guangdong, Zhejiang, Heilongjiang, Shanghai, Xinjiang, Sichuan, and Liaoning, as shown in Figure 6-12. Among provinces, autonomous regions, and municipalities directly under the central government, the gap in data sharing and utilization remains prominent. The number of query/verification interface calls of Guangxi, Jiangsu, and Shandong outstrips the total number of the other twenty-eight provinces, autonomous regions, and municipalities directly under the central government.

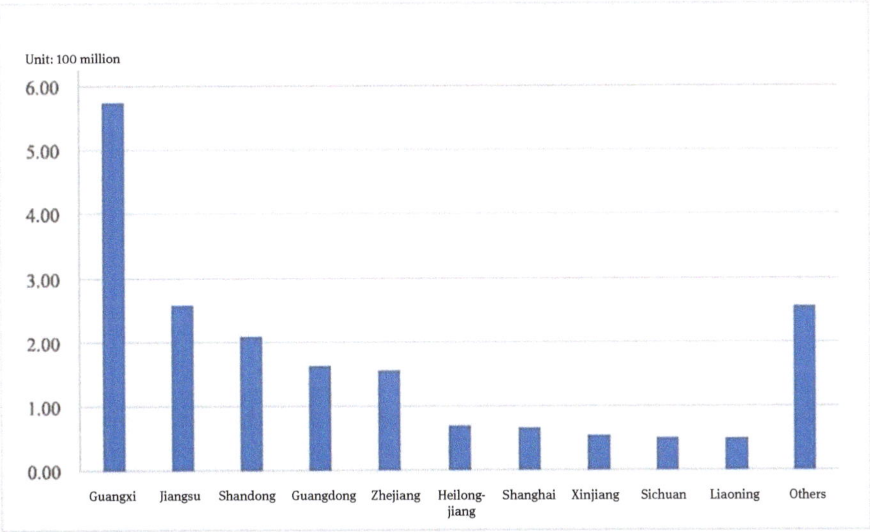

Figure 6-12 Number of query/verification interface calls on National Data Sharing and Exchange Platform by various provinces, autonomous regions, and municipalities directly under the central government from July 2022 to June 2023.

Source: National Data Sharing and Exchange Platform.

In the sharing of data between departments, from July 2022 to June 2023, the State Taxation Administration ranked first in the data sharing list in the total number of queries/verifications for basic information of natural persons, when it conducted special additional deductions in personal income tax, with an average of more than 90 million monthly calls. In the number of data interface calls, the State Taxation Administration, the Department of Publicity of the CPC Central Committee, the Ministry of Human Resources and Social Security, the National Development and Reform Commission, and the General Office of the State Council ranked among the top five, as shown in Figure 6-13.

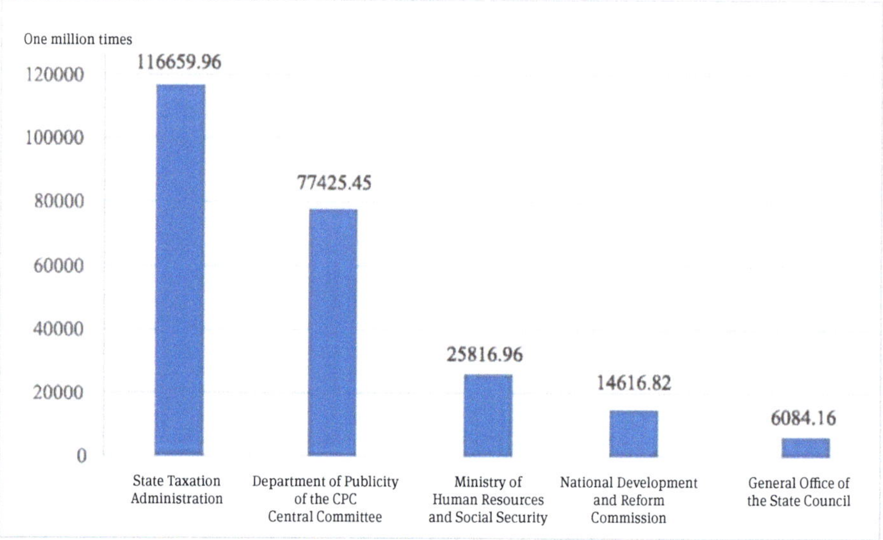

Figure 6-13 Top five departments in the total number of data interface calls from July 2022 to June 2023.

Source: National Data Sharing and Exchange Platform.

The construction of data sharing and exchange systems in various regions accelerates. According to a survey conducted by the School of Public Policy & Management, Tsinghua University, among thirty provincial-level regions surveyed, seventeen have achieved full coverage of data sharing and exchange platforms at the provincial, municipal, and county levels, and thirteen have achieved coverage of data sharing and exchange platforms at the provincial and municipal levels. Twenty-seven regions have established real-time data exchange systems, of which twenty-four regions have achieved minute-level real-time data exchange. Various regions strive to achieve the connection to vertical business management systems of the State Council. Currently, fourteen regions have achieved the connection between data sharing and exchange platforms and some vertical management systems, and seven regions have achieved the connection with several vertical management systems. Basic data such as population, legal persons, geographic information, credit, and licenses, as well as data on tax, health, education, natural resources, and market regulation, constitute the data that various regions hope to receive from relevant departments. Data sharing and exchange platforms provide effective support for data circulation and sharing between departments and regions.

6.3.4 The level of data openness is continuously improved

The openness of government data helps to unleash data energy, stimulate innovation, promote the development of the digital economy, and enhance the capability and level of governance. In recent years, governments at various levels have continuously accelerated the construction of platforms for data openness and promoted access to government data. By October 2022, 208 provincial and municipal governments in China had launched platforms for access to government data, including 25 provincial-level platforms, 12 subprovincial-level platforms and 171 prefecture-level platforms. Compared to the second half of 2021, there were 15 new local platforms, including one provincial-level platform and 14 municipal-level platforms, growing by about 8 percent.

Figure 6-14 shows the trend of the number of local platforms for access to government data in China from 2012 to 2022. Figure 6-15 shows the proportion of platforms for access to government data at various levels and in various regions.

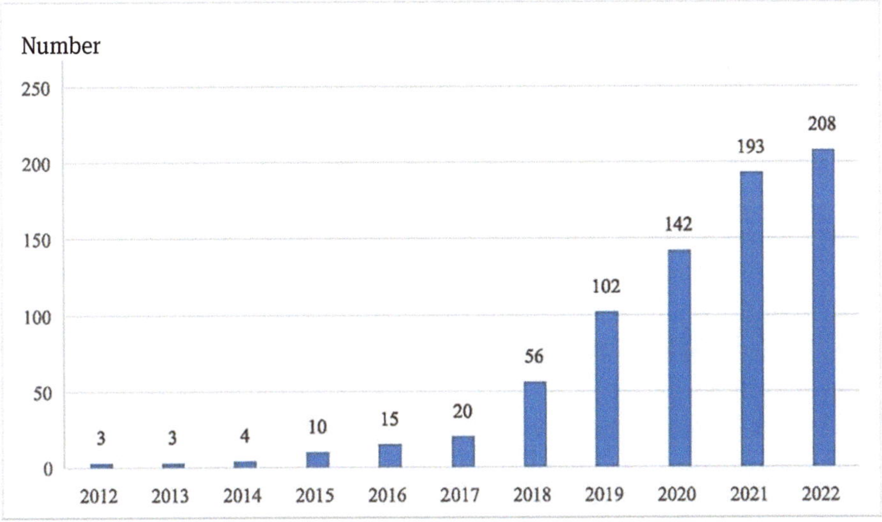

Figure 6-14 Trend in the number of local platforms for access to government data in China from 2012 to 2022.

Source: Report on the Opening of Local Government Data in China 2022.

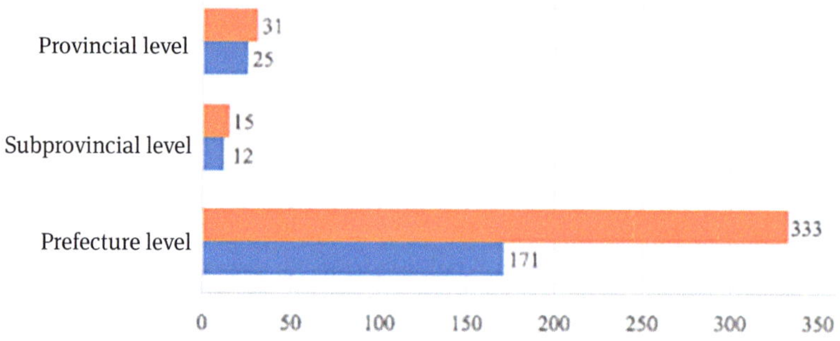

	Prefecture level	Subprovincial level	Provincial level
Total number of local governments	333	15	31
Number of platforms	171	12	25

Figure 6-15 Proportion of platforms for access to government data at various levels and in various regions.

Source: Report on the Opening of Local Government Data in China 2022.

6.4 Capabilities of Digital Service and Regulation are Further Consolidated

With the continuous development and wide application of information technology, digital transformation as an idea and a method has been deeply integrated into the work of governments. By continuously optimizing online services, vigorously promoting digital regulation, and solidly advancing the construction of the information infrastructure, various regions significantly improve the efficiency of digital service and regulation and provide strong support for governmental performance.

6.4.1 The level of online services is significantly raised

Governments at various levels and in various regions actively build ubiquitous, accessible, intelligent, convenient, fair, and inclusive digital service systems. China reaches a high level in online services. According to the United Nations *E-Government Survey 2022*, China ranked 43rd in the world in e-government (45th in 2021). Specifically, China ranked among the top in the "Online Services" index in the world and took the lead in the level of government services. Shanghai ranked tenth in the comprehensive analysis of 86 indicators among 193 cities worldwide, and its digital services reached a leading level internationally.

The service capability of the National Integrated Government Service Platform is continuously improved, and the construction of "one-stop government services" and "cross-provincial government services" is continuously deepened. The National Integrated Government Service Platform connects thirty-one provinces, autonomous regions, and municipalities directly under the central government, Xinjiang Production and Construction Corps, as well as forty-six platforms of departments of the State Council. Standardized services are initially achieved for more than 5.5 million policies and more than 10,000 widely used applications in local departments. 90.5 percent of provincial-level administrative licensing matters can be accepted online, without the need for a second visit. By the end of March 2023, the number of real-name users of the National Integrated Government Service Platform exceeded one billion, with more than 86 billion visits.

The services and applications of the National Integrated Government Service Platform are continually innovated, and the degree of satisfaction and sense of gain of enterprises and the public are continuously enhanced. The evaluation system of government services continues to be improved, which raises the level of government services in various regions and departments. Relevant regions and departments build and improve "helping ease enterprises' burden" section in the National Integrated Government Service Platform, promote the "whole-process handling online" of government service matters for more enterprises, actively explore services and applications of big data and AI, and provide 1.6 million incidents of policy inquiry, matching self-test, precise service push, and online handling for enterprises. Relevant regions and departments launch a "livelihood services" section to provide temporary assistance application, maternity service, social security, and medical insurance for special groups such as people with various difficulties and the elderly. Relevant regions and departments realize online handling of value-added tax refunds for international liquefied natural gas (LNG) imports, improve the "single window" section for international trade, establish the "electricity service" section, and stimulate the vitality of business entities. Relevant regions and departments build and improve "handling one affair one time" and "cross-provincial government services" sections in the National Integrated Government Service Platform, pilot and demonstrate "cross-provincial government services" and "regional government services" in the Yangtze River Delta, the Pan-Pearl River Delta, southwestern China, and other regions, and formulate relevant standards for projects. The cumulative number of the visits to "cross-provincial government services" section exceeds 20 billion times.

Various regions introduce relevant plans for the construction of government service platforms and actively promote the digital integration of government services. Thirty-one provinces, autonomous regions, and municipalities directly under the central government, as well as the Xinjiang Production and Construction Corps, have all built government service platforms. Government service platforms from thirty regions have covered five levels, i.e., provinces, cities, counties, towns, and villages. The proportion of online government services with "five-level connectivity" reaches as high as 93.75 percent. Government services in villages keep expanding to grassroots and rural areas. For example, Beijing promotes the whole-process online and electronic handling of business approval, which reduces application materials and handing deadlines for government services at the municipal and district levels by 74 percent and 71 percent, respectively. The average visit for administrative permits at the municipal level is reduced to less than 0.1 times. Jiangsu focuses on the needs of enterprises and citizens, and launches "handling one affair one time" for thirty common affairs such as starting enterprises, deregistration of enterprises, registration of real estate, approval of construction projects, mortgage registration of real estate and movable property, registration of newborns and marriage, which reduces the procedures, materials, and time limits by more than 60 percent, and significantly enhances the sense of achievement of enterprises and citizens in the reform. Zhejiang relies on the government service platform, streamlines online business procedures of subsidy policies, monitors the whole process of approval and distribution of subsidies, and achieves direct access and benefit of policies and the prevention and control of risks. Take two subsidy policies for disabled people as an example. The distribution list is updated in a timely manner via centralized data review, and a total of 101,700 risky payments are prevented. Guangdong optimizes and integrates the demand response platform for small and medium-sized enterprises, as well as the demand platform for the industrial chain and supply chain guarantee section, builds a unified "business entity demand response platform,", and meets the demands of and receives suggestions from nearly 700,000 enterprises and individual businesses in the province. Chongqing launches *Yu Kuai Ma*, which comprehensively integrates all kinds of information on cards, codes, and certificates, connects more than 2,000 types of application scenarios and services, and covers multiple environments in culture, tourism, and medical care, such as libraries, exhibition halls, tourist buses, as well as online appointments and QR code scanning in hospitals.

In the Yangtze River Delta, southwestern China, and the Pan-Pearl River Delta, cross-provincial government services and regional government services are continuously enhanced. "Three Provinces and One City" in the Yangtze River Delta, i.e., Shanghai, Jiangsu, Zhejiang, and Anhui, utilize the National Integrated Government Service Platform, launch a total of 148 types of cross-regional services, handle more than 6.42 million affairs online, achieve the sharing and mutual recognition of 37 types of commonly used electronic certificates, issue more than 14.3 million electronic certificates, and share and exchange more than 800 million pieces of data, which effectively promote regional integration and high-quality development of the Yangtze River Delta, and accumulate useful experience for national cross-provincial government services. Through the National Integrated Government Service Platform, Beijing, Tianjin, Hebei, and Xiong'an New Area complete 128 affairs related to cross-provincial government services, launch online handling nationwide of 112 affairs such as the transfer and continuation of pension insurance and unemployment insurance applications, as well as 142 commonly used services, realize the handling of 231 affairs such as housing provident fund and social security in "Beijing-Tianjin-Hebei + Xiong'an," release 153 unified standards for the same affairs in Beijing-Tianjin-Hebei Free Trade Zone in three groups, and support the national strategy of coordinated development of the Beijing-Tianjin-Hebei region. Nine regions in the Pan-Pearl River Delta, such as Guangdong, Fujian, and Jiangxi, rely on government service platforms, integrate more than 2,400 commonly used affairs and 200 commonly used government services in various regions and departments, achieve cross-provincial government services in the Pan-Pearl River Delta, and handle 56 government services in Guangdong in Hong Kong and Macao. Sichuan and Chongqing release 297 affairs that can be handled in the two regions in three groups, and a total of more than ten million affairs have been handled.

6.4.2 The capability in digital regulation is tremendously improved

In recent years, the digitization and modernization of governmental performance at various levels and in various regions in China have been significantly improved. In the field of regulation, various regions accelerate the construction of models of digital regulation and promote "smart regulation" and "targeted regulation." Presently, business collaboration is basically achieved among multiple departments such as market regulation, human resources and social security, customs, and commerce, which reduces the burden on enterprises. Data is analyzed and applied to support urban unified online management and emergency response and improve the scientific, precise, and intelligent level of urban governance. The construction of a national "Internet + regulation" system was initially completed in 2020. Various regions and departments accelerate the construction of regional and departmental Internet + regulation systems, promote the connection with the national regulation system, and carry out law enforcement based on the system.

The influence of the Internet + regulation platform and applet of the State Council continues to expand. The platform and applet enlarge the channel for collecting and giving information on regulation, enrich regulatory approaches, improve regulatory effects, and solve common and urgent problems among the masses and enterprises, which thoroughly implements major decisions and arrangements of the CPC Central Committee and the State Council. From January 1, 2022 to March 31, 2023, the Internet + regulation platform of the State Council received more than 8.6 million comments and more than 83 million visits, and transferred more than 1.2 million problems or clues to relevant regions and departments in an appropriate way. The Regulation Office of the General Office of the State Council has directly dispatched personnel to check more than 5,000 problems or clues, which are also included in on-site investigations organized by the State Council or relevant departments in national regulation or department regulation. This effectively solves the most pressing difficulties of high concern to business entities and citizens and fully implements various policies and measures for benefiting enterprises and citizens issued by the CPC Central Committee and the State Council. In order to actively respond to the concerns of the masses and receive the supervision of the masses, the Internet + regulation platform of the State Council has released eighty-eight issues of "feedback on regulation," which give public feedback on the opinions of the masses, and urge relevant regions and departments to systematically carry out the rectification of their work; this has won wide support among the public.

6.4.3 The level of support and guarantees is evidently enhanced

The infrastructure of digital government improves. The coverage of the WAN of the national e-government platform further expands, fully connecting thirty-one provinces, autonomous regions, and municipalities directly under the central government, as well as the Xinjiang Production and Construction Corps, achieving full coverage of cities and counties, as well as 96.1 percent of towns and villages, and providing basic support for building ubiquitous, accessible, intelligent, convenient, fair, and inclusive digital service systems. Significant results are made in the intensive construction of government cloud platforms. The construction of a government cloud platform has been basically completed in thirty-one provinces, autonomous regions, and municipalities directly under the central government, as well as the Xinjiang Production and Construction Corps. More than 80 percent of prefecture-level cities have built or applied government cloud platforms. Governments at various levels and in various regions have transferred digital government systems and platforms to the cloud in a large scale. The intensive construction and supply pattern of computing and storage resources in digital government has initially taken shape.

The requirements for the security of digital government are further standardized. In recent years, multiple laws and regulations, such as *Cybersecurity Law of the People's Republic of China*, *Data Security Law of the People's Republic of China*, *Personal Information Protection Law of the People's Republic of China*, and *Regulations on Security Protection of Critical Information Infrastructure*, have been successively issued. Several policies and documents, such as *Measures on Cybersecurity Review*, *Measures on Security Evaluation of Cloud Computing Service*, and *Measures on Security Evaluation of Data Outbound Transfer*, have been successively released. A number of important systems, such as cybersecurity review, the security evaluation of cloud computing services, the management of data security and personal information protection have been basically established. State organs are required to follow the principles of "synchronous planning, synchronous construction and synchronous use" in governmental work and strictly ensure security, which lays a solid foundation for security protection in the construction of digital government.

10.2478/9788367405867-008

Chapter 7
Construction of a Digital Society

The digital society is a product of the deep integration of digital technology and social transformation and is a new social form following the development of an agricultural society, an industrial society, and an information society. Accelerating the construction of the digital society serves as fundamental support for meeting the needs of people for a better life and accords with the requirement for promoting better and faster development of socialist modernization.

As a systematic project, the construction of the digital society not only boosts the transformation of social production, life, and operations but also involves the adjustment of the structure of society and the mix of social interests. The CPC Central Committee and the State Council issue *Overall Layout and Planning for the Construction of Digital China*, which regards "achieving significant results in precise, inclusive and convenient digital society" as one of the goals of the construction of digital China, and determines the direction for accelerating the construction of the digital society.

Since 2022, various departments and regions have adhered to the guidance of Xi Jinping Thought on Socialism with Chinese Characteristics for a New Era, centered on the decisions and arrangements of the CPC Central Committee as well as the goals of building a digital China into a country with cyber strength; all have systematically designed and comprehensively promoted the construction of digital society. The digital society has become more balanced and inclusive. In digital livelihoods, the goal of "digital society meets the needs of citizens" has been basically achieved. Phased results have been made in the development of a digital countryside, with a new landscape of digital communities online and offline. The standards of digital life have arrived at a new stage, and the governance of digital society has reached a new level, signaling phased progress in the construction of a precise, inclusive, and convenient digital society.

7.1 That "Digital Society Meets the Needs of Citizens" is Basically Realized in Digital Livelihoods

Digitization empowers people's livelihood, makes digital education accessible, and improves the quality of the development of digital healthcare. Digital social security facilitates the services for people's livelihood, and digital sport thrives. That "digital society meets the needs of citizens" is basically realized in digital livelihoods, which continuously meet the needs of people for a better digital life.

7.1.1 Digital education becomes more inclusive and convenient

The development environment of digital education is continually optimized. By February 2023, the networking rate of national compulsory education schools had reached 100 percent. Multimedia classrooms had been built in 99.5 percent of primary and secondary schools.[1] In the management of schools, the completion rate of information-empowered schools and the systems of cybersecurity had reached a high level. Nearly 85 percent of schools had formed systems for cybersecurity management.[2] China Education Television broadcasts all courses of various grades through television channels, and the "TV + education" model accelerates the development of digital education. The action plan for the Internet-based Intelligence Development Project is continuously carried out. Special training classes on information-based education for directors of educational departments and schoolmasters of primary and secondary school are organized in 160 key counties that receive assistance in pursuing rural revitalization, aiming to cultivate leading talents for the development of digital education.[3]

The opening and sharing of digital educational resources are achieved. The National Smart Education Public Service Platform was launched in 2022. As the largest educational and teaching resources library in the world, the platform has three resources platforms, one service hall, nine themed sections, and fifteen local platforms. It gathers 44,000 types of resources of primary and secondary schools, 1,173 professional teaching resources libraries for vocational education, 27,000 high-quality MOOCs for higher education, more than 6,700 excellent online courses, and more than 2,200 open video courses, covering about 600 majors and providing 26 types of high-quality government services, with 215 VR demonstration and training base cultivation projects throughout the country.[4] Relying on the National Smart Education Public Service Platform, nearly 55 percent of teachers in vocational schools nationwide carry out blended learning and explore the use of emerging technologies

1 Huai Jinpeng. "Digital Transformation and the Future of Education: A Keynote Speech at World Digital Education Conference," February 2023.

2 China National Academy of Educational Sciences. *Blue Book of Smart Education in China 2022*, February 2023.

3 Information Technology Center of Ministry of Agriculture and Rural Affairs. *China Digital Countryside Development Report 2022*, February 2023.

4 Huai Jinpeng. "Digital Transformation and the Future of Education: A Keynote Speech at World Digital Education Conference," February 2023.

such as VR and digital twins to create teaching scenarios and solve problems in internship and training. Many remote rural areas in central and western regions launch online and offline classrooms, which improve the quality and level of teaching. For example, Jinzhai County in Anhui Province focuses on the construction of smart classrooms in most remote teaching venues and integrates 55 original main online classrooms and 177 receiving classrooms into smart classrooms, ensuring that remote teaching venues enjoy smart education first. In July 2022, the OUC Lifelong Education App was launched. Currently, the platform has provided 630,000 types of course resources, including 570,000 types of course resources from well-known third-party platforms, 60,000 audio-video courses developed by OUC, and 7,705 courses (79,993 audios and videos) collected from 3,351 universities and educational institutions.[5] Since its launch, the OUC Lifelong Education Platform has provided more than twenty-six million occurrences of learning services to learners and organized nearly thirty themed events, with more than five million users. The cumulative learning time spent by users exceeds 15,000 hours. The number of cooperative colleges and institutions for learning resources reaches 1,000. In July 2022, under the guidance of the Office of the Central Cyberspace Affairs Commission and the Party School of the CPC Central Committee (National Academy of Governance), the National Digital Literacy and Skills Enhancement Platform was launched, aiming to urge relevant research institutes, industrial enterprises, and social organizations to open and share digital educational resources to/with the public through the platform. The digitization of educational resources continues to expand the coverage of high-quality educational resources, foster balanced development of education, promote educational equity, open a path to smart education, and improve the supply of digital educational resources.

7.1.2 The quantity and quality of digital healthcare improve

The scale of digital healthcare is growing steadily. The National Health Commission actively improves remote medical service network at the five levels (i.e., province, city, county, town, and village), with a coverage rate of more than 90 percent at the county level. By June 2023, the number of Internet healthcare users in China had reached 364 million, with an increase of 1.62 million over December 2022, accounting for 33.8 percent of the total number of Internet users, as shown in Figure 7-1.[6] The digital healthcare industry is in full swing. In 2022, the penetration rate in the digital

5 "The One-year Anniversary of the Launch of OUC Lifelong Education Platform: Digitalization Empowers Lifelong Education for All." Accessed June 2023. https://www.ouchn.edu.cn/News/zbxw/93ceabd8a07f41f284012e7d168fa4ca.htm.

6 CNNIC (China Internet Network Information Center). The 52nd Statistical Report on China Internet Development, August 20.

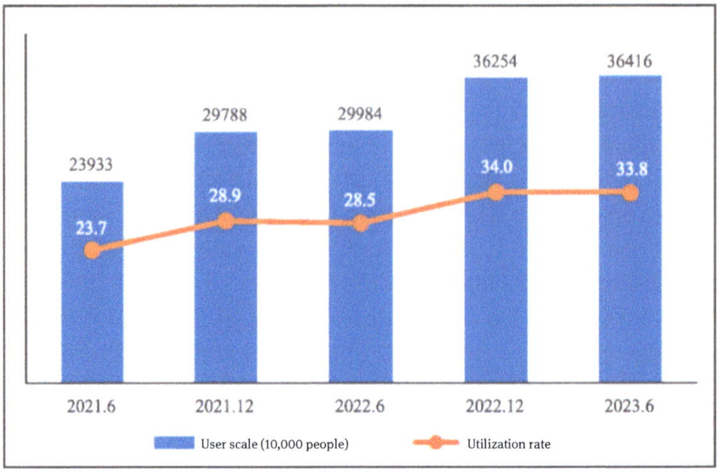

Figure 7-1 Scale and utilization rate of Internet healthcare from June 2021 to June 2023.

Source: The 52nd Statistical Report on China Internet Development.

healthcare market in China increased from 38 percent to 70 percent. As predicted, the scale of the digital healthcare market in China would climb to 43.6 billion *yuan* in 2023, showing a trend of exponential growth in the next five years. In particular, Internet enterprises successively enter the medical industry, forge advantages in such fields as Internet diagnosis and treatment, and retail drugs, explore the deep integration of online and offline business models, and focus on the layout of medical e-commerce and online medical consulting based on physical healthcare.[7] For example, in September 2022, JD Health and Omron reached a strategic cooperation agreement. The two parties announced that they would launch in-depth cooperation in multiple fields such as the innovation on service models as well as digital and intelligent marketing.[8]

Digital healthcare continuously advances, with the level of standardization improved. Since 2022, IoT, AI, big data, and other advanced technologies have been intensively applied in medical care and health, and new models and forms such as remote consultation, Internet hospitals, and smart healthcare develop rapidly. The number of patent applications in the field of digital healthcare grows quickly. In the past five years, a total of 154,000 patents related to digital healthcare have been applied for in more than fifty countries and regions worldwide. China, the

7 "Zero Power Intelligence Industry Research Institute: Prediction Report on the Competition Pattern and Development Trends of the Digital Healthcare Industry in China 2022–2026," March 2022.

8 "JD.com Announces Third Quarter 2022 Results." Accessed November 2022. https://ir.jd.com/system/files-encrypted/nasdaq_k/assets/2022/11/18/18-19-23/JD.com%20Announces%20Third%20Quarter%202022%20Results.pdf.

United States, and South Korea rank in the top three, with 66,000, 29,000, and 10,000 patent applications, respectively.[9] In digital healthcare, technological innovation remains active in China. In the number of patent applications in globally digital healthcare, among the top ten corporations, three come from China, two come from Japan, and five come from Switzerland, the United States, Germany, the Netherlands, and South Korea. Simultaneously, relevant departments formulate policies to guide the standardized development of the digital medical industry and optimize the regulatory framework of Internet diagnosis and treatment and Internet drug sales. In September 2022, the National Medical Products Administration issued *Measures on the Regulation of Online Drug Sales*, which stipulates the management of online drug sales, the responsibilities of platforms, and the measures on supervision and inspection and legal responsibilities, aiming to improve the governance of online drug sales.

7.1.3 Digital social security and employment better guarantee people's lives

In China, the digitization of social security continually improves, and the application scenarios continuously expand. In June 2023, the Ministry of Human Resources and Social Security issued *Implementation Plan for the Construction of Digital Human Resources and Social Security*, which aims to comprehensively promote digital reform of human resources and social security; optimize the services in digital social security, employment, and human resources; achieve integrated business, precise service, intelligent regulation, scientific decision-making and ecological development; and lead and support the high-quality development of human resources and social security. In 2022, thirty-one provinces, autonomous regions, and municipalities directly under the central government supported the payment of social security through WeChat Pay, with an annual payment of more than 880 million *yuan*, up by more than 16 percent compared to 2021.[10] Twenty-seven provinces, autonomous regions, and municipalities directly under the central government provided a convenient and efficient channel on the WeChat applet for handling social security. In addition to the payment service of social security, users can apply for electronic social security cards, use medical insurance vouchers, register for medical treatment, and print social security vouchers through WeChat City Services. By May 2023, 715 million people applied for and used electronic social security cards in China. In particular, electronic social security cards are quickly promoted and applied in rural

---

9 Patsnap. Analysis Report on Technological Innovation Index in the Field of Digital Healthcare in 2022, December 2022.
10 CNNIC. The 51st Statistical Report on China Internet Development, March 2023.

areas, providing convenient services such as insurance registration, social security payment and inquiry, and treatment certification and distribution for rural residents. Currently, thirty-one provinces, autonomous regions, and municipalities directly under the central government distribute financial subsidies for agricultural affairs through social security cards.[11]

Digital social security enhances the happiness of vulnerable groups. Because of the national elderly care service information system, unified management and targeted service are available for the information of left-behind elderly people in rural areas. The information system for monitoring people at risk of returning to poverty is continuously improved, and the timeliness and accuracy of the monitoring are continuously enhanced. Since 2022, among 681,100 people monitored in central and western provinces, 98.5 percent have obtained assistance, and 5,208 people have eliminated the risk of returning to poverty.[12] Based on national children welfare management information system, information ledgers for left-behind children in rural areas, orphans and *de facto* unattended children, children infected with the AIDS virus, and left-behind women in rural areas can be formed so as to achieve online and offline coordination, establish a long-term assistance and relief mechanism, and protect the growth of minors.

Digital technology creates job opportunities. The development of digital technology catalyzes a variety of employment modes such as content creation, an Internet advertising agency, live streaming e-commerce, etc. A new recruitment model of the "live stream interview" quickly emerges, in which employers interact with job seekers in live streaming rooms, and recruitment shifts from "face-to-face" to "screen to screen." The live stream interview becomes a new mechanism for promoting employment in various regions. More people are seeking employment through short videos and live streaming. In 2022, the proportion of blue collar workers who obtained jobs in this way increased by 12.4 percent.[13]

7.1.4 Digital sport shows a trend of robust development

Digital sport takes a quantum leap. By December 2022, the number of online fitness users in China had reached 380 million, accounting for 35.6 percent of the total number of Internet users. Specifically, users of mobile apps for fitness accounted for 18.9 percent, users of smart devices for fitness accounted for 17.4 percent, and users of online training accounted for 14.6 percent, as shown in Figure 7-2. Among online

---

11 Cyberspace Administration of China. *Digital China Development Report 2022*, April 2023.

12 Information Technology Center of Ministry of Agriculture and Rural Affairs. *China Digital Countryside Development Report 2022*, February 2023.

13 China New Employment Forms Research Center. *Research Report on the Employment of Blue Collars in China 2022*, December 2022.

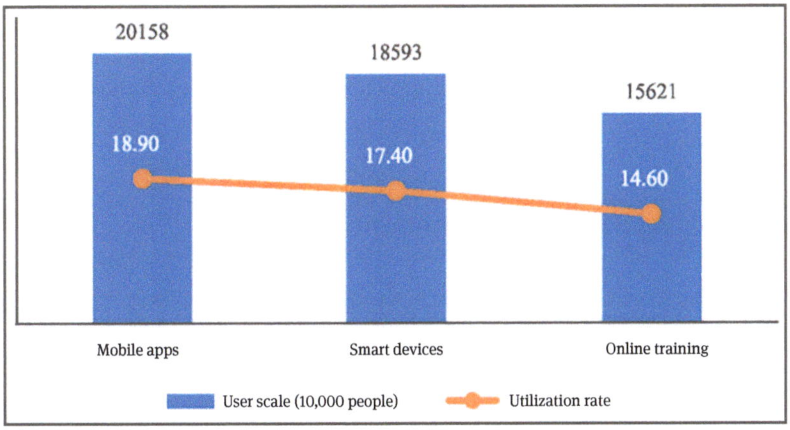

Figure 7-2 Scale and utilization rate of online fitness in various ways in December 2022.

Source: The 51st Statistical Report on China Internet Development.

fitness users, the proportion of users who exercised at low frequency (1–3 times a month), medium frequency (1–3 times a week), and high frequency (4 or more times a week) was 40.0 percent, 41.2 percent, and 18.8 percent, respectively.[14]

New forms of digital sport continue to emerge. Online fitness becomes an important channel to promote national fitness. The number of online fitness users grows rapidly, and various models of online fitness take shape. The National Fitness Online Games sponsored by the General Administration of Sport of China received positive responses from major Internet platforms. By July 2022, the number of direct participants exceeded ten million. In 2023, National Fitness Online Games were held. The number of direct participants exceeded 2.3 million, with more than 1.7 million completion certificates issued for various events within one month. Additionally, online fitness represented by online training attracts a large number of Internet users. Some celebrities become coaches of online fitness and have millions of fans. With live streaming, millions of fans watch online.

7.2 Phased Achievements are Made in the Construction of a Digital Countryside

As digital technology and digital talents quickly flow to rural areas, the digital foundation for rural revitalization is continuously consolidated. Digital technology

14 CNNIC. The 51st Statistical Report on China Internet Development, March 2023.

facilitates the development of smart agriculture, and new digital forms and models in rural areas mushroom. In China, phased achievements are made in the development of a digital countryside, which accelerates rural revitalization in an all-round way.

7.2.1 Top-level design is further optimized

In recent years, the Office of the Central Cyberspace Affairs Commission, together with relevant departments, has conscientiously implemented the decisions and arrangements of the CPC Central Committee, launched the development action of the digital countryside, and formulated or issued a series of policies and documents. In August 2022, the Office of the Central Cyberspace Affairs Commission, the Ministry of Agriculture and Rural Affairs, the Ministry of Industry and Information Technology, and the State Administration for Market Regulation, alongside relevant departments, formulated *Guidelines for the Construction of Standard System for Digital Countryside*, which proposes a model framework for a standard system and accelerates the construction of standards for a digital countryside. In April 2023, the Office of the Central Cyberspace Affairs Commission, the Ministry of Agriculture and Rural Affairs, the National Development and Reform Commission, the Ministry of Industry and Information Technology, and the National Rural Revitalization Administration jointly issued *Key Points for the Development of Digital Countryside in 2023*, which deploys twenty-six key tasks with ten targets, including consolidating the foundation for the development of rural digitalization, strengthening digital guarantee of food security, and improving the effectiveness of online assistance.

7.2.2 The digital infrastructure of rural revitalization is continuously consolidated

In rural areas, network infrastructure has achieved full coverage, and the penetration rate of the Internet has improved in both quantity and quality. By the end of 2022, the proportion of broadband access in administrative villages nationwide reached 100 percent, and the proportion of fiber optic and 4G access both exceeded 99 percent, basically realizing "same network and same speed" in rural and urban areas. 5G quickly extends to rural areas and covers all counties. By August 2022, a total of 1.968 million 5G base stations had been built and opened nationwide, and 5G network had covered all prefecture-level urban areas and county-level urban areas, as well as 96 percent of towns. By the end of 2022, the total number of rural broadband users in China had reached 176 million, with a net increase of 18.62 million throughout the year, up by 11.8 percent over 2021, 2.5 percent higher than that of urban broadband users in growth rate.[15] The number of rural Internet users had reached 308 million, accounting for 28.9 percent of total Internet users, with an increase of 24 million over December 2021, up by 1.3 percent. To be specific, the users of online education and Internet healthcare accounted for 31.8 percent and 21.5 percent of the total number of rural Internet users, up by 2.7 percent and 4.1 percent over 2021, respectively. In the popularization rate of information-based communication and video entertainment apps, the number of users in rural areas is basically on par with that in urban areas. The utilization rate of short videos in rural areas is 0.3 percent higher than in urban areas, and the utilization rate of instant messaging in rural areas is 2.5 percent lower than in urban areas.[16] By June 2023, the penetration rate of the Internet in rural areas had reached 60.5 percent.[17]

The digital transformation of rural infrastructure, such as roads, water conservancy, the power grid, and cold-chain logistics in the areas of agricultural products continuously advances. The quality of information services continually improves. The digital transformation of rural roads aims to achieve "smart management and maintenance." Various regions quickly realize the digital functions of rural roads, i.e., "presented with network, performed on cloud, shared via database, and supervised by platform," and gradually form digital platforms for comprehensive management and maintenance of rural roads featuring "separate records of roads and bridges." Longchang City, Sichuan Province, builds a comprehensive transportation dispatching and commanding platform, which basically achieves data access and video monitoring of transportation vehicles such as buses and general cargo, as well as key infrastructure such as highways, bridges, and tunnels in the city. The digital level of water conservancy and the power grid in rural areas continues to improve. Various regions establish online monitoring systems of water quality, information-based management and control systems of water plants, monitoring systems of pipeline networks and scientific dispatching and commanding, information-based management and control systems of power plants, monitoring systems of power grids and scientific dispatching and commanding, as well as intelligent charging systems. Zhashui County, Shangluo City, Shaanxi Province builds an information-based management and control center for water conservancy, which achieves online monitoring of water quality and intelligent management and control of water plants. The digital transformation of the industrial chain of agricultural product accelerates. By the end of 2022, the Agricultural Products Warehousing and Preservation Cold Chain Logistics Project had supported the construction of about 69,000 facilities and added a storage capacity of more than 18 million tons[18]. Cixi City, Zhejiang Province

---

15 *Statistical Bulletin on the Communications Industry in 2022.* Accessed January 2023. https://www.miit.gov.cn/gxsj/tjfx/txy/art/2023/art_77b586a554e64763ab2c2888dcf0b9e3.html.

16 CNNIC. The 51st Statistical Report on China Internet Development, March 2023.

17 CNNIC. The 52nd Statistical Report on China Internet Development, August 2023.

18 Information Technology Center of Ministry of Agriculture and Rural Affairs. *China Digital Countryside Development Report 2022*, February 2023.

promotes the digital application of "sharing cold storage," which dynamically displays the condition of cold-chain facilities through a network and increases the comprehensive utilization rate of cold storage by 15 percent. In addition, information serves are provided for villages and households. By the end of 2022, a total of 467,000 information service societies had been built and operated nationwide, providing 363 million instances of public information services and 686 million instances of daily information services for farmers and new agricultural operators.

7.2.3 The level of agricultural intelligence is continually raised

Significant results are made in the integration of digital technology and agricultural machinery and agronomy. The Ministry of Agriculture and Rural Affairs continues to implement the projects in digital agriculture and support the construction of eight national digital agriculture innovation centers and subcenters and forty-one national digital agriculture innovation and application bases. According to monitoring data of the Ministry of Agriculture and Rural Affairs, in 2022, the national information rate of agricultural production reached 25.4 percent, with a year-on-year increase of 2.9 percent. The number of drones for plant protection reached 160,000. More than 600,000 tractors and combine harvesters were equipped with operation monitoring and intelligent control terminals based on the Beidou Navigation Satellite System. Unmanned farms or farms with a few people are effectively implemented in Wuhu, Anhui, the Great Northern Wilderness, and the Jiansanjiang Reclamation Area. Digital technologies such as intelligent agricultural machinery and automated seedling cultivation are widely integrated into agricultural production. Digital application scenarios, such as digital fields and smart farms (animal husbandry and fishing), continuously expand, providing support for the development of the entire chain of agriculture. As the data shows, intelligent agricultural machinery can perform the function of continuous and full-time operation, raising the operational efficiency by 20 percent-60 percent.[19] The construction of agricultural and rural big data platform steadily progresses. Electronic maps of national functional areas for grain production and protected areas for the production of important agricultural products are completed. The National Agriculture Remote Sensing Application and Research Center carries out remote-sensing monitoring of the growth of important agricultural products, soil moisture status, crop yield, and other aspects at home and abroad, and continuously produces high-quality monitoring reports.

Smart planting promotes the intelligent development of the entire industrial chain from farmland to dining table. By the end of 2022, the national information

19 "China Releases the First Roadmap for Smart Agricultural Machinery Technology and Will Form a Group of Commercial Unmanned Farms by the End of the 14th Five-Year Plan." Accessed June 2023. https://m.gmw.cn/baijia/2022-05/18/1302952764.html.

rate of field planting exceeded 21.8 percent. In particular, the information rate of the production of three major grain crops (wheat, rice, and corn) reached 39.6 percent, 37.7 percent, and 26.9 percent, respectively.[20] For example, in the wheat field at Danji Town, Tongshan District, Xuzhou City, an intelligent yield-measuring harvester measures yield while harvesting. The large screen on the field ridge generates a real-time spatial distribution map of wheat yield of the field, providing a "digital map" for the planting during the next season. A "Wheat Growth Inspection Robot," equipped with multispectral sensors with a depth camera, laser radar, and visible light, moves back and forth. It can not only intelligently inspect twenty-four hours a day, but also accurately perceive the field environment and crop growth.

The digital transformation of forestry, animal husbandry, and fishery quickens. Various regions accelerate the construction of space-air-ground integrated perception and application systems for forestry, establish new models of resources regulation through aerial observation, ground patrol, and online inspection, and achieve new pattern of vertical-horizontal connectivity of forestry data. In fishery, the technology and equipment for real-time monitoring of hydroponic environment, automatic oxygenation, automatic and precise feeding of bait, disease monitoring and warning, and treatment and control of circulating water are quickly upgraded, achieving healthy aquaculture and energy conservation and consumption reduction. Through the implantation of precise systems, feed waste is reduced by 30 percent to 40 percent, and feeding accuracy is raised from 60 percent to 90–95 percent. In the breeding industry of cows, hens, and pigs, digital transformation of technology and equipment, such as precise regulation and intelligent management of the breeding environment, precise feeding, intelligent egg-picking, intelligent inspection and disinfection of the breeding environment, automatic treatment of waste, and remote intelligent diagnosis of livestock and poultry, accelerates. For example, the system of "smart pastures" is used by more herdsmen in Urumqi, Changji, Ili, Altay, and other regions. Livestock wear collars with BDS and have electronic ID cards. Herdsmen only need to download the smart pasture app on their mobile phones to remotely watch and operate. This achieves intelligent grazing and provides an important basis for product quality and safety traceability.

7.2.4 New digital business forms and models continue to emerge in rural areas

Agricultural products are sold through online live streaming. New service forms that assist farmers with live streaming develops quickly, and many cities that help to sell a

---

20 Information Technology Center of Ministry of Agriculture and Rural Affairs. *China Digital Countryside Development Report 2022*, February 2023.

variety of agricultural products emerge. This accelerates the circulation of agricultural products, increases rural incomes, and enriches the supply of agricultural products. Simultaneously, the form of "short video +live streaming" enhances consumptive power, improves agricultural productivity, empowers agriculture, rural areas, and farmers in a digital way, and promotes high-quality development of agriculture. *Kuaishou Report on the Consumption Trends of Agricultural Products & 2022 Chinese Farmers' Harvest Festival* presents a panoramic view of new consumption trends of agricultural products. More middle and low-end cities become famous via online live streaming, directly bringing more high-quality and inexpensive agricultural products to urban and rural households.

Rural e-commerce gains momentum. The Ministry of Agriculture and Rural Affairs continuously implements the "Internet + " project for agricultural products shipped out to urban households. The Ministry of Commerce implements the Digital Commerce for Rural Revitalization Project. In 2022, national rural online retail sales reached 2.17 trillion *yuan*, with a year-on-year increase of 3.6 percent, and online retail sales of agricultural products reached 531.38 billion *yuan*, with a year-on-year increase of 9.2 percent, 6.4 percent higher than in 2021.[21] In September 2022, "Chinese Farmers' Harvest Festival & Golden Autumn Consumption Season" was launched in Beijing, in which the total sales of agricultural products on relevant e-commerce platforms exceeded 50.7 billion *yuan*. Farmers expand their knowledge on e-commerce and optimize their marketing strategies. In December 2022, a special training course on agricultural and rural e-commerce was successfully held on the "cloud smart agriculture" online platform, which focused on topics such as accelerating agricultural and rural modernization with smart agriculture; promoting high-quality development of the Internet + project for agricultural products shipped out to urban households by upgrading e-commerce, rural financial services, e-commerce law, building agricultural brands and developing rural industries; increasing the number of e-commerce live streaming rooms; and developing and applying integrated media and e-commerce content. This facilitates the development of rural e-commerce and the launch of agricultural products.

7.3 The Digital Life of Citizens Reaches a New Level

Digital technology creates new opportunities for cultivating digital literacy and skills of the masses, and the service scenarios for digital life become more diverse.

21 "Head of E-commerce Department of Ministry of Commerce Introduces the Development of the Online Retail Market in 2022." Accessed June 2023. http://m.mofcom.gov.cn/article/xwfb/xwsjfzr/202301/20230103380919.shtml.

In particular, digital technology gives more opportunities for digitally vulnerable groups to integrate into digital society, and generally enhances their sense of happiness and gains from a digital life.

7.3.1 Smart community displays a new appearance

The construction of the smart community accelerates, with its efficiency improved. In May 2022, the Ministry of Civil Affairs and other eight departments jointly issued *Opinions on Deepening the Construction of Smart Community*, which clarifies key tasks such as intensively building smart community platforms, creating a new landscape of digital community life, forming convenient and inclusive smart-life service circles, and facilitating digital community life with multi-end connections, multi-party interaction, and intelligent sharing. Since 2022, the construction of urban smart-community infrastructure has been accelerated. Integrated community management platforms seamlessly connect to residents. Unmanned logistics and delivery enter communities, which promotes the digitization of various living scenarios such as community shopping and consumption, domestic life, public cultural life, leisure and entertainment, and transportation and travel.

The functions and services of a smart community become more complete. Various digital scenarios, such as shopping and consumption, payment, domestic life, transportation and travel, and business promotion quickly expand. Services such as employment, health, hygiene, medical care, social assistance, elderly care, assistance for disabled people, childcare, and protection of minors can be handled on mobile phones, via online platforms, and at nearby service centers, which tremendously facilitates citizens' handling of their personal affairs. Online group buying and digital community shops serve as new infrastructure of community economy. Services for community life become more precise, convenient, and diverse.

7.3.2 National digital literacy and skills enhancement are implemented

Digital literacy and skills of citizens improve. From July to August 2022, the Office of the Central Cyberspace Affairs Commission and other thirteen departments jointly hosted the "2022 National Digital Literacy and Skills Enhancement Month." Twenty-six thousand themed activities were planned and organized nationwide, directly involving more than twenty million participants and covering more than four hundred million people. There were 222,000 types of digital resources, with more than 41,000 promotional articles and nearly 1.26 billion online views. The event effectively evoked the enthusiasm of all sectors of society and enhanced national digital literacy and skills. In July 2022, a national digital literacy and skills enhancement platform was officially launched. In April 2023, "2023 National Digital Literacy and Skills Enhancement Month" was launched. The activity of digital literacy cultivation for teachers and students in the campus environment is continuously promoted. Nearly 80 percent of students in primary and secondary schools reach a qualified level or above in digital literacy. The digital literacy of teachers in primary and secondary schools is comprehensively improved. More than 86 percent of teachers reach a qualified level or above. A digital literacy and skills cultivation system that covers urban and rural areas is basically established, and the digital literacy and skills of various occupational groups are rapidly improved. For example, a series of activities of "National Digital Literacy and Skills Enhancement Month" in Shanghai covered 215 subdistricts and towns in 16 districts as well as 63 universities. A total of 1,381 activities were carried out, covering 6.969 million people online and offline.[22] According to data from the Ministry of Agriculture and Rural Affairs, various regions continually train farmers in the skills of using mobile apps, organize "Mobile Phone Skills Training for Farmers Week," optimize online training platforms and offline training systems, and enrich training content. Over the past seven years, more than 185 million people have received the training.

The digital literacy and skills of the disabled and elderly people are steadily rising. In "National Digital Literacy and Skills Enhancement Month," various regions take measures to help disabled and elderly people to bridge the digital divide. The top-level design for the construction of barrier-free environment for information exchange is continuously improved. In cooperation with "Barrier-free Transformation of Internet Applications Action," the Disabled Persons' Federation at various levels launch "Action to Improve the Digital Professional Competence of Disabled People," advance barrier-free transformation of Internet applications, implement digital public welfare actions, and enable disabled people to share in the achievements of digital development. According to data from the real-name registration system of the China Disabled Persons' Federation, currently disabled people who find jobs through the Internet mainly engage in information technology, software services, e-commerce services, and other industries. About 68,000 people are employed each year. More than 200,000 disabled people start online businesses on various e-commerce platforms. As digital literacy and skills are enhanced, the employment of disabled people is improved in both quality and quantity. Empowered by digital technology, elderly people use the Internet freely. For example, Jing'an District in Shanghai formulates *Standards and Guides of Jing'an District for Elderly People to Bridge the Digital Divide*, targets the downsides of digital learning of elderly people and continuously improves their digital literacy and skills.

22 "2022 National Digital Literacy and Skills Enhancement Month in Shanghai Ends." Accessed June 2023. https://www.shyp.gov.cn/shypq/jntsy-bmdt/20220822/413567.html

7.3.3 The elder-friendly and barrier-free level of digital public services is quickly improved

The penetration rate of barrier-free public service websites continues to increase. *Law on the Construction of Barrier-free Environment of the People's Republic of China* was passed in June 2023. As stated, Internet websites, service platforms, and mobile Internet apps that are built with government funds are required to meet the standards of barrier-free website design and the standards of barrier-free access to national information. Mobile Internet enterprises attach great importance to the barrier-free transformation of apps. Nearly 100 apps launch the elder-friendly model with large fonts, large icons, high contrast, and simple functional interfaces. This basically meets the needs of elderly and disabled people to socialize, shop, and obtain information through websites. In December 2022, the China Consumers Association evaluated 104 commonly used apps. As revealed, 76 percent of the apps met the requirements for the elder-friendly transformation of apps, and 76.2 percent of the respondents were generally satisfied with elder-friendly apps.[23]

"Smart Assistance for Elderly People" continues to be carried out, which helps elderly people to bridge the digital divide and enables them to share in digital dividends. By the end of 2022, the China Aging Development Foundation had launched "Technology-empowered Assistance for Elderly People" in twenty cities. In April 2023, the Ministry of Transport issued *Working Plan for Continuously Improving Elderly-friendly Barrier-free Transport and Travel Services in 2023*, which clearly requires the expansion of coverage of "one-button call" services for taxi call and online ride-hailing, carry out the "love reservation" service of urban rail transit, and provide reservation services for elderly and disabled people and other passengers through WeChat official accounts, applets, and other channels. In April 2023, the first site of "Free Travel for Elderly People" initiated by the China Aging Development Foundation was opened at Banquan Sports Park, Yanqing District, Beijing. Technology empowers the elder-friendly upgrading of traditional scenic areas, creating barrier-free and intelligent scenic areas that facilitate the travel of elderly people.

7.4 The Governance Capability of Digital Society is Continuously Enhanced

Since 2022, a new pattern of the governance of a digital society has been basically formed in China. The National governance system of digital society has been

23 China Consumers Association. *Research Report on the Consumption Supervision and Evaluation Project of Elderly-Friendly Apps*, December 2022.

continuously optimized, and the efficiency of digital governance in rural areas has been continually improved. The governance of the digital community has been accelerated, and the digitization of the whole society has been upgraded. These have laid a solid foundation for promoting the modernization of the national governance system and governance capability.

7.4.1 The Governance System of Digital Society is Continually Optimized

The institutional foundation for the governance of digital society is continuously consolidated. Since 2022, China has issued a series of laws, regulations, policies, and documents, constructed a national governance system for the digital society, strengthened the governance of big data and algorithms and the regulation of platforms, and deepened the development of digital governance. For example, in February 2023, the CPC Central Committee and the State Council issued *Overall Layout and Planning for the Construction of Digital China*, which proposes to promote the governance of digital society, toimplement the development of the digital countryside, and to empower rural industrial development, rural construction, and rural governance with digitization. Simultaneously, various departments and regions have formulated high-quality policies, laws, and regulations, established basic institutional standards for key links in the governance of digital society, formed complete institutional solutions, determined specific and detailed implementation plans, effectively implemented institutional standards, integrated systems and innovation, and provided stronger support for the construction of the digital society at the institutional level.

The infrastructure for the governance of digital society is rapidly upgraded. An integrated intelligent social security prevention and control system, an integrated intelligent public security system, and an emergency information-based system that combines routine exercises and actual emergency response take shape nationwide. Digital technologies represented by the IoT, big data, AI, and blockchain quickly empower the governance of digital society, and optimize and upgrade the basic environment for the governance of digital society. For example, since 2022, more than twenty provinces in China have developed and applied intelligent mobile mediation systems, which gather nearly 20 million pieces of data and information on people's mediation cases, and provide residents with online mediation services such as intelligent consultation, online application, and online mediation. Hangzhou utilizes AI technology to construct a "city brain" that empowers digital urban governance, strives to build the "first city of digital governance," develops comprehensive perception-based urban intelligent infrastructure that integrates data aggregation, intelligent computing and decision analysis, and optimizes urban governance.

7.4.2 The digital level of rural governance is continuously promoted

Party building leads to the digitization of rural governance. Led by Party building, various regions accelerate digital rural governance and integrate "Party building + grassroots governance + digitization." With Party members playing a leading role, various regions fully leverage the advantages of digital platforms, regularly publish the information on Party organizations and the activities of Party branches, provide digital platforms for Party members in rural areas to learn and exchange, promote the deep integration of education and management of Party members and daily work in rural areas, and accelerate the digital transformation, optimization and upgrading of rural governance. For example, at the Caicun Village Party and Masses Service Center, Caicun Town, Hunyuan County, Datong City, Shanxi Province, the "Leading Role of Party Building" section connects to the *San Jin Xian Feng* platform and develops characteristic applications for rural grassroots Party organizations, including New Era Civilization Practice Station and Wishes of the Masses. The center adopts online and offline forms to regularly carry out political and ideological education for Party members, especially mobile Party members.

The construction of a smart governance network in rural areas is accelerating. Various regions actively promote the digital construction of rural governance and the opening and sharing of data resources, comprehensively collect data on administrative villages (communities) and grids based on the principle of data collection for multiple parties, continuously explore the combination of the human resources network in grids and the cloud network of big data, and accelerate the construction of comprehensive smart governance networks in rural areas. Deqing County, Zhejiang Province promotes the network of the digital countryside in the county, and creates a twin countryside in the cloud, which covers twenty-two key scenarios such as remote-sensing monitoring, opinions of villagers, management of chronic disease and health code, and achieves comprehensive perception of rural production, life, and ecology as well as overall smart governance. Digital platforms break the restrictions of time and space, allow villagers who work outside and have difficulties in walking to know various work in villages promptly, offer suggestions on the work and supervise the work, and connect external funds, technologies, and markets with village resources. For example, Huangqitan Village, Shibatai Town, Zhuozi County, Ulanqab City, Inner Mongolia Autonomous Region, actively uses the "Village Farmers" applet and the Village Affairs Management Platform guided by the Ministry of Agriculture and Rural Affairs to improve rural governance with the help of Internet tools. Liaozhong District, Shenyang City, Liaoning Province, relies on the Internet Platform for the Regulation of Funds, Assets and Resources in Rural Collective Economy, and achieves the whole-process regulation of funds, assets, and resources in rural areas. Since its founding, the platform has covered 186 administrative villages (communities), 226 village-level accounting units, and 224 joint-stock economic cooperatives, with a total of 324,454 pieces of fund information and a total recorded asset value of 515.4143 million *yuan*. Simultaneously, various regions implement campaigns for digital rural governance and vigorously combat Internet financial crimes involving rural banks, rural credit, P2P online loan platforms, illegal online payments, etc. In addition, digital rural governance continuously empowers the management of vulnerable groups such as left-behind children. By the end of 2022, because of the Children Welfare Management Information System, various regions had investigated care-service targets in rural areas nationwide, and collected information on a total of 755,000 left-behind children.[24]

Online services for public law and social assistance are quickly popularized. Administrative villages and communities commonly establish legal aid stations, promote remote service models such as online application for legal aid and video legal consultation, and improve the service of smart legal aid. The work of "Internet + village (community) legal advisers" continuously advances, and nearly 530,000 administrative villages nationwide all have legal advisers. Rural legal advisers and grassroots legal service workers provide online legal advice, legal aid and legal publicity for rural residents and village Party branch committees and villagers committees. For example, in Zibo City, Shandong Province, a smart court platform covers major villages and provides services such as self-service contact with judges, legal consultation, online filing, online mediation, and circuit trials. Villagers who have disputes will first seek resolution through smart court platforms.

7.4.3 The governance of smart communities enters the fast lane

The governance model of smart communities is continually reinvented. With the governance model of "big data + grid," the smart community efficiently gathers, integrates, optimizes, and distributes connected information and resources in the community grid. It ollects information on public demands and emergencies in the grid in a timely fashion, monitors dynamic resources in the grid, and provides accurate and targeted social governance services for the public. Digital technology continuously empowers the last mile of community governance, optimizes community governance, and enriches service scenarios. Residents play an active role in community governance, with governance forms reshaped and governance models innovated. For example, the Qingpu District, Shanghai, innovatively launches a digital path for the transformation of grassroots governance that combines an offline community center (as physical form) and an online "Happiness cloud" system (as information hub), and further promotes the innovation in urban governance model,

---

24 Information Technology Center of Ministry of Agriculture and Rural Affairs. *China Digital Countryside Development Report 2022*, February 2023.

reform in urban governance methods, and the reconstruction of urban governance systems. By building a unified integrated platform for digital community governance, Zhongtian Community, Jinshan Street, Fuzhou City, actively promotes the deep integration of "Internet + digital governance + service system." People, things, and the environment of the community have been comprehensively managed, which effectively improves the speed and quality of community services.

The capability of smart emergency response in the smart community is enhanced. Digital technology empowers the construction of emergency response systems in modern communities, and the pattern of "security, emergency response, and disaster relief" takes shape. Urban communities continue to enhance the capabilities of response to major natural disasters and emergencies, as well as the effectiveness of emergency management, disaster prevention and relief, and monitoring and early warning. For example, Qiuxian County, Handan City, accelerates the construction of the new smart city and explores the path of urban governance empowered by digital technology. Xiangshan District, Huaibei City, develops "Xiangshan e-governance" to optimize grid-based urban governance. Shuangliu District, Chengdu City, builds an online mass line service platform. These cases are included in *2023 List of Typical Cases of Innovative Social Governance* jointly released by the *People's Daily Online* and the Party School of the CPC Central Committee (National Academy of Governance). Yuhang District, Hangzhou City, establishes a "1 + 1 + N" organizational structure for community emergency forces (one emergency fire control working group, one emergency fire control administrator, and N members from the grid), forms an efficient community emergency mechanism that combines routine exercises and actual emergency response, promotes the construction of a micro fire station, disaster resettlement site, material warehouse, and publicity center with high standards, and creates a Yuhang model for modern community emergency systems.

10.2478/9788367405867-009

Chapter 8
Building a Digital Culture

The report of the 20th CPC National Congress stresses that "To build a modern socialist country in all respects, we must develop a socialist culture with Chinese characteristics and be more confident in our culture. In our efforts to turn China into a country with a strong socialist culture, we will focus on upholding socialism with Chinese characteristics, rallying public support, fostering a new generation of young people, developing Chinese culture, and better presenting China to the world. We will develop a sound, people-oriented socialist culture for our nation that embraces modernization, the world, and the future. We will ignite the cultural creativity of the entire nation and build a powerful source of inspiration for realizing national rejuvenation." Empowered by national policies and digital technologies, digital culture, as a form of digital technology in the cultural field, endows the creation, production, presentation, dissemination, and consumption of cultural products with significant digital characteristics. Guided by socialist core values, digital culture enriches the form of socialist culture, enhances the dissemination of Chinese culture, promotes the construction of socialist cultural system with Chinese characteristics, and fosters the development of contemporary socialist culture with the innovation in ideas, approaches, forms, content, and technologies.

Over the past year, digital culture has been advancing in policy, content, industry, and technology. Polices on digital culture have been successively implemented, and laws and regulations on digital culture have been continuously improved, providing legal support for the development of digital culture. High quality and positive energy become core words in the content of digital culture. A group of digital cultural works that demonstrate high quality and disseminate positive energy continue to emerge. The development of the digital culture industry gains momentum, coming to a stage of high-quality development. New-generation revolution of digital technology that centers on AI technology advances, which spurs the digital transformation of the cultural industry and enhances cultural innovation. The construction of a digital culture always adheres to the development of a socialist culture with Chinese characteristics, strives to achieve the creative transformation and innovative development of excellent traditional Chinese culture, enhances cultural awareness, cultural confidence, and cultural self-improvement, continuously bolsters China's cultural soft power and the influence of Chinese culture, and contributes spiritual power to building up China's cultural strength.

8.1 Policies Promote and Consolidate the Development of a Digital Culture

In China, the development of the digital culture industry is driven by new technologies and new cultural forms. Currently, new ideas and policies accelerate the development of the digital culture industry. Over the past year, relevant departments focused on cutting-edge issues and long-term development, continuously strengthened top-level design, consolidated the foundation of digital culture, and fostered the high-quality development of the digital culture sector and industry.

8.1.1 The overall plan for building a digital culture is coordinated and promoted

In February 2023, the CPC Central Committee and the State Council issued *Overall Layout and Planning for the Construction of Digital China*, which incorporates the construction and development of a digital culture industry into the national strategy of digital China and provides overall layout and top-level design for the development of digital culture. Focusing on vigorously developing online culture, promoting cultural digitization, and enhancing the service capability of digital culture, *Overall Layout and Planning for the Construction of Digital China* aims to enrich digital cultural products, stimulate cultural stock resources, develop new cultural forms, and cultivate new models of cultural consumption. By deepening supply-side structural reform in the cultural field with digital technology, *Overall Layout and Planning for the Construction of Digital China* makes the supply of cultural products better adapt to the cultural needs of people in the digital era and meets the growing spiritual and cultural needs of people at a higher level. In 2022, the General Office of the CPC Central Committee and the General Office of the State Council issued policies and documents such as *Opinions on Promoting the Implementation of National Strategy of Cultural Digitalization* and *The 14th Five-Year Plan for Cultural Development*, which determine the direction for the layout of cultural digitization.

Building a rural digital culture meets the intrinsic requirement to implement the strategy of digital China, takes into consideration the development of digital culture industry, and plays a key role in comprehensively promoting rural revitalization. In January 2023, the CPC Central Committee and the State Council issued *Opinions on Comprehensively Promoting the Key Work of Rural Revitalization in 2023*, which proposes to cultivate new rural industries and new business forms, including implementing the plan for rural revitalization empowered by the cultural industry, rural leisure tourism, the project of "Digital Commerce for Rural Revitalization," and the Internet + project for agricultural products shipped out to urban households. In April 2023, the Office of the Central Cyberspace Affairs Commission and four other departments jointly issued *Key Points for the Development of Digital Countryside in 2023*, which requires the integration of digital culture industry with rural revitalization and empowers rural industrial development, rural construction, and rural governance. As clarified, China will innovate and develop rural digital culture, including creating an environment for the prosperity and development of rural online culture and promoting the digitization of rural resources and cultural relics. The construction of the digital countryside continuously advances, which improves multidimensional digital capabilities (including rural digital culture) and forges a more diverse and prosperous cultural landscape of a digital China.

8.1.2 Policies on digital culture focus on new business mdels and usher in a new era for the governance of a digital culture

Over the past year, digital culture, as a new form of cultural industry, showed a growth trend. As digital economy thrived, the operation of digital culture industry was continuously standardized by a series of policies. In 2023, the Ministry of Culture and Tourism issued policies and documents such as *Notice of Ministry of Culture and Tourism on Regulating the Business Activities of Online Dramas (Festivals) and Promoting the Healthy and Orderly Industrial Development* and *Opinions of Ministry of Culture and Tourism on Promoting the High-quality Development of Online Tourism Market*, and guided the China Association of Performing Arts to formulate *Outline of Online Streamers Training Service System*, which provide a policy-related basis for the operation of the digital culture market and the management of personnel, strengthen support and guidance, and promote the high-quality development of the digital culture industry. In August 2023, the State Administration for Market Regulation and Standardization Administration issued *Requirements for Corporate Intellectual Property Compliance Management System (GB/T 29490-2023)*, which provides standards for digital culture enterprises to prevent risks to intellectual property and realize the value of intellectual property.

Intelligent digital technology represented by generative AI produces opportunities for the development of digital culture, but spawns new problems simultaneously. The policies on digital culture are successively implemented, ushering in a new era for the governance of digital culture. In January 2023, *Regulations on the Management of Deep Synthesis in Internet Information Services* jointly issued by the Office of the Central Cyberspace Affairs Commission, the Ministry of Industry and Information Technology, and the Ministry of Public Security officially took effect. In August, the Office of the Central Cyberspace Affairs Commission, together with the National Development and Reform Commission, the Ministry of Education, the Ministry of Science and Technology, the Ministry of Industry and Information Technology, the Ministry of Public Security, and the National Radio and Television Administration released *Interim Measures on the Management of Generative Artificial Intelligence Services*. This further strengthens the regulation of new technologies, applications, and business forms; coordinates development and security; promotes the reasonable and effective utilization of AI technology according to law; and bolsters the healthy development of digital culture.

8.1.3 Policies on digital culture guide new social trends

Guided by socialist culture and empowered by emerging digital technology, the digital culture industry plays an important role in building a digital China, developing a digital economy, boosting cultural confidence, securing new successes in socialist culture, and building China into a country with a strong socialist culture. Over the past year, relevant departments continuously introduced policies on digital culture and guided new social trends with core socialist values. In August 2022, *The 14th Five-Year Plan for Cultural Development* was issued, which emphasizes the prosperity of cultural and artistic creation and production, including encouraging and guiding the creation and production of online culture, developing a positive and healthy online culture, strengthening the protection of digital copyright, etc. In October, the State Administration for Market Regulation, the Office of the Central Cyberspace Affairs Commission, and other five departments jointly issued *Guiding Opinions on Further Regulating the Endorsements by Celebrities*, which effectively strengthened the rectification of the failures of endorsements by celebrities, as well as the events that seriously disrupt market order and pervert social morals. In August 2023, the National Radio and Television Administration held a symposium on the high-quality development of TV dramas in the new era. As proposed, China continues to strengthen service guarantees, purify the industrial ecosystem, and create a favorable environment for the creation and development for high-quality works, including promoting the integration of online and offline video-audio works, providing more stages and channels for the dissemination of excellent works, launching comprehensive governance in the cultural and entertainment field, and guiding wholesome and positive social trends.

8.2 Positive Energy Prevails, and the Content of Digital Culture Flourishes

In June 2023, at the Symposium on Cultural Inheritance and Development, General Secretary Xi Jinping stressed that "It is our new cultural mission in the new era to further promote cultural prosperity and develop a great culture in China and a modern Chinese civilization from a new starting point. It is imperative to have greater confidence in our own culture, shoulder the mission, work diligently and proactively, and make concerted efforts to create a new culture of our times and build a modern

Chinese civilization."[1] Digital culture plays an important part in modern civilization of the Chinese nation. Over the past year, positive energy prevailed in the construction of digital cultural content, injecting the vitality of innovation into ideals and beliefs education. Relevant departments effectively promoted the creative transformation and innovative development of excellent Chinese culture, strengthened the governance of the ecology of digital culture, adhered to the integration of technological innovation and industrial regulation, and jointly built a clean, harmonious, and healthy ecology of digital cultural content.

8.2.1 Building a digital culture injects the vitality of innovation into ideals and beliefs education

Ideals and beliefs are like the basis and calcium for the faith of the CPC members. Since the 18th CPC National Congress, General Secretary Xi Jinping has made a series of important statements and profoundly elaborated on the theoretical connotation and meaning of ideals and beliefs. With diverse forms, rich content, and technological innovation, digital culture empowers the inheritance and dissemination of red culture, creates a red culture that follows mainstream ideology and integrates subjective initiatives, and injects the vitality of innovation into ideals and beliefs education.

The Museum of the Communist Party of China uses cutting-edge technologies such as AR, VR, and AI to completely restore the scenes in which the Red Army fought bitterly at the Xiangjiang River, fought their way across the Wujiang River, and seized the Luding Bridge during the Long March. A variety of environmental effects are combined, which enables the audience to really understand the difficulties the Red Army faced in the Long March. The museum reflects the extraordinary over-100-year journey the CPC has traveled in an all-round, whole-process, panoramic, and epic way, and strengthens the learning and understanding of the history of the CPC. By September 2023, the museum had received more than two million visitors from all sectors of society. In July 2023, the Shanghai Fourth CPC National Congress Memorial Hall launched "Digital Technology-Empowered Ideological and Political Education: A Metaverse-based Exhibition Area of Shanghai Fourth CPC National Congress Memorial Hall." Visitors can scan the code to connect to the applet, watch the AR scenes of sixteen districts in Shanghai, and have a panoramic view of 612 revolutionary sites in Shanghai, including pictures and texts. iFLYTEK utilizes AI to empower Party building. It enriches learning methods and improves learning efficiency via new AI technologies, such as virtual anchors giving Party lessons,

1 "General Secretary Xi Jinping Attended the Symposium on Cultural Inheritance and Development and Delivered an Important Speech." Accessed June 2023. https://www.gov.cn/yaowen/liebiao/202306/content_6884316.htm.

robot-assisted Party building, the voice tool on *Xue Xi Qiang Guo* platform, and an AI notebook for Party members' education. Digital technology promotes ideological and cultural construction among Party members and the masses, and helps Party members and cadres to boost their ideals and beliefs, enhance their ideological pursuits, and strengthen their Party consciousness.

A technology-empowered digital education platform and learning tool fully embody the organic unity of the wisdom of the times and technological innovation, provide new communication forms and channels for continuously studying Party history, disseminating red culture and inheriting revolutionary traditions, and inject the power of innovation into firmly upholding the correct political direction, the right tone in public opinion, and the correct value orientation, and giving play to the role of ideals and beliefs as the anchors of online civilization.

8.2.2 Digital culture provides a new path for the creative transformation and innovative development of traditional Chinese culture

Excellent traditional Chinese culture forms the foundation and source for the construction and development of digital cultural content. The organic unity of cultural content and digital technology transforms the forms of content production, management, interaction, and dissemination in the creative transformation and innovative development of traditional Chinese culture.

1. Digital technology transforms the forms of cultural resources

Cultural resources epitomize the national spirit and cultural confidence of the Chinese nation and constitutes an important source of digital cultural content. With the popularization and application of digital technology, digitization has become an innovative form for promoting cultural resources. Optimizing the management and utilization of cultural resources promotes the transformation, dissemination, and inheritance of traditional culture. By the end of 2022, Dunhuang Academy had completed a digital photography project that collected images of 278 caves, image processing of 164 caves, 3D reconstruction of 145 colored statues and seven large archaeological sites, panoramic-roaming programs of 162 caves, and digitization of more than 50,000 archival films. Additionally, blockchain technology was used to build "Digital Dunhuang Open Material Database," an authorization and utilization system of cultural heritage and digital resources, which now includes more than 6,500 high-definition archives of digital resources from the Mogao Caves and other cave sites, as well as literature on the Library Cave. Dunhuang Academy integrates various digital technologies to achieve comprehensive intelligent management of Dunhuang cultural resources and to promote digital inheritance and innovation in cultural content.

In intangible cultural heritage, digital technology is also used to reinvent the form of cultural resources. By the end of 2022, more than 200 public cultural cloud platforms at various levels had been built nationwide, with total library resources of 1,504 TB, 588,757 collections and 218,025 hours, covering art categories such as literature, dance, film, folk art, calligraphy, etc. In June 2023, the Ministry of Culture and Tourism issued a series of industrial standards such as *The Collection and Record of Digital Resources for the Digital Protection of Intangible Cultural Heritage*, which guides and standardizes the collection and record of digital resources of representative projects of various categories of intangible cultural heritage in China, and clarifies cultural and industrial standards for the collection and record of digital resources of intangible cultural heritage.

2. Intelligent technology creates new scenarios of cultural experience

Core socialist values and traditional Chinese culture provide value orientation and content framework for the development of digital culture, and the integration and application of intelligent technology create new 3D immersive scenarios of cultural experience for the innovative development of digital cultural content. In January 2023, in the "Online Spring Festival Gala," the China Media Group set up a Cyber Traditional Style Metaverse Venue. Users can choose personal images of a digital human and enjoy singing performance of Xiao C, a digital anchor of CCTV, which reshaped the traditional audiovisual experience of evening parties. In April 2023, Weibao Bookstore, located on the central axis of Beijing, introduced the Central Axis Cultural Information Digital Aggregation Platform. In line with the spatial layout of the central axis of Beijing, the interior design and AR device of Weibao Bookstore bring visitors to an interesting space. In addition, AI technology creates a space jointly built by human and machine, giving the public a new experience to create central-axis art with an AI entity. In June 2023, the Xi'an City Wall Scenic Area held Forest of Steles & Old City Wall Digital Heritage Exhibition, which created a space for experiencing digital cultural heritage based on ZTE's XRExplore platform and enabled visitors to see the old city wall and the Forest of Steles in digital and realistic ways.

Digital transformation combines the space of traditional culture with scenarios of digital technology, creates an immersive space for cultural experience with cultural and technological characteristics, and produces a new experience of digital culture.

3. Information technology empowers new channels of cultural dissemination

Information technology boosts cultural development, expands new paths of cultural dissemination, and provides more diverse and efficient channels for the dissemination of digital cultural content. First, information technology accelerates the aggregation of high-quality cultural content in the cloud. In July 2022, the China Media Group launched the construction of the Central Museums Digital Platform. With national cultural strategic resources, the platform presents cultural relics, artworks, and aesthetic courses from institutions such as the National Museum of China and the Palace Museum in the cloud and provides the public with a space of digital culture that combines cultural heritage and convenient service. Second, information technology enhances the dissemination of excellent cultural content in an interesting way. At the 2022 China (Shenzhen) International Cultural Industries Fair, *A Painting of Jinling*, a digital scroll of customs in Nanjing at Jiangsu Hall, allowed visitors to experience the prosperity of Jinling with 533 people in an immersive way. With traditional style of Chinese painting, *Poetic Jining*, a digital artwork of Jining, Shandong, adopted digital visual processing technology and interactive programming technology, integrated cultural technology and poetic atmosphere in a creative form, and empowered online dissemination and vivid presentation of the canal culture. Third, information technology enables various groups to access cultural resources. In December 2022, the Youku Barrier-free Theater was officially launched. After registration at the China Disabled Persons' Federation, visually impaired users can watch film and TV works in the theater for free. Digital technology empowers traditional communication channels and gives care to special groups. This embodies humanistic care in the practice of digital cultural communication.

8.2.3 Comprehensive governance of a digital culture adheres to the model of "regulation + guidance + service"

Digital culture signifies a form of culture that features digitization, networking, and intelligence. Currently, technologies such as big data, cloud computing, AI, and blockchain are developing rapidly, which provides technological support and great opportunities for innovation in digital cultural content and breeds new business forms and problems in digital culture industry. It is an urgent task to improve the governance system and capability in the cultural field, tackle the relationship between digitization and culture, development and security, joint contribution and shared benefits, autonomy and openness, and inheritance and innovation, and build a scientific and efficient modern governance system of digital culture.

The Internet is not a place beyond the rule of law. Since 2023, the Office of the Central Cyberspace Affairs Commission has continuously launched "Clean up" campaigns, focusing on nine areas such as standardizing We Media, combating the manipulation of information content by an online water army, regulating the communication order of major traffic links, correcting wrong information content on life service platforms, guiding the information content in short videos, purifying the online environment for minors on summer vacation, and combating cyber violence. The abuse of digital technology disrupts the digital cultural market and undermines cyberspace. In response to the concerns of Internet users, the Office of the Central

Cyberspace Affairs Commission strengthens the regulation of online platforms and guides the wholesome and positive ecology of digital cultural content.

The governance of digital cultural content requires Internet platforms and enterprises to actively perform their responsibilities. In May 2023, Tencent released *The White Paper on Compliance Governance of WeChat Channels*, which systematically introduces the measures and achievements of WeChat Channels in the governance compliance and ecology from six dimensions, i.e., platform rule systems, content ecosystems, minor protection systems, personal information protection systems, institutional user control systems, and intellectual property protection systems.[2] In June, Douyin published *Report on the Transparency of Security Governance in the First Quarter of 2023*. According to the data, in the first quarter of 2023, Douyin punished 2,900 accounts for illegal dissemination of false information, handled 1.58 million videos, and sent 1.35 million warning notes.[3] Internet platforms guide creators to follow platform rules in the production of digital content, participate in the governance of platforms with governmental regulation, and promote the construction of positive ecology of digital cultural content.

In the construction of digital cultural platforms, governmental departments strengthen the awareness of serving the masses and establish channels for feedback and communication, which enhance the governance awareness of Internet users, form a governance model of "regulation + guidance + service," and build a multiparty collaborative governance system. On the home page of its portal, the Palace Museum designs a prominent icon, "My Comments," and actively interacts with Internet users who express their views on the digital presentation of cultural relics. Various Internet platforms improve their governance systems. The complaint and appeal mechanism widely attracts Internet users to participate in the construction of the content and ecology of digital platforms.

8.3 The Digital Culture Industry Sees High-Quality Growth and Development

As an emerging industry, the digital culture industry centers on cultural and creative content. In the digital culture industry, digital technology promotes the production, dissemination, and service of digital content and helps to cultivate new supply and lead new consumption. In 2023, the digital culture industry entered a new stage of high-quality growth and development. According to data from the National Bureau

2 Tencent. "The White Paper on Compliance Governance of WeChat Channels," May 2023.

3 "Douyin Released *2023 Q1 Security Transparency Report* and Punished 2,900 Accounts for Illegal Dissemination of False Information." Accessed September 2023. https:/wap.peopleapp.com/article/mh35786357/rmh35786357.

of Statistics, in the first half of 2023, among cultural enterprises above a designated size in China, sixteen industries that featured new business forms of digital culture achieved a revenue of 2,358.8 billion *yuan*, with a year-on-year increase of 15.0 percent, 7.7 percent higher than all cultural enterprises above a designated size.

8.3.1 The digital culture industry and social scenarios are integrated and interembedded, and new opportunities are explored in diverse fields

In rural revitalization, in September 2022, the China Media Group launched "2022 Online Harvest Evening Party," the first immersive online harvest festival, which not only allowed farmers to fully enjoy their festival, but also made more Internet users understand new agriculture, the countryside, and farmers. In February 2023, *Do Farm Work*, an online reality show, was launched. It recorded the rural life of contemporary young people, showcased new atmosphere of rural areas in the new era, evoked the enthusiasm of young people for agriculture and rural areas, and explored new paths for rural revitalization with digital literary and artistic works. According to *Data Report on Rural Culture and Tourism*, over the past year, various platforms saw an increase of more than 459 million topics on rural areas, with more than 2,390.1 billion views, up by 65 percent year on year. There were more than 41.5 billion likes, more than 2.8 billion reposts, and more than 5.8 billion comments.[4] The development of the digital culture industry enables Internet users to record rural life, build and disseminate rural culture, and contribute to rural culture and tourism, thus promoting rural culture.

In the protection of our cultural heritage, the digitization of intangible cultural heritage resources in traditional villages continues to advance in China. In 2022, 126 new village libraries were added, and a total of 839 village libraries were completed, forming a database of traditional villages that covered multiple modalities and data types. Online e-commerce facilitates the protection and development of cultural heritage by expanding economic revenue. According to the *2022 Intangible Cultural Heritage Consumption and Innovation Report* released by the Culture and Tourism Industry Index Laboratory, in 2022, there were 32,853 stores on intangible cultural heritage on the Taobao platform, with an increase of 9.5 percent compared to 2020. The transaction volume on intangible cultural heritage increased by 11.6 percent compared to 2020.[5] Additionally, online platforms provide digital paths for the

4 "'Live Stream + Culture & Tourism' Upgrades New Industrial Momentum, and Presents a Landscape of 'Poetry and the Distance.'" Accessed September 2023. https://h.xinhuaxmt.com/vh512/share/11645877?d=134b2a5.

5 Culture and Tourism Industry Index Laboratory and Ali Research. *Intangible Cultural Heritage Consumption Innovation Report 2022*, October 2022.

publicity and dissemination of intangible cultural heritage. In June 2023, the China Association of Performing Arts, alongside eight online platforms including Tencent Video, co-organized "Intangible Cultural Heritage on Cloud Image Exhibition," which displayed more than 3,000 videos. The event was lengthened, and selected videos were free of charge for a limited time on various online platforms, which lowered the threshold for the public to watch high-quality cultural content.

In tourism, the Sichuan Giant Panda National Park and the Wawu Mountain Museum utilizes new digital technologies like AR to design and construct the first penetrating natural view-borrowing museum in Sichuan, achieving the organic unity of tourism development and natural protection. Besides, short video and online live streaming not only provide tourists with diverse choices of content in "tourism via the cloud," but also cultivate an integrated model of attracting tourists for various tourism enterprises. According to the official data from Douyin, in the first quarter of 2023, the number of users who published travel-related content on the Douyin platform ranked second in the industry, up by 7.3 percent year on year. By the end of March 2023, the average growth rate of accounts of tourism enterprises on various platforms exceeded 20 percent. In particular, the accounts of hotels, business travel-ticketing agents, and tourist attractions grew robustly, with a year-on-year growth of 61.5 percent, 46.0 percent, and 35.5 percent, respectively.[6]

In cultural heritage and museums, museums in various regions focus on such areas as development concepts, a technological approach, and business innovation, and explore a series of new forms for the innovation and development of museums such as "exhibitions via the cloud," "XR immersive exhibitions," digital collections and "archaeological blind boxes." A number of cultural and artistic institutions, such as the National Museum of China, Art Exhibitions China, and Dunhuang Academy, successively launch virtual images of digital humans, which provides a new idea for the operation of museums while attracting young people. In April 2023, the Great Bao'en Temple in Nanjing created a realistic connected communication space. In the temple, visitors can enter the "Metaverse of the Grand View of Great Bao'en Temple" with their personal virtual digital images and have a novel experience of on-site travel and a virtual shuttle.

8.3.2 The digital culture industry boosts online and offline interaction, with breakthroughs in cultural innovation

In the field of publishing, according to data from the National Bureau of Statistics, in the first half of 2023, the revenues of the digital publishing industry grew by

6 "Recovery, Evolution and Reconstruction: *Douyin Tourism Industry White Paper 2023.*" Accessed June 2023. https://trendinsight.oceanengine.com/arithmetic-report/detail/947.

16.1 percent. In March 2023, People's Publishing House launched an integrated media book *Report on the Work of the Government 2023* (video-picture-text edition), which covers report on the work of the government, as well as the explanations of relevant experts of the report in the form of video, picture, and text. QR codes connect the book and digital audios and videos, accelerating the deep integration and development of traditional and emerging publishing. In addition, immersive scripts, audiobooks, and other digital cultural forms provide new industrial tracks and innovative directions for digital publishing.

In the field of digital collections, digital collections derived from technologies such as blockchain and digital copyright promote digital publishing and resources utilization of physical cultural relics and taps the value of cultural and creative industries. The *China Digital Collection Industry Development Report 2022* reports hat in 2022, the monthly circulation of digital collections exceeded one million, and that the cultural industry boasts most diverse application scenarios and the greatest development potential.[7] By January 2023, there were 2,449 digital collection platforms in China, with 1,274 newly added platforms in the second half of 2022.[8]

In the field of online literature, the high-quality development of mainstream online literature in China accelerates. *Xinhua Cultural Industry IP Index Report 2022*, compiled by the China Economic Information Service, states that the publication of realistic online literature is on the rise, with diverse and complementary subjects, be it the modern adaptations of ancient society or fantasy worlds in works on industrial subject and infrastructure, or the utilization and recognition of traditional Chinese culture in works on our intangible cultural heritage and traditional style.[9] Online literature has become an important source of IPs in the digital culture industry. In the "Top 50 of Comprehensive List of IP Value in Chinese Cultural Industry" in *Xinhua Cultural Industry IP Index Report 2022*, there are 26 IPs that belong to the category of "literature," accounting for 52 percent. More than 20 IPs come from online literature.

In the field of games and animation, the Fourth Animation Award of China Government Award for Culture and Arts was given to 20 works, including *Nezha: Birth of the Demon Child* and *White Cat Legend (Season 1)*, which reflect the highest artistic level of the animation industry in China, the contribution of the industry to national development, and the zeitgeist of China in the journey to modernization. Major domestic ACGN exhibitions, such as ComiCup, BiliBili World, and ChinaJoy, are successfully held, which build platforms for offline communication among

---

7 On-chain Industry Blockchain Research Institute and Blockchain Branch of China Federation of Logistics & Purchasing. *China Digital Collection Industry Development Report 2022*, September 2022.

8 "Analysis of the Current Situation and Development Trends of the Digital Collection Industry Market in China in 2023: Scenic Area IP Promotes the Distribution of Digital Collection." Accessed September 2023. https://bg.qianzhan.com/report/detail/300/230721-d7b6c4a9.html.

9 China Economic Information Service. *Xinhua Cultural Industry IP Index Report 2022*, November 2022.

ACGN enthusiasts. Excellent game works expedite the creation and dissemination of cultural IPs, enhance the cultural confidence of the Chinese people, and augment the dissemination and influence of Chinese culture at home and abroad. In 2022, the market share of Chinese games in the United States, Germany, the United Kingdom, and other countries all exceeded 20 percent. Genshin Impact and other games were included in the "List of 122 National Cultural Export Key Projects" released by the Ministry of Commerce.

8.3.3 Concerted efforts are made in the online audiovisual industry, which demonstrates the vitality of the digital culture market

Over the past year, the online audiovisual industry innovated on the basis of tradition, with a trend toward the dissemination of mainstream public opinion, the creation of high-quality content, and the standardization of the market order. The digital culture market was optimized, the industrial pattern was continuously expanded, the industrial form was continually enriched, and the industrial scale was enlarged year by year, which promoted the development of high-quality digital culture. By June 2023, the number of online video (including short video) users in China reached 1.044 billion, with a utilization rate of 96.8 percent.[10]

The market for short videos and online live streaming accounts for half of the online audiovisual industry. According to the *Research Report on the Development of Online Audio-video Industry in China 2023*, in 2022, the market share of the online audio-video industry was 727.44 billion *yuan*, with an increase of 4.4 percent compared to 2021. Specifically, the market share for the field of short videos was 292.83 billion *yuan*, accounting for 40.3 percent, making a great contribution to industrial growth. The market share for the field of online live streaming was 124.96 billion *yuan*, accounting for 17.2 percent, an important force driving the growth of the market of the online audio-video industry.[11]

In the field of short videos, the mainstream media creates a matrix of accounts of short video platforms and build their own platforms, jointly promoting the digital dissemination of high-quality cultural content. At the beginning of 2023, *Chinese Classics (Season 2)* produced and launched a series of original short videos. Episode 5 of *The History of Kingdom Yue* was viewed more than 15 million times on various platforms. Episode 8 of *The Classic of Tea* received 3.4 million likes within 24 hours on a third-party account of CCTV 1, with more than ten million views on WeChat Channels.

10 CNNIC (China Internet Network Information Center). *The 52nd Statistical Report on China Internet Development*, August 2023.

11 China Netcasting Services Association. *Research Report on the Development of Netcasting in China 2023*, March 2023.

In April 2023, Douyin and Tencent Video announced that they would cooperate on the promotion of short and long videos and the follow-up creation of short videos to realize the coordinated development of short and long videos.

In the field of online live streaming, n 2022, the Palace Museum produced more than fifty online live streaming shows, with a total viewership of nearly 190 million. Via online live streaming, famous writers sell new books and recommend good books, enlarging online sales and digital dissemination of excellent literary works. On Kuaishou, there are more than 20 million online live streams on intangible cultural heritage and folk art, including 2.48 million on opera. On average, more than 40,000 streamers engage in traditional culture, including inheritors of intangible cultural heritage who live stream on Kuaishou every day.[12]

Additionally, digital cultural brands are built in integrated video, OTT/IPTV, online audio, and other industries. For example, in August 2022, Mango TV collaborated with more than ten automotive brands in exploring vehicle-screen video entertainment services. In 2023, Ximalaya stepped up efforts to expand all scenarios, develop AI technology, and implement IP sourcing, aiming to build a more intelligent digital audio brand.

8.4 Technology Enters a New Round of Development, and Digital Culture Faces New Opportunities

The iteration and innovation of digital technologies such as big data, VR, IoT, metaverse, and AI break the limitations of time and space, shape new features, models, and forms of the digital culture industry, and provide new momentum for improving the quality and efficiency of the development of digital culture. Currently, technology enters a new round of transformation. Big data and IoT technology mature, VR technology has more diverse application scenarios, AI and metaverse technology see breakthroughs in generative AI, and digital culture empowered by digital technology faces new opportunities for development.

8.4.1 Data management technology connects the entire chain and fosters the creation of cultural databases

As a new type of production method, data forms the foundation for digitization and networking. Data is quickly integrated into production, distribution, circulation,

12 China Culture Daily. *Fast and Slow: 2023 Kuaishou Intangible Cultural Heritage Ecology Report*, June 2023.

consumption, and social service management, and deeply alters lifestyles and social governance. The *National Strategy for Cultural Digitalization* stresses the need to coordinate and utilize the achievements of digital projects and databases that have been built or are under construction in the cultural field and create databases on Chinese culture.

In the resources on excellent traditional Chinese culture, historical and cultural heritage plays an important part and serves as a cultural gene bank of the over-1,000-year history of the Chinese nation, which can be transformed into a cultural database of Chinese people and Chinese nation via digital technology. Data management technology means a set of digital technology that integrates the functions of data collection, data storage, data management, and data application. Through technologies such as photography, scanning, sound recording, video recording, and 3D modeling, cultural relics and intangible cultural heritage can be collected from all directions (720 degree) and multiple modalities and transformed into the form of data for storage. Simultaneously, a digital archive management system is built by using technologies such as IoT, blockchain, and knowledge graphs, forming a database of Chinese culture with clear copyrights and links. Presently, the Palace Museum and Dunhuang Academy have established the Palace Museum Digital Cultural Relics Library and the Digital Dunhuang Resources Library.

In the formation of the database of Chinese culture via data correlation, identification resolution technology supports the realization of data connection and interoperability. While securing distributed data storage without changing data ownership, identification resolution technology connects the data of cultural resources at various levels, in order to achieve data correlation and sharing in an all-round way. First, underlying correlation service engines and application software are deployed in data centers of cultural institutions. In line with the principles of physical distribution and logical correlation, data resources such as cultural relics, ancient books, arts, operas, and cultural heritage sites are collected, the construction of gene banks of red culture is carried out, and existing or ongoing cultural databases are connected. Second, technological systems that provide identification code registration and resolution services are deployed in the computer rooms of cable television network companies.[13] The two sides connect existing data resources and create and manage the databases of Chinese culture that are entirely interconnected, fully presented, and shared by the public. The national cultural big data system can be established, which is physically distributed, logically linked, quickly connected, efficiently searched, fully shared, and comprehensively integrated. By March 2023, twenty-four provincial-level libraries had launched the construction of smart library knowledge warehousing platforms. Public libraries at various levels have started the construction of basic digital resources on characteristic collection resources and open

13 Gao Shusheng. "Technological Strategy and Implementation Path of National Cultural Digitalization Strategy." *Cyberspace Administration in China*, 2023 (4): 43–46.

courses. Technologies such as the semantic web and knowledge graphs were used to carry out fine-grained construction of knowledge resources as well as indexing of these resources.

8.4.2 Wide application of extended reality (XR) technology drives innovation in digital culture

XR technology refers to the use of modern high-tech methods centered on computers to create a digital environment that combines reality and virtuality, which provides a new type of human–machine interaction and brings seamless immersion between the virtual world and the real world to users. It is also a collective term for various technologies such as AR, VR, and MR. In recent years, XR technology has been widely applied in the innovation in cultural products in the digital culture industry, becoming a growth point for digital cultural creativity in multiple industries such as culture and tourism, cultural heritage, gaming and online audio-video.

Aiming to bridge the gap between the physical and virtual worlds, XR technology possesses technological advantages in digital restoration and protection of cultural relics, digital interaction in cultural space, and digital dissemination of cultural content. 3D scanning, 3D modeling, motion capture, panoramic shooting, and other technological means in XR technology can easily solve the problem that traditional photography and videography have: they cannot record a full picture of cultural heritage. AI technology can be used to restore the original appearance of cultural relics while protecting their existing forms, and even present the appearance of cultural relics that changes over time. In the field of cultural relics, XR technology creates a digital scene that combines virtual and real elements and allows users to obtain a richer and more complete sensory experience through wearable devices such as controllers and tactile sensors, thereby enhancing the interactive experience of traditional cultural space and better conveying cultural content and spirit. In April 2023, Dunhuang Academy released the Digital Library Cave, which uses digital scanning, gaming engines, and other technologies to complete the reproduction of cultural relics in a 1:1 millimeter scale to vividly represent the historical scene of the Library Cave and its more than 60,000 volumes of precious cultural relics stored in the cave a century ago. Additionally, the combination of XR and AI technologies not only achieves 1:1 digital reproduction of cultural relics, but also empowers the innovative forms of dissemination such as XR digital exhibition, allowing diverse and colorful Chinese treasures to be appreciated by the public at home and abroad in digital form, and promoting domestic and international cultural exchanges. At the 2023 Beijing China Art International Fair, nearly 10,000 cultural relics and artworks were displayed and traded online. An offline interactive experience area was established to provide a space of comprehensive exhibition and sales for cultural relics collectors at home and abroad, in online and offline ways.

Currently, owing to technological costs, the wide use of XR technology has not been realized. However, the multidimensional, multimodal, and multi-ensory features of XR technology provide an approach to the construction of digital cultural venues and the dissemination of digital cultural content.

8.4.3 Breakthroughs are made in AI technology, and innovations are made in the production of digital culture

At the end of 2022, cutting-edge AI technology represented by generative AI entered a new stage of development. As a form of technological integration, AIGC establishes patterns through existing data and generates relevant content with its appropriate generalization capability, based on natural language processing, generative algorithms, pretrained models, and multimodal technology. AIGC innovates the production process and logic of traditional digital cultural content. While reducing production costs, AIGC possesses content-generation capability that reaches the average level of humans in specific fields and performs much better than previous intelligent machines in terms of autonomy.

In the production of digital culture, generative AI improves the production of content and demonstrates strong adaptability in multitask, multimodality, and multilanguage settings. Generative AI plays an important role in content generation, especially in the cross-modal text-to-image model represented by MidJourney, as well as the GPT-series model with a development trend of universal AI. Industries with high level of digitization and strong demand for content are important scenarios of AIGC. Currently, the application scenarios of AIGC in media, film and television, gaming, music, and e-commerce become mature, and technological breakthroughs breed innovation and new applications.[14] Intelligent applications such as short video editing, script rewriting, music creation, and virtual anchoring have been commercialized.

In the environment of the Chinese language, AI has entered a stage of rapid development. By September 2023, "ERNIE Bot" of Baidu, "Tongyi Qianwen" of Alibaba, "Yunque" of Douyin, "Hunyuan" of Tencent, "Zidong Taichu" of the Chinese Academy of Sciences, "SenseNova" of SenseTime, and "Intern" of Shanghai Artificial Intelligence Laboratory, had been launched and opened. Cultural digitization, cultural big data, and cultural AI fully utilize the valuable resources of Chinese culture and significantly improve the efficiency and effectiveness of cultural institutions. Local large language models based on Chinese data may adapt to the production and creation of Chinese cultural content and contribute to the innovation and development of Chinese culture.

---

14 Guo Quanzhong and Zhang Jinyi. "AI + Culture: The Development Trends of AIGC." *Journalism Lover*, 2023 (3): 8–14.

10.2478/9788367405867-010

Chapter 9
Exchanges and Cooperation in International Governance in Cyberspace

In 2023, the complexity, instability and uncertainty in cyberspace intensified in the postpandemic era, and the international landscape became complex and turbulent. The United States overstated ideological factors in international governance in cyberspace, conspired to transfer crises by stoking national security threats and ideological confrontation, and sought to redesign a set of rules beneficial to the US through political means, in terms of international governance in cyberspace. As the competition among powers becomes more intense, the militarization of cyberspace accelerates. Major countries around the world vied to strengthen capabilities in cyber warfare and scrambled for strategic leadership in cyberspace. The arena of strategic competition among major countries evolved toward the field of technological power, and the contest for dominance over the supply chain of chip heightened. Some countries politicized technological issues, which undermined the stability of the global chip industrial chain and supply chain.

Meanwhile, it is the shared aspiration of the international community to improve the mechanism of international governance in cyberspace, promote the formulation of international rules in cyberspace that are universally accepted by all parties, and strengthen peaceful cooperation in cyberspace. In the field of digital trade, various countries expect to revise the paradigms of multilateral negotiations and the existing rules of the WTO. Chapters of e-commerce are added in regional and bilateral trade agreements, including the issue of digital trade within the scope of rulemaking.[1] In the field of technology, most countries represented by China unanimously oppose unilateralism and technological bullying, secure the stability of international industrial chain and supply chain, and jointly boost the recovery and development of the global economy.

Confronted with a complex international landscape in cyberspace, China upholds the tenets of extensive consultation, joint contribution, and shared benefits, continuously expands or deepens the cooperation in digital economy, cybersecurity, network technology, and other fields, actively partakes in cyberspace governance, and promotes global inclusive development. In November 2022, the State Council

1 "On the Construction and Trends of International Rules on Digital Trade." Accessed April 2023. https://baijiahao.baidu.com/s?id=1722422618787635365&wfr=spider&for=pc.

Information Office released the white paper *Jointly Building a Community with a Shared Future in Cyberspace*, which introduces the concept and practice of Internet development and governance in China in the new era and shares China's positive achievements in promoting building a community with a shared future in cyberspace. The white paper calls on the international community to conform to the development trends in the information era and in human society, and to respond to the risks and challenges to cyberspace, which demonstrates China's commitment to human progress and world harmony, and conveys China's aspiration to strengthen cooperation in Internet development and governance with countries around the world.

9.1 Situation on China's Participation in International Governance in Cyberspace

In 2023, the "double-edged sword" effect that arose from the innovation and application of new technologies attracted global attention. The international community remains vigilant against the potential risks of new technologies and ensures the healthy development and standardized application of new technologies by making international rules, enacting laws, and formulating policies. The competition for dominance in the supply chain of chip intensifies, which profoundly reshapes the global supply chain system of the semiconductor industry in an accelerated way. Globally, unified rules on digital trade have not been established; there are wide divergences among various parties concerning the formulation the rules on digital trade. It is an important task for various countries to lay down rules on digital trade that meet the requirements for domestic economic development.

9.1.1 Much attention is attached to the potential risks to the innovation and application of new technologies

New technologies represented by AI, big data, and the IoT are quickly upgraded and widely applied, having a far-reaching impact on the development of global economy, the models of social governance, and the daily life of people. Simultaneously, the double-edged sword of new technologies arouses widespread attention from the international community. On the one hand, the abuse of technology further exacerbates such issues as data abuse, content infringement, and false information, breeding the risks to such areas as privacy protection, data security, and ethics, and making regulation increasingly difficult and complex. On the other hand, as the Ukrainian crisis continues, intelligent, automated, and weaponized approaches of cyberattacks appear in new guises, triggering a new round of arms race dominated by the militarized application of disruptive technologies, and accelerating the militarization of cyberspace.

The international community attaches great importance to the potential risks of digital technology. The formulation of international standards that address the risks to the application of new technologies has been carried out for many years. In 2023, international organizations made progress in the regulation of AI. In April 2023, UNESCO called on the world to implement ethical standards for AI to ensure the achievement of the goals of *Recommendation on the Ethics of Artificial Intelligence*, a global agreement on the ethics of AI.[2] In February 2023, the Organization for Economic Cooperation and Development proposed ten principles for AI, stressing that the developers and users of AI must bear necessary responsibilities for the normal operation of technological systems.

Major countries and regions around the world successively promote legislation and take other measures to ensure the security, fairness, and transparency of the applications of new technologies. For example, in the regulation of AI technology, the European Union vigorously promotes the formulation of the *AI Act* and accelerates the legislative process. In March 2023, the UK government released *A Pro-innovation Approach to AI Regulation*, which proposes to strengthen regulatory principles for AI such as security, transparency, fairness, accountability, and governance to secure AI innovation and application. In July 2023, the Office of the Central Cyberspace Affairs Commission and other six departments jointly issued *Interim Measures on the Management of Generative Artificial Intelligence Services*, which ensures the healthy development and standardized application of the AI industry and provides a useful framework for global exploration of AI governance.

9.1.2 Competition for dominance in the chip supply chain intensifies

As the arena of strategic competition among major countries evolves toward the field of technological power, chips become key strategic resources in the digital era. The competition for dominance in the chip supply chain turns white-hot and quickly reshapes the global supply chain system of the semiconductor industry.[3] On the one hand, various countries adjust laws and policies on the chip industry in a bid to promote the development of domestic semiconductor industry. The US introduces the *CHIPS and Science Act*, which provides huge subsidies to the domestic chip industry

2 "UNESCO Calls to Implement Ethical Standards for AI." Accessed May 2023. http://www.legaldaily.com.cn/international/content/2023-04/03/content_8840255.html.

3 "Chip 4: The Strategic Pillar for Supply Chain Alliance." Accessed April 2023. https://www.icc.org.cn/trends/mediareports/796.html.

and requires any companies receiving US subsidies to manufacture chips domestically in the US. The European Union adopts *The EU Chips Act*, aiming to increase its share in the global semiconductor manufacturing market from 10 percent to at least 20 percent by 2030. Japan defines eleven areas, including chips, as key resources, intending to ensure the supply of strategic resources directly related to economic security but heavily dependent on overseas sources. South Korea passes the *Korean Chips Act*, which regards chips as national security assets and core technologies.

On the other hand, several countries have started to build "supply chain alliances" based on strategic alliances rather than the industrial ecosystem, forge competitive advantages in the supply chain of semiconductors, and politicize technological issues. As the largest technological powerhouse, the US plays a leading role in forming cliques like Chip 4 and coerces other countries into decoupling from global technological and industrial chains as well as the supply chain. The US, Japan, and the Netherlands reach an agreement on restricting the export of some advanced chip-manufacturing devices to China. India, as an emerging country, strengthens its connection with developed countries and accelerates the construction of a resilient, diverse, and secure supply chain in the semiconductor industry via the QUAD mechanism.

9.1.3 Formulation of rules on global digital trade shows a trend of diversified development

Against the backdrop of digital globalization, the rules on digital trade become an important issue in global economic and trade negotiations. Currently, owing to the diverse goals and demands for building an international rule system for digital trade, as well as complex and interwoven concerns, the formulation of rules on digital trade progresses slowly and shows a trend of fragmentation. Various countries take multiple paths to participate in the formulation of rules on digital trade.[4] First, various countries expect to revise the paradigms of multilateral negotiations and the existing rules of the WTO and make breakthroughs in the negotiations on e-commerce. By February 2023, the WTO's multilateral negotiations on e-commerce expanded to eight-nine member states, and the trade volume between the WTO members accounted for 90 percent of global trade volume. Second, some countries sharing common goals reach high-level agreements and seek multilateral negotiation outcomes. In November 2022, the G20 Leaders' Summit was convened in Bali, Indonesia.

4 Foreign Economic Affairs Research Branch of Development Research Centre of the State Council and China Academy of Information and Communications Technology Research Group. "Development and Cooperation of Digital Trade: Current Situation and Trends." *China Policy Review*, 2021 (6): 53–64.

The summit released *G20 Bali Leaders' Declaration*, which lays stress on inclusive international cooperation in digital trade and calls for international cooperation in trade and investment. Lastly, regional trade agreements have a stronger influence on global economy and play a leading role in the formulation of global rules on digital trade. Middle powers such as Japan and Singapore explore frameworks of rules on digital trade independent of China, the US, and Europe. Singapore accelerates the advancement of the *Digital Economy Partnership Agreement* (DEPA) and invites China, South Korea, Canada, and others to join DEPA. Presently, China, South Korea, and Canada have completed technical consultations and established "working groups to advance talks on joining the DEPA." Additionally, trade agreements such as the *Comprehensive and Progressive Agreement for Trans-Pacific Partnership* (CPTPP) and the *Regional Comprehensive Economic Partnership* (RCEP) strengthen the compatibility of domestic and regional mechanisms for data regulation among contracting parties, help to establish industrial chains and ecosystems for the development of digital trade, and deepen cooperation and common development in global digital trade.

9.2 Hot Topics in International Governance in Cyberspace and Practices in China

Currently, the world is undergoing profound changes unseen in a century, and the information revolution is an irresistible trend that continuously shapes the landscape in international governance in cyberspace. In 2023, hot topics in cyberspace continued with new changes and development. Technology governance, data governance, and digital trade governance were key fields that attracted great attention from various countries. The competition among major powers in these fields further intensified, posing a big challenge to global governance in cyberspace. China stands at the strategic height of the future and destiny of mankind, actively participates in world Internet development and governance, contributes its approaches to promoting the development of cyberspace, and demonstrates its determination to firmly move forward and assume responsibilities in building a community with a shared future in cyberspace.

9.2.1 China puts out a call to jointly safeguard the security of the industrial supply chain and fights against the politicization of technological issues

Against the background of the technological revolution, emerging technologies are deeply integrated into various fields of economy and society, become an important lever for countries to promote economic and social transformation, foster new economic drivers, and forge new competitive advantages. Currently, major economies around the world attach great importance to shaping local technological advantages and accelerate progress in the fields of semiconductor, quantum, 5G/6G, and AI. In order to augment their absolute advantages in the military and economic fields, several countries continue to broaden the concept of "national security," politicize technological issues, and disrupt the global industrial ecosystem of emerging technologies, by abusing export control measures, determining key technology lists, and strengthening the scrutiny of emerging technologies. In addition, to address the potential risks to security of innovation and application of new technologies, various countries take measures to enhance the regulation and legislation of new technologies and promote both development and standardization.

The Chinese government has always opposed politicizing technological issues, repeatedly emphasizing that the international community should abandon unilateralism and protectionism, uphold openness and integration as well as the spirit of sticking together in times of adversity, and take concerted efforts to keep industrial and supply chains secure and unclogged. In November 2022, during a meeting with US President Biden in Bali, Indonesia, Chinese President Xi Jinping clearly stated that: "Starting a trade war or a technology war, building walls and barriers, and pushing for decoupling and severing supply chains run counter to the principles of market economy and undermine international trade rules. Such attempts serve no one's interests." In November 2022, the State Council Information Office released the white paper *Jointly Building a Community with a Shared Future in Cyberspace*, stressing that the Chinese government opposes politicizing technological issues, abusing state power, violating the principles of market economy and the rules on international economy and trade, and resorting to any means to suppress and contain foreign enterprises.

Simultaneously, China attaches great importance to the development and governance of new information technology and introduces a series of supporting policies to enhance the competitiveness of national information technology industry. In August 2022, six departments, including the Ministry of Science and Technology and the Ministry of Industry and Information Technology, issued *Guiding Opinions on Accelerating the Innovation in Scenarios and Promoting High-quality Economic Development through High-level Application of Artificial Intelligence*. This provides policy guidance and institutional arrangements for coordinating and promoting innovation in AI scenarios, solving major problems in the application and industrialization of AI, and comprehensively improving the quality and level of the development of AI. In December 2022, the CPC Central Committee and the State Council issued *Outline of the Strategic Plan for Expanding Domestic Demand 2022-2035*, which proposes to comprehensively enhance the core competitiveness of the information technology industry, and boost technological innovation and application in AI, advanced communications, integrated circuits, new displays, advanced computing, and other fields.

9.2.2 China actively promotes the development and utilization of data elements and strengthens the exploration of cross-border data flow

As data elements are a focus of their digital strategies, various countries raise strict requirements for data regulation domestically, actively promote the development and application of data elements, and explore international cooperation in cross-border data flow. First, many countries generally accelerate the process of data legislation. Asian, African, and Latin American countries represented by Thailand, Indonesia, and Argentina officially introduced laws on personal data protection. Singapore, France, and other countries release normative documents such as guidelines on personal data protection in specific technological fields such as AI and blockchain. Second, many countries further the development and application of data through a series of measures such as improving basic systems of data element markets, promoting the circulation and utilization of data elements, and regulating the competition in digital markets. Third, the idea of the governance of cross-border data flow is recognized by more countries in the world, and cross-border cooperation in data transfer in areas such as digital trade and law enforcement is continuously launched.

The effectiveness of data governance relates to the construction of a digital China and the modernization of national governance. China continues to consolidate a data governance framework that balances security and development, promotes the full release of the value of data elements, and strengthens the exploration of cross-border data flow. In December 2022, the CPC Central Committee and the State Council issued *Twenty Articles on Data*, which determines the direction for accelerating the construction of a basic system of data, further releasing the value of data elements, and stimulating the potential of data elements. In September 2022, *Measures on Security Evaluation of Data Outbound Transfer* officially took effect, which stipulates the scope, conditions, and procedures for security evaluation of data outbound transfer, provides an operable and implementable legal basis for data outbound transfer, helps to balance development and security, and makes the rules for cross-border data flow and management in practice.

9.2.3 China accelerates the development of the digital economy and plays a positive role in the formulation of relevant international rules

The digital economy becomes a focus for countries around the world to seize the opportunities for development and forge new advantages in international competition. At present, the international community has not reached a consensus on the governance rules on the digital economy. In alignment with the needs for security and development, various countries accelerate the layout of the framework of digital trade rules and strive for leadership in formulating digital trade rules. For example, the US initiates the Indo-Pacific Economic Framework, prioritizing the governance and cooperation in digital trade, especially shaping digital trade rules, with Indo-Pacific digital economic cooperation. Additionally, the trend of forming alliances in global digital trade continues to be strengthened. The US plays a leading role in establishing the Cross-Border Privacy Rules (CBPR) in APEC, incorporating Japan, South Korea, Singapore, and other countries. The European Union focuses on protecting data privacy and continues to strengthen its ties with data allies. Japan continuously promotes Data Free Flow with Trust (DFFT), attempting to build a digital circulation circle among the US, Europe, and Japan.

China thoroughly implements the strategies of building a country with cyber strength and national big data, and successively issues *The Strategy for the Development of Digital Economy* and *The 14th Five-Year Plan for the Development of Digital Economy* in order to accelerate digital industrialization and industrial digitization and realize the robust development of the digital economy.[5] In February 2023, the CPC Central Committee and the State Council issued *Overall Layout and Planning for the Construction of Digital China*, which requires the deep integration of digital technology with the "Five-sphere Integrated Plan" for progress in the economic, political, cultural, social, and eco-environmental fields, comprehensively empower economic and social development, and strengthen, optimize, and expand the digital economy.

Chinese President Xi Jinping stresses that "We should carry out bilateral and multilateral cooperation in digital governance, and maintain and improve the multilateral governance mechanism of digital economy." Guided by the concept of building a community with a shared future in cyberspace, China actively participates in the formulation of standards and rules for organizations engaged in digital economy. In June 2022, China played an active role in the WTO MC12 and contributed to the achievement of a package of agreements, fully demonstrating that China assumes responsibilities in maintaining multilateral trading systems and in promoting the construction of an open world economy. In August 2022, the Digital Economy Partnership Agreement (DEPA) Joint Committee established a working group on China's accession to DEPA, comprehensively advancing relevant negotiations and accelerating the connection between China and high-standard international economic and trade rules.

5 "Report of the State Council on the Development of Digital Economy." Accessed April 2023. http://www.gov.cn/xinwen/2022-11/28/content_5729249.htm.

9.3 China Actively Engages in International Exchanges and Cooperation

Over the past year, under the guidance of General Secretary Xi Jinping's idea of building a community with a shared future in cyberspace, China gave full play to the role of bilateral and multilateral cooperation mechanisms, continually deepened and expanded global partnerships, and strengthened practical cooperation in digital economy, cybersecurity, Internet basic resources, technological standards, data security, online culture, and other fields. This fully demonstrates that China performs its responsibilities in fostering the fair and rational development of global cyberspace governance.

9.3.1 Building a platform for international exchanges and cooperation in cyberspace

China actively plays its role as a responsible major country, deeply participates in building global and regional multilevel Internet governance platforms, urges governments, enterprises, and civil societies in the world to express their views, strengthen communication, and deepen cooperation in the field of international Internet governance, shares the achievements of Internet development with the world, forges consensus on global cyberspace governance, and makes positive contributions to reforming the global Internet governance system and building a community with a shared future in cyberspace.

Since 2014, China has successfully hosted several sessions of the World Internet Conference (WIC) Wuzhen Summit, continuously pooled wisdom and consensus among all parties, and deepened digital cooperation. WIC becomes a high-end platform for an Internet shared and governed by all and global exchanges and cooperation in the digital economy, which is of high concern for all parties in the international community. In July 2022, the WIC international organization was officially established. In November 2022, the 2022 World Internet Conference (WIC) Wuzhen Summit opened at Wuzhen, Zhejiang. Chinese President Xi Jinping sent a congratulatory letter, profoundly interpreting the opportunities and challenges brought by digitization to human society, and clearly expressing China's sincere desire to work together with countries around the world to build a community with a shared future in cyberspace, which was highly recognized by the international community. As the first annual meeting of the WIC international organization, the Wuzhen Summit, with the theme of "Toward a Shared Digital Future in a Connected World: Building a Community with a Shared Future in Cyberspace," covered four topics: cooperation and development, technology and industry, culture and society, and governance and security; the Summit invited more than 2,100 guests from more than 120 countries and regions to attend online and in person. "Excellent Cases on Jointly Building a Community with a Shared Future in Cyberspace" were staged. Twelve representative cases were selected from more than 100 countries and regions around the world and more than 200 participating parties showcased practices of various parties in five fields, i.e., the construction of network infrastructure, online cultural exchanges, the innovation and development of the digital economy, cybersecurity guarantees, and international governance of cyberspace.

Under the framework of the Wuzhen Summit, "Global Development Initiative Digital Cooperation Forum," "International Rules on Cyberspace: Practice and Exploration," and "Forum on Jointly Building a Shared Digital Economy in the New Era" were successfully held. *Non-paper on Global Development Initiative Digital Cooperation*, *Compilation of the Achievements of International Seminars on "Building a Community with a Shared Future in Cyberspace"* (co-edited by more than 100 global experts and scholars), and *Common Vision of a Digital World: Global Think Tanks on Jointly Building a Community with a Shared Future in Cyberspace* (collection of papers) were published. These gathered consensus on digital cooperation and development from all parties, elaborated on the concept and proposition of building a community with a shared future in cyberspace, and contributed China's strength to promoting building a community with a shared future in cyberspace.

From June 25 to 27, 2023, WIC Nishan Dialogue on Digital Civilization kicked off at Nishan, Qufu, Shandong, under the theme of "The Age of AI: Building a Digital World of Exchanges, Mutual Learning and Inclusiveness." About 400 representatives from governments, enterprises, universities, and academia worldwide participated in the dialogue through in-person and online means. They discussed the opportunities and challenges brought by AI technology to human civilization, explored feasible paradigms for global governance of AI, jointly promoted the exchanges, mutual learning, and inclusiveness among human civilizations in the age of AI, and worked together to build a community with a shared future in cyberspace.

Additionally, China gives full play to important platforms like think tanks in promoting international exchanges and cooperation. In 2022, the China Academy of Information and Communications Technology signed memorandums of cooperation with nearly twenty international organizations, universities, and think tanks in Africa and ASEAN to jointly build an international cooperation network through a digital think tank, deepen cooperation among think tanks in the Internet field, strengthen mutual trust and consensus on ideas, and make positive contributions to serving national diplomatic strategies and promoting the construction of a new development pattern.

9.3.2 Participating in the process of governance under the UN framework

China firmly safeguards the international system with the United Nations at its core, always upholds the UN's role as the main channel in international governance of cyberspace, and actively participates in the exchanges and cooperation in cyberspace under the UN framework. Since 2022, the Chinese government has actively implemented the United Nations' "Our Common Agenda" and offered relevant opinions and suggestions to the "New Agenda for Peace" led by the United Nations. China has urged the UN General Assembly (UNGA) to adopt the resolution *The Development of the ICT Field from a Perspective of International Security*, and include the Chinese approach to "building a community with a shared future in cyberspace" in the UNGA's resolution for the third time. China has constructively participated in the work of the United Nations Open-ended Working Group on Information Security, first proposing that major countries should set an example in complying with "Norms of Responsible State Behavior in Cyberspace," successfully incorporating it into relevant UN reports. China has proactively participated in the consultation on cyberspace affairs among special agencies or mechanisms such as the International Telecommunication Union, the negotiations on *The United Nations Convention Against Cybercrimes*, UNESCO, the United Nations Human Rights Council, and the United Nations Economic and Social Council, as well as activities on international platforms sponsored by the United Nations, such as WSIS (World Summit on the Information Society) and IGF (Internet Governance Forum). In addition, international organizations as well as Chinese communities and research institutions, including World Internet Conference, China IGF, the China Academy of Information and Communications Technology, and the Chinese Academy of Social Sciences, have actively taken part in the negotiation and formulation of the UN *Global Digital Compact* and made positive contributions to the sharing of digital technology by people around the world.

The International Telecommunication Union (ITU) serves as a special agency of the United Nations responsible for ICT affairs. The quadrennial ITU Plenipotentiary Conference is the highest authority and policy-making body of the ITU. From September to October 2022, the ITU Plenipotentiary Conference was held. China was successfully re-elected as a member of the ITU Cheng Jianjun, director of State Radio Regulation of China, was elected as a member of the new session of Radio Regulations Board (RRB) of the ITU. During the conference, China actively participated in discussions on Internet governance, AI, digital pandemic prevention, smart cities, and other topics, supported developing countries to bridge the digital divide, and assisted the ITU in playing a greater role in global Internet governance.

As a body of UNGA, the United Nations Human Rights Council (HRC) stays committed to protecting human rights in all countries. Over the years, China has actively participated in activities in the field of human rights sponsored by the UN and contributed Chinese wisdom to global governance of human rights. In September 2022, the Beijing Children's Legal Aid and Research Center, the Child Law International Alliance (CLIA), the China NGO Network for International Exchanges, and the China Association for NGO Cooperation jointly hosted the 51st Meeting of the HRC under the theme of "Strengthening National Legislation in the Digital Era to Protect Children from Cyberbullying." Representatives from countries and organizations such as

China, Austria, Switzerland, and UNICEF were invited to attend the meeting and deliver speeches, sharing their respective practices and beneficial experiences to better protect the legitimate rights and interests of children in cyberspace.

The United Nations Economic and Social Council is the only body of the United Nations in which nongovernmental organizations participate in the formal framework. In December 2022, the United Nations Economic and Social Council officially gave special consultative status to the China Federation of Internet Societies. Currently, there are more than 6,300 nongovernmental organizations with consultative status worldwide, and more than 90 come from China (including Hong Kong, Macao, and Taiwan). The China Federation of Internet Societies is the first social organization in the field of cyberspace affairs in China to obtain consultative status.

The World Summit on the Information Society (WSIS) is the largest and highest-level annual summit in the world in the field of ICT organized by the UN. In March 2023, the WSIS Awards Ceremony was held in Geneva, Switzerland. China Mobile's *"Material Supermarket" Revitalization Solution for Enterprises and Institutions* won the highest project award, which was the only award received by Chinese enterprises at this summit. The project "Age Friendliness of Mobile Internet Applications" recommended by the China Academy of Information and Communications Technology, which aims to solve the difficulties of the elderly in using intelligent technology, won the C10 Information Society Ethics Champion.

The Internet Governance Forum (IGF) of the UN is an open forum on Internet governance, with open forums, seminars, exhibitions, and other supporting activities. China has participated in the platform activities for many consecutive years, gathered the strength of domestic Internet industries and communities, and contributed to the process of global Internet governance. In personnel appointments, Xue Lan from Tsinghua University was elected as a member of the leading group of IGF, and Zhang Xiao from the China Internet Network Information Center was elected as a member of the experts group of IGF, making positive contributions to promoting global Internet governance. In international exchanges and cooperation, in December 2022, the Cyberspace Administration of China held a number of open forums, seminars, and other activities at the 17th IGF and actively introduced China's experiences and practices centering on digital economy, AI, data security, and other topics. The International Cooperation Bureau of Cyberspace Administration of China and the Cyber Security Association of China jointly hosted an open forum with the theme of "Deepening International Cooperation in Digital Economy, Achieving Connectivity and Common Prosperity," focusing on in-depth discussions on topics such as the digital economy and digital connectivity for all, digital and data governance in the digital economy, as well as China's experience in promoting international cooperation in the digital economy. The China Federation of Internet Societies, the Communication University of China, and UNICEF jointly hosted the release and award conference on "AI as a Draft Standard and Typical Case of the Children's Industry," invited AI experts from various countries to give constructive suggestions on the optimization and upgrading of *Guidelines for the Construction of Internet Applications for Minors Based on AI Technology*, and discussed the network service models and effects on minors based on AI technology in combination with enterprise cases. The Cyber Security Association of China and the Fuxi Institution jointly hosted a seminar on "Ensuring the Digital Rights and Data Security of Vulnerable Groups: Exploration and Realization of Data Security and Personal Information Protection for the Elderly," focusing on the digital rights and security protection of the elderly in the digital era, exploring the concepts and practices on legal and social governance in various countries, and urging the international community to formulate policies and rules for data security and personal information protection for the elderly.

In March 2022, the UN Secretary-General established the High-Level Advisory Board on Effective Multilateralism, aiming to strengthen the efficiency of multilateral governance, implement the recommendations of "Our Common Agenda," and respond to major issues of common concern to the UN member states. Xu Bu from the China Institute of International Studies was invited to serve as a member of the advisory board. In April 2023, the UN Secretary-General António Guterres sent a special letter thanking the China Institute of International Studies for its outstanding contribution to the UN report *A Breakthrough for People and Planet: Effective and Inclusive Global Governance for Today and the Future.*

9.3.3 Deepening the partnership in the digital economy

China adheres to the principles of extensive consultation, joint contribution, and shared benefits in global governance, proactively participates in international negotiations on the digital economy, actively initiates bilateral and multilateral dialogues and cooperation in the field of the digital economy, and makes important contributions to maintaining and improving the governance mechanism of digital economy and exploring new drivers of world economic growth.

China actively participates in consultations and negotiations on the digital economy via multilateral platforms such as APEC, G20 and BRICS. APEC is the highest level, most extensive, and most influential economic cooperation mechanism in the Asia Pacific region. China deeply engages in APEC cooperation in the digital economy and promotes the implementation of *APEC Internet and Digital Economy Roadmap* in a comprehensive and balanced way. The APEC Digital Economy Steering Group (DESG) and the APEC Business Advisory Council (ABAC) play an important part in APEC cooperation and serve as major platforms for participating in economic and trade cooperation and rulemaking in the Asia Pacific region. The Chinese government vigorously recommends Chinese personnel to hold the post of vice chairman of DESG againand takes an active part in consultations and negotiations on the digital economy. Via the ABAC platform, the China Council for the Promotion of International Trade (CCPIT) and other social organizations enable the Chinese business community to partake in discussions on digital issues. In January 2023, representatives of governments and industrial associations from the Cyberspace Administration of China and the China Association for Standardization actively participated in Sustainable Development and Digital Economy Innovation Practical Cases Seminar of the APEC Women Leadership Forum and introduced and interpreted China's policies and practices in the digital economy and privacy protection. From 2021 to 2023, the Cyberspace Administration of China successively held the APEC Digital Poverty Reduction Seminar, the Digital Capacity Building Seminar, and the Digital, Green, and Coordinated Transformation and Development Seminar, via which China shares practical experience in the construction of the digital economy and deepens the consensus on APEC cooperation in the digital economy.

China participates in the G20 Leaders' Summit, the G20 Ministers' Meeting on Digital Economy, the G20 Digital Economy Working Group, the G20 Digital Economy Development Group, and other meetings and activities, deepening practical cooperation in the field of the digital economy. In November 2022, at the 17th G20 Leaders' Summit, Chinese President Xi Jinping proposed "three upholdings" to promote global digital cooperation: upholding multilateralism and strengthening international cooperation, upholding development first and bridging the digital divide, and upholding innovation-driven development and fostering postpandemic economic recovery. He underscored that all parties should stimulate the vitality of digital cooperation and make the development achievements of the digital economy benefit people of all countries. At the summit, China proposed *Action Plan for the G20 Digital Innovation and Cooperation*, aiming to boost international cooperation in digital industrialization and industrial digitization and unleash the potential of the digital economy in driving global growth. In September 2022, the G20 Digital Economy Ministers' Meeting was held in Bali, Indonesia. Representatives of the Chinese government actively participated in discussions on various topics such as digital connectivity, digital literacy, and data flow, and proposed practical measures to strengthen cooperation among industrial organizations in the digital field, cultivate ICT talents, and enhance the innovation and application of digital technology. In addition, the CCPIT B20 Working Group enthusiastically participates in the consultations on B20 issues related to India and Indonesia, and researches and proposes business initiatives in the fields of digitization, trade, and investment so as to bolster the development of digital trade, enhance the security of digital space, and strengthen the construction of digital infrastructure.

BRICS functions as an important multilateral cooperation mechanism represented by emerging economies and developing countries. China attaches great importance to the BRICS cooperation mechanism and actively deepens the implementation of BRICS cooperation based on the achievement documents such as *The BRICS Digital Economy Partnership Framework*. In 2022, the Ministry of Industry and Information Technology hosted the BRICS Industrial Internet and Digital Manufacturing Development Forum, the First Digital BRICS Forum, and the Fourth BRICS Future

Network Innovation Forum. Exchanges and discussions were carried out on topics such as mobile communications, AI, the industrial Internet, digital transformation, the application of digital technology, and cooperation in digital governance. *The BRICS Digital Transformation Cooperation Initiative for Manufacturing* was released, putting forward ten propositions such as building accessible digital infrastructure, fully stimulating the value of data elements, jointly building a new open and collaborative ecosystem, and building a multilateral international cooperation mechanism. In June 2022, the China Council for the Promotion of International Trade held the BRICS Business Community Forum online and in person. In the forum, a special seminar was organized under the theme of "Embracing Digital Economy and Promoting the New Industrial Revolution Partnership among BRICS."Representatives from BRICS and "BRICS + " countries were invited to attend and engaged in extensive exchanges on strengthening cooperation in the digital economy and promoting the construction of partnerships. Additionally, *Beijing Initiative of BRICS Business Community* was released, aiming to gather strength to promote global economic recovery. In July 2022, the Ministry of Industry and Information Technology staged the 8th Meeting of BRICS Communications Ministers. Under the theme of "Using ICT to Advance the 2030 Agenda for Sustainable Development, Deepening Cooperation to Achieve More Robust, Greener, and More Balanced Development," the meeting invited ministerial officials from BRICS countries and heads of international organizations to participate in the exchanges, and published *Declaration of the 8th Meeting of BRICS Communications Ministers*. The meeting further consolidates the BRICS strategic partnership, deepens practical cooperation in the field of ICT among BRICS countries, and injects strong momentum into achieving the high-quality development of BRICS countries.

The Mobile World Congress (MWC) is one of the most influential exhibitions in the field of mobile communications worldwide. From February to March 2023, MWC 2023 & Ministerial Conference: Digital Leaders Roundtable was held in Barcelona, Spain. The secretary-general of the World Internet Conference was invited to attend, delivering a speech around the driving forces of digital innovation and transformation and the groundbreaking innovations in the digital field.

2023 sees the tenth anniversary of the proposal of the "Belt and Road Initiative." Relying on the joint construction of the "Belt and Road," China has strengthened cooperation in the field of the digital economy with the BRI countries, making important contributions to promoting the economic and social development of various countries. China and ASEAN seize the opportunity of digital transformation, continuously build China-ASEAN Digital Economy Cooperation Partnership, and lead China-ASEAN comprehensive exchanges in cyberspace. In June 2022, Singapore and China signed two memorandums of understanding in Geneva, Switzerland, aiming to strengthen cooperation in the fields of green development and the digital economy and provide new momentum for the two countries to explore new areas of cooperation in the digital economy and the green economy. In July 2022, with the support of the Cyberspace Administration of China and the Ministry of Foreign Affairs, ASEAN-China Centre held a press conference on China-ASEAN digital cooperation, introducing China's ideas on digital cooperation to ASEAN envoys in China, and making China-ASEAN cooperation in the digital economy deeper and more practical. In September 2022, the 5th China-ASEAN Information Harbor Forum, co-sponsored by the Cyberspace Administration of China, the National Development and Reform Commission, the Ministry of Industry and Information Technology, and the Guangxi Zhuang Autonomous Region People's Government, was held in Nanning. Under the theme of "Jointly Building the Digital Silk Road and Sharing the Digital Future," the forum conducted exchanges and discussions around the development of the digital economy, intelligent connectivity, data exchanges, and cooperation and mutual benefit, helping China-ASEAN Information Harbor to accelerate the construction of platforms for infrastructure, information sharing, technological cooperation, economic and trade service, and cultural exchanges. In the forum, an exhibition on the achievements of digital technology was organized, covering such fields as new 5G applications, AI, and the metaverse. In October 2022, the Second ASEAN-China Cyber Dialogue was held in Singapore. Various parties had in-depth exchanges on the overall landscape in cyberspace, the protection of critical infrastructure, the construction of policy mechanisms, and practical cooperation. All parties reached a consensus on strengthening solidarity and cooperation, upholding multilateralism, and ensuring peace, security, and resilience in cyberspace. In November 2022, the 25th ASEAN-China Summit was held in Phnom Penh, Cambodia, releasing *ASEAN-China Joint Statement on Strengthening Common and Sustainable Development*. As stated, the two sides will promote cooperation in the fourth industrial revolution and digital transformation, implement *China-ASEAN Plan of Action on a Closer Partnership of Science, Technology and Innovation for Future 2021-2025*, and expand cooperation in scientific and technological innovation. The two sides will implement the achievements of the China-ASEAN Digital Economy Cooperation Year, and further strengthen cooperation in areas such as e-commerce, smart cities, and digital transformation. In February 2023, the Third China-ASEAN Digital Ministers' Meeting was held, which reviewed the achievements of China-ASEAN cooperation in the digital field since 2022, exchanged the latest digital development and policies, and discussed the *China-ASEAN Digital Cooperation Plan in 2023*. China and ASEAN countries expressed their expectations of strengthening cooperation within the framework of *The Plan of Action on the Implementation of the China-ASEAN Digital Economy Partnership 2021-2025* and agreed to renew *Memorandum of Understanding on China-ASEAN Digital and ICT Cooperation*.

China-Africa cooperation in the Belt and Road Initiative enters a stage of high-quality development. China actively participates in the construction of the African digital economy, expands the coverage of the "Digital Silk Road," bridges the digital divide, and boosts bilateral trade. In October 2022, the Nigerian Africa-China Media Center and the Nigerian Institute of International Affairs jointly hosted the Africa-China

Economic Partnership Agenda Conference, with the theme of "China's Participation in the Construction of African Digital Economy." Chinese and Nigerian scholars from Renmin University of China, the Chinese Academy of Social Sciences, and the Nigerian Institute of International Affairs discussed topics such as the development of the African digital economy, China-Africa cooperation in the digital economy and China-Africa cooperation in media. In November 2022, the Africa-China Alliance for Poverty Alleviation Inaugural Ceremony and the 2022 FOCAC Africa-China Poverty Reduction and Development Conference were held, with the theme of "Deepening the Partnership for Poverty Reduction and Development, Promoting High-quality Development of Africa-China Cooperation." Representatives discussed topics such as "Continuously Deepening Africa-China Partnership for Poverty Reduction and Development," "Continuously Strengthening Africa-China Policy Exchanges on Poverty Reduction and Development," and "Continuously Promoting the Practice of Africa-China Cooperation in Poverty Reduction and Development." At the conference, the *Declaration on the Founding of Africa-China Alliance for Poverty Alleviation* was announced, and knowledge products such as the *Annual Report on African Poverty Reduction 2022* and *Case Collection of China-Africa Cooperation in Poverty Reduction and Development 2022* were released. In November 2022, the Chinese ambassador to South Africa was invited to attend the unveiling ceremony of "Huawei-Rain-Wits 5G Laboratory" and delivered a speech expressing China's firm support for South Africa's development of its digital economy.

China and Arab States make solid progress in jointly building the Belt and Road Initiative, and the cooperation in the digital economy reaches a new level. In December 2022, Chinese President Xi Jinping attended the First China-Gulf Cooperation Council (GCC) Summit and proposed five key areas of China-GCC cooperation for the next three to five years. Specifically, measures would be taken to promote the innovation and development of the digital economy, such as jointly building big data and cloud computing centers, strengthening 5G & 6G technological cooperation, establishing a number of incubators for innovation and entrepreneurship, and implementing ten digital economy projects around the cooperation in cross-border e-commerce and the construction of a communications network. In the same month, Chinese President Xi Jinping paid a state visit to Saudi Arabia. China and Saudi Arabia issued a joint statement stressing that both sides would strengthen cooperation in the fields of communications and the digital economy. The two countries signed outcome documents such as *Memorandum of Understanding on Cooperation in the Field of Digital Economy*.

The China-Russia cooperation in the field of digital economy continues to deepen, becoming a highlight of bilateral cooperation. In December 2022, during the 27th regular meeting of Chinese and Russian prime ministers, the two countries signed an outcome document emphasizing that the two sides would strengthen cooperation in the field of the digital economy and align their positions on digital economy issues within the frameworks of BRICS and Shanghai Cooperation Organization (SCO).

In November 2022, the China-Russia Digital Economy Summit Forum, hosted by the China Association for Science and Technology, the Russian Union of Scientific and Engineering Associations (RUSEA), and the Heilongjiang Provincial People's Government was successfully held in person and online. With the theme of "Open Source and Openness for a Digital Future," the forum focused on the innovation and development of the digital economy between China and Russia and injected new momentum into deepening bilateral cooperation between China and Russia.

The China-CELAC, China-Belarus, and China-Europe relations are continually improved and upgraded. In July 2022, the China-Latin America Digital Technology Anti-Pandemic Cooperation Forum and the First China-Latin America Digital Technology Cooperation Forum were held, providing platforms for policy exchanges and practical cooperation between China and Latin America on the latest development of digital technology, the role of digital technology in fighting the pandemic, resuming work and production and promoting economic recovery, as well as strengthening new infrastructure construction, AI, 5G, and other fields. In March 2023, the president of Belarus paid a state visit to China. The two countries signed and issued a joint statement emphasizing that the two sides would implement the memorandum of understanding on bilateral e-commerce cooperation and actively carry out cooperation in the field of the digital economy. In the same month, 2023 China-Europe Track-II Digital Dialogue co-organized by the Cyber Security Association of China and the European Union Chamber of Commerce in China was held in Beijing. The dialogue focused on topics such as "Exchanges of Regulatory Rules for Cross-border Data Flow between China and Europe," "Opportunities for Global Digital Cooperation and China-Europe Digital Cooperation," and "China-Europe Cooperation in Talents Training in the Digital Field," which deepened understanding and mutual trust between China and Europe and promoted practical cooperation in the digital field.

Digital currency, as a new infrastructure in the financial field, boosts the development of the digital economy. In 2022, many countries accelerated the research and deployment of central bank legal digital currencies. China actively explored feasible solutions for cross-border central bank digital currencies and made positive progress in m-CBDC Bridge. In October 2022, BIS HKC, the Hong Kong Monetary Authority, the Bank of Thailand, the Central Bank of the UAE, and the Digital Currency Research Institute of the People's Bank of China successfully completed real transaction pilot tests based on digital currencies in four countries or regions for the first time on the m-CBDC Bridge platform. Twenty commercial banks from the Chinese mainland, China's Hong Kong, Thailand, and the United Arab Emirates concluded more than 160 multi-scenario payment and settlement businesses for their clients on cross-border trade through m-CBDC Bridge, achieving breakthroughs in the cross-border field of e-CNY. Additionally, the People's Bank of China exchanges and discusses cutting-edge issues related to legal digital currencies with monetary and fiscal regulatory authorities in various jurisdictions, multinational financial institutions, and top universities around the world. It actively participates in the formulation of standards on legal digital currencies within the framework of international organizations and jointly constructs an international standard system.

9.3.4 Continuously launching international cooperation in cybersecurity

Maintaining cybersecurity is a shared responsibility of the international community. China actively fulfills its international responsibilities, constructively participates in regional cybersecurity processes such as BRICS and SCO, strengthens partnerships in the field of cybersecurity, deepens international cooperation in cybersecurity emergency response, jointly combats cybercrimes and cyber terrorism, proactively propagates the important idea of building a community with a shared future in cyberspace, and continuously consolidates and expands its influence in the field of cybersecurity.

China energetically promotes cooperation in the field of cybersecurity among BRICS countries. In June 2022, Chinese President Xi Jinping presided over the 14th BRICS Leaders' Summit via video in Beijing and announced the adoption of *XIV BRICS Summit Beijing Declaration*, emphasizing the importance of establishing a legal framework for cooperation among BRICS countries to ensure the security of the use of ICT. As stated, various parties should implement *Roadmap for Practical Cooperation in Cybersecurity among BRICS Countries* and the work of the Cybersecurity Working Group and continue to facilitate practical cooperation among BRICS countries. This demonstrates the common position of major developing economies in the world on a series of major issues in the field of cybersecurity.

China actively contributes to the information security process under the framework of SCO. In September 2022, Chinese President Xi Jinping attended the 22nd Meeting of the Council of Heads of State of the Shanghai Cooperation Organization and delivered an important speech, "Ride on the Trend of the Times and Enhance Solidarity and Cooperation to Embrace a Better Future." He welcomed all parties to participate in the implementation of the *Global Security Initiative*, to expand security cooperation, and to address the challenges to global security.

China continues to participate in multilateral platforms such as APEC and ITU, and conducts extensive exchanges with all parties on cybersecurity issues. During the 64th and 65th plenary sessions of APEC TEL, experts from the China Academy of Information and Communications Technology served as conveners and initiated the Security and Prosperity Steering Group (SPSG) Meeting. They publicized progress in China's data security governance, participated in seminars on data security and new technology security, and strengthened policy exchanges and mutual trust with various economies. At the ITU Global Cybersecurity Index (GCI) Conference, Chinese experts and their counterparts in the world exchanged ideas, discussed GCI models and indicators, and contributed Chinese wisdom.

China continues to strengthen bilateral and multilateral dialogues on cybersecurity. Since 2022, the Chinese government has fully seized the opportunities such as "Regular Meeting of Chinese and Russian prime ministers," "China-Russia Information Security Consultation Mechanism," "China-ASEAN Network Affairs Dialogue," and "Singapore International Cyber Week." China exchanges views with all parties on the global cybersecurity landscape, proposes practical suggestions for continuing and deepening bilateral dialogue and cooperation in the field of cybersecurity, and calls on all parties to jointly safeguard the security and stability in cyberspace. Social organizations and research institutions represented by the Cyber Security Association of China and the China Academy of Information and Communications Technology give full play to the role of track-II diplomacy, actively promote bilateral and multilateral exchanges on cybersecurity issues, and contribute to building a community with a shared future in cyberspace. In the cooperation with CERT organizations, by May 2023, China had established "CNCERT International Partnerships" with 285 CERT organizations in 82 countries and regions, and signed cybersecurity cooperation memorandums with 33 of them. In August 2022, CNCERT/CC participated in the "2022 Asia Pacific Cybersecurity Emergency Exercise" initiated by APCERT and successfully completed various exercise tasks. In October, CNCERT/CC participated in the 2022 APCERT Annual Meeting, in which CNCERT/CC successfully ran for re-election as vice chairman unit of APCERT for the fourth time and as a member of the APCERT Steering Committee for the sixth time. In December, CNCERT/CC hosted a seminar on China-ASEAN cybersecurity emergency response capability building, and had extensive exchanges with CERT organizations in ASEAN countries on emergency response processes, capability building, and other related work. In the same month, CNCERT/CC sponsored the 2022 CNCERT International Partners Conference with the theme of "Taking Concerted Efforts to Create a New Future for Security Cooperation," with seminars on "Cross-border Collaboration" and "Technical Experience." Participants exchanged ideas on cooperation and experience in cybersecurity in regions such the BRI countries, Arab States, and ASEAN countries. In addition, China makes new contributions to talent cultivation in the field of cybersecurity in developing countries. The China International Development Cooperation Agency actively plans and implements training programs such as the Mobile Internet Development Seminar for Developing Countries, the Cybersecurity and Information Countermeasure Seminar for Developing Countries, and the China-Africa Cybersecurity Training Course, which train a large number of professionals in the field of cyberspace affairs, especially cybersecurity.

China has always contributed to combating cybercrimes, formulating global conventions under the UN framework, and continuously advancing consultation processes in this field through international and regional mechanisms. The ad hoc committee of *The United Nations Convention against Cybercrimes* has sponsored five negotiation meetings. The Chinese delegation actively promotes the *Global Security Initiative*, calling on all countries to strengthen international cooperation in combating cybercrimes and contributing to building a community with a shared future in cyberspace. The Supreme People's Procuratorate of China plays an active role in international multilateral platforms such as BRICS, SCO, China-ASEAN Prosecutors-General Conference, and the International Association of Prosecutors, and consults with relevant countries on combating cybercrimes and reaches consensus with them. The Supreme People's Procuratorate of China urges relevant parties to sign bilateral and multilateral agreements in combating cybercrimes, strengthens criminal justice assistance, and continuously deepens cross-border law enforcement and judicial cooperation in cybersecurity. The Supreme People's Procuratorate of China augments legislation in the field of foreign affairs as well as the research on the extraterritorial application of domestic law, organizes the translation of relevant extraterritorial materials, and improves training and exchanges. The Supreme People's Court of China actively dispatches representatives to participate in the formulation and negotiation of *The United Nations Convention Against Cybercrimes*, as well as the 31st Session of the United Nations Commission on Crime Prevention and Criminal Justice. Based on the work of combating cybercrimes, the Supreme People's Court of China publicizes China's judicial concepts and practices and urges relevant countries and regions to actively cooperate in the field of combating cybercrimes. The Ministry of Public Security of China vigorously takes part in international mechanisms such as INTERPOL, promotes the implementation of the *Global Security Initiative* proposed by President Xi Jinping, and contributes Chinese strength to maintaining global security and development. From March to June 2022, Chinese public security organs, under the framework of INTERPOL, stepped up efforts to crack down on telecom and online fraud. Launching the "Shuguang Campaign," Chinese police worked with police from seventy-six countries to combat fraud, leading to the discovery of 1,770 hideouts located in various countries, the apprehension of more than 2,000 suspects, and the interception of more than 50 million US dollars in illicit funds,[6] accumulating successful experience in combating telecom and online fraud around the world.

9.3.5 Strengthening exchanges and cooperation in the feld of Internet basic resources

Chinese government and technological communities actively participate in the work of international organizations and platforms in the field of Internet basic resources, such as IETF (Internet Engineering Task Force), ICANN (Internet Corporation for Assigned Names and Numbers), and APNIC (Asia-Pacific Network Information

6 "Public Security Organs Strengthen International Law-enforcement and Advance the 'Shuguang Campaign.'" Accessed June 2023. http://www.legaldaily.com.cn/legal_case/content/2022-09/14/content_8781627.html.

Center), and make positive contributions to building a community with a shared future in cyberspace. In June 2022, Wang Aijun from the China Telecom Research Institute was successfully elected as chairman of the IETF SAVNET Working Group. Currently, he is the only chairman of IETF working group from Chinese telecom operators. From June to July 2022, Chinese government and research institutions actively participated in the 74th and 75th sessions of ICANN, as well as GAC (Governmental Advisory Committee) meetings held simultaneously, carrying out in-depth discussions on issues such as the opening of new gTLD and domain name abuse. In October 2022, the Internet Governance Research Center of the China Academy of Information and Communications Technology and ICANN jointly held the Chinese Community Summary and Exchanges Meeting of the 75th ICANN Conference, and invited representatives from governmental departments, domain name registration management and service institutions, legal service institutions, research institutions and universities, who discussed the participation of the 75th ICANN Conference and the latest progress of ICANN in international policies. The conference helps Chinese communities to deeply participate in ICANN and related affairs in Internet governance and enhances the cohesion and influence of Chinese communities. In March 2023, Wang Lang from CNNIC and Duan Haixin from Tsinghua University were elected as vice chairmen of ICANN GAC and UASG, respectively, fully demonstrating China's growing strength and influence in the Internet field. In the same month, Hu Anlei from CNNIC was successfully elected as a new executive committee member of Asia Pacific Network Information Center, which helps to further develop community relations and deepen regional cooperation in the Asia Pacific region.

9.3.6 Promoting the formulation of international rules in the fields of information technology and standards

China plays an active role in the construction of international rules and standards in the field of information technology and elevates China-led innovation achievements to international standards. In recent years, China has continued to participate in standards organizations such as ISO (International Organization for Standardization) and International Electrotechnical Commission (IEC), as well as communications agencies such as ITU. Hundreds of international standards undertaken and drafted by China have been officially approved or released. In March 2023, Chinese research institutions participated in the 45th plenary meeting of the ISO/IEC JTC1/SC6. Two proposals on WLAN that were previously approved became international standards that would be released as ISO/IEC international standards within the year. The standard on fiber optics formulated by the China Electronics Standardization Institute and the China Information Communication Technologies Group has been officially released by the IEC. The standard boasts the first IEC international standard led by China in the field of active devices for optical communication. In November 2022, five international standards formulated by the China Information Communication Technologies Group were approved and released by the ITU. Two of them involved the integration of network technology and AI and provided needed guidance in this regard. China makes remarkable headway in the standards on information security. Three China-led international standards on cybersecurity, including quantum key distribution and the security of mobile devices for biometric recognition, have been released or will be released. The international standard on quantum information (ISO/IEC 23837) developed by the China Information Technology Security Evaluation Center will be released. In China, the professional team for international standardization of cybersecurity continues to grow. By March 2023, there were 157 registered experts in international standardization of cybersecurity in China, of which 45 experts served as conveners of working/consulting groups and project editors, contributing Chinese strength to the international standardization of cybersecurity.

Additionally, China actively participates in bilateral and multilateral dialogue and provides Chinese solutions for formulating international standards. The State Cryptography Administration enthusiastically participates in informal meetings of the Committee on Technical Barriers to Trade (TBT) of WTO, WTO e-commerce negotiations, GAMS (Governments/Authorities Meeting on Semiconductors), and other international conferences, actively interprets China's policies on cryptography management to the international community via various platforms, and continuously strengthens the understanding and recognition of other countries. The China Branch and Brazil Branch of the BRICS Institute of Future Networks have signed a cooperation agreement to carry out exchanges and cooperation on policies, regulations, and technical standards in the field of information and communications.

9.3.7 Fostering international cooperation in the field of global data security

Currently, the risks to global data security keep increasing. It is an important and urgent task for the international community to make the rules on global data security and promote global data governance. In recent years, China has actively participated in the governance of international data ecosystem security based on the *Global Data Security Initiative*. In March 2023, China constructively participated in the meetings of the United Nations Open-ended Working Group on Information Security and urged various countries to develop international rules to address the risks and challenges to data security, based on the *Global Data Security Initiative*.

China vigorously promotes dialogue and cooperation in the field of data security between China and Cuba, China and Arab States, China and Russia, and China and ASEAN. In November 2022, China and Cuba issued a joint statement unanimously stressing that data security plays a crucial role in national security and socioeconomic development in various countries, that Cuba supports China's

Global Data Security Initiative, and that the two sides will develop rules on global digital governance based on the initiative. In December, Chinese President Xi Jinping attended the First China-Arab States Summit, and proposed "eight major cooperation initiatives" for pragmatic cooperation between China and Arab States in the next three to five years, calling for the joint implementation of the *China-Arab States Data Security Cooperation Initiative*, establish China-Arab States exchanging mechanism for cyberspace affairs, and strengthen exchanges and dialogue in areas such as data governance and cybersecurity. The summit passed the *Riyadh Declaration of the First China-Arab States Summit*, announcing that China and Arab States will continue to deepen cooperation and jointly promote global cyberspace governance. In March 2023, China and Russia signed and issued a joint statement, emphasizing that the two sides will implement China's *Global Data Security Initiative*. In addition, at the Third China-ASEAN Digital Security Forum hosted by China, representatives from ASEAN countries, Chinese governmental departments, and relevant institutions engaged in in-depth exchanges on digital security, which facilitated bilateral cooperation in the digital security industry, and helped to jointly build a secure and trustworthy regional digital economy ecosystem.

9.3.8 Promoting international exchanges and mutual learning of online culture

China firmly seizes the development opportunities for digital technology, gives full play to the role of the Internet as the main channel of international communication, and makes new progress in international exchanges and mutual learning of online culture. In the exchanges of digital cultural heritage, China actively advances international cooperation in the protection and utilization of digital cultural heritage. In April 2023, representatives of Ambassade de France en Chine signed a letter of intent with Wuhan University and unveiled Centre Franco-Chinois de la Culture Digitale du Patrimoine. The center was jointly established by Wuhan University and École Nationale des Chartres. As one of the first group of six Sino-French centers in China, it focuses on the research and utilization of digital cultural heritage in China and France and aims to make new contributions to educational and cultural exchanges between China and France. In the same month, the Overseas Chinese Affairs Office of the Guangxi Zhuang Autonomous Region and the Guangxi Overseas Chinese School launched the "Chinese Culture Experience Camp for Overseas Chinese Youth." More than 140 overseas Chinese youth from Thailand, Cambodia, Laos, Indonesia, Vietnam, and Myanmar ltook courses on intangible cultural heritage and Dong culture in Guangxi online and in person, leaving students with a deep understanding of traditional Chinese culture.

In Internet media communication, China actively builds platforms for communication and cooperation between domestic and foreign Internet media. In

April 2023, the China Internet Media Forum was held in Nanjing, with a parallel forum, Chinese Narrative: Building a New Paradigm for International Communication. The forum invited representatives of foreign media from five continents around the world, as well as relevant leaders from media websites, social media platforms, and other institutions. Centering on three topics, i.e., "emphasizing media diversity, building new forces in international communication," "promoting mutual learning of civilizations, innovating new discourses in international communication," and "reforming media forms, building new patterns in international communication," participants discussed media cooperation and development and explored the construction of a Chinese narrative system that integrates China and foreign countries.

China regularly holds the China Internet Civilization Conference every year, which creates a platform for disseminating China's ideas on Internet civilization, exchanging experiences in Internet civilization, showcasing achievements in Internet civilization, and promoting international mutual learning of Internet civilization. In July 2023, the International Exchanges and Mutual Learning Forum on Internet Civilization of the Internet Civilization Conference was held in Xiamen, Fujian, with the theme of "Strengthening Exchanges, Mutual Learning and Co-existence of Internet Civilization, Jointly Building a Community with a Shared Future in Cyberspace." At the conference, foreign representatives or experts and scholars from the US, the United Kingdom, Belgium, the Middle East, and Central Asia discussed the exchanges, mutual learning, and coexistence of Chinese and foreign civilizations via the Internet. The forum aims to create a platform for online cultural exchanges and sharing, to strengthen cultural exchanges and mutual learning in cyberspace, and to contribute to building a community with a shared future in cyberspace and promoting the progress of human civilization.

10.2478/9788367405867-011

Postscript

Today, digital technology, as a leading force in the technological revolution and the industrial transformation of the world, is deeply integrated into the entire process of economic and social development and profoundly alters the models of production, lifestyle, and social governance. Since the 18th CPC National Congress, China has made remarkable achievements in cyberspace affairs and made a new leap forward in building China into a country with cyber strength. Mainstream public opinion in cyberspace has been consolidated and developed, a comprehensive Internet governance system has been basically formed, and the capability and system for safeguarding cybersecurity has been improved. The leading role of information technology as a driving force for development has been given full play, the rule of law in cyberspace has been constantly improved, and a louder voice in international affairs and the influence in cyberspace have been gained and strengthened. In October 2022, the 20th CPC National Congress was successfully held in Beijing. The congress formulated strategic plans for building a modern socialist country in all respects and advancing the great rejuvenation of the Chinese nation on all fronts and made overall arrangements for carrying out the "Five-sphere Integrated Plan" and the "Four-pronged Comprehensive Strategy" in a coordinated manner. The report of the 20th CPC National Congress stresses that China will cultivate new growth engines such as next-generation information technology and AI, accelerate the development of the digital economy, further integrate it with the traditional economy, and build internationally competitive digital industry clusters. These important statements determine the direction and provide action guidance for building a digital China into a country with cyber strength. The *China Internet Development Report 2023* (hereinafter referred to as *The Report*) focuses on the practice of learning and implementing the spirit of the 20th CPC National Congress in the field of cyberspace affairs, publicizes and interprets the latest theoretical achievements of Xi Jinping's Thought on Socialism with Chinese Characteristics for a New Era, especially his important thought on building China into a country with cyber strength, comprehensively showcases Chinese Internet development over the past year, systematically summarizes the experiences and practices of Chinese Internet development, and scientifically forecasts trends in Internet development. We hope that by exploring China's Internet development, we introduce experience and contribute wisdom to Internet development and governance in various countries around the world.

Meeting of Directors of Office of the Central Cyberspace Affairs Commission (OCCAC) attaches great importance to the compilation of *The Report*, and leaders of OCCAC give us considerable guidance. Bureaus and units of OCCAC provide us with substantial support. Relevant ministries and commissions, including the General Office of the State Council and the Ministry of Industry and Information Technology, as well as the Office of Cyberspace Affairs Commission in provinces, autonomous regions, and municipalities directly under the central government, give us strong support with relevant data and materials. *The Report* is launched by the Chinese Academy of Cyberspace Studies (CACS). Main contributors are: Xia Xueping, Xuan Xingzhang, Li Yingxin, Qian Xianliang, Liu Ying, Zou Xiaoxiang, Jiang Yang, Liao Jin, Jiang Wei, Yin Hong, Li Bowen, Cheng Yifeng, Jiang Shuli, Li Wei, Long Qingzhe, Deng Jueshuang, Chi Haiyan, Xu Yanfei, Zhang Yang, Li Can, Wu Xiaolu, Wu Jieqiong, Xiao Zheng, Zhao Gaohua, Liu Chaochao, Li Xiaojiao, Wang Yitong, Ye Bei, Chen Jing, Jia Shuowei, Yuan Xin, Shen Yu, Cai Yang, Li Yangchun, Yang Xiaohan, Tian Yuan, Liu Yao, Lu Dan, Long Chaoze, Li Jingyi, Meng Qingshun, Song Shouyou, Lin Hao, Wang Pu, Wang Meng, Yang Shuhang, Zhang Can, Zhai You, Cai Lin, Zhang Chan, Yang Xintong, Lin Zhiping, Liu Jiapeng, Yang Xuecheng, Sui Yue, Jin Zhong, Jin Qiong, Ding Fang, Meng Qingguo, Wang Lida, Guo Quanzhong, Zhang Jinyi, Jiang Qiaolei, Chen Zonghai, Tian Zhihong, Xu Huajie, Xu Peixi, Shang Xixue, etc.Experts and scholars, including Zhang Li, Zhao Guojun, Chen Qi, Li Guangqian, Wang Limei, Zhang Yuqiang, Lü Yongqiang, Cui Jinggui, Dong Yuanyuan, Shen Weixing, Wang Dongkun, and Zhang Yuling contribute their valuable suggestions.

The Report, albeit successfully published thanks to the strong support and considerable help from all sectors of society, is inadequate in terms of perspective and insight due to a tight deadline. Therefore, we ardently welcome valuable opinions and suggestions from governmental departments, international organizations, research institutes, Internet corporations, and social organizations across different sectors, home and abroad, to help us produce better reports in the future and contribute more wisdom and strength to world Internet development and governance.

Chinese Academy of Cyberspace Studies (CACS)
October 2023

Bei Fragen zur Produktsicherheit wenden Sie sich bitte an:
If you have any questions regarding product safety,
please contact:

Walter de Gruyter GmbH
Genthiner Straße 13
10785 Berlin
productsafety@degruyterbrill.com